AF600598

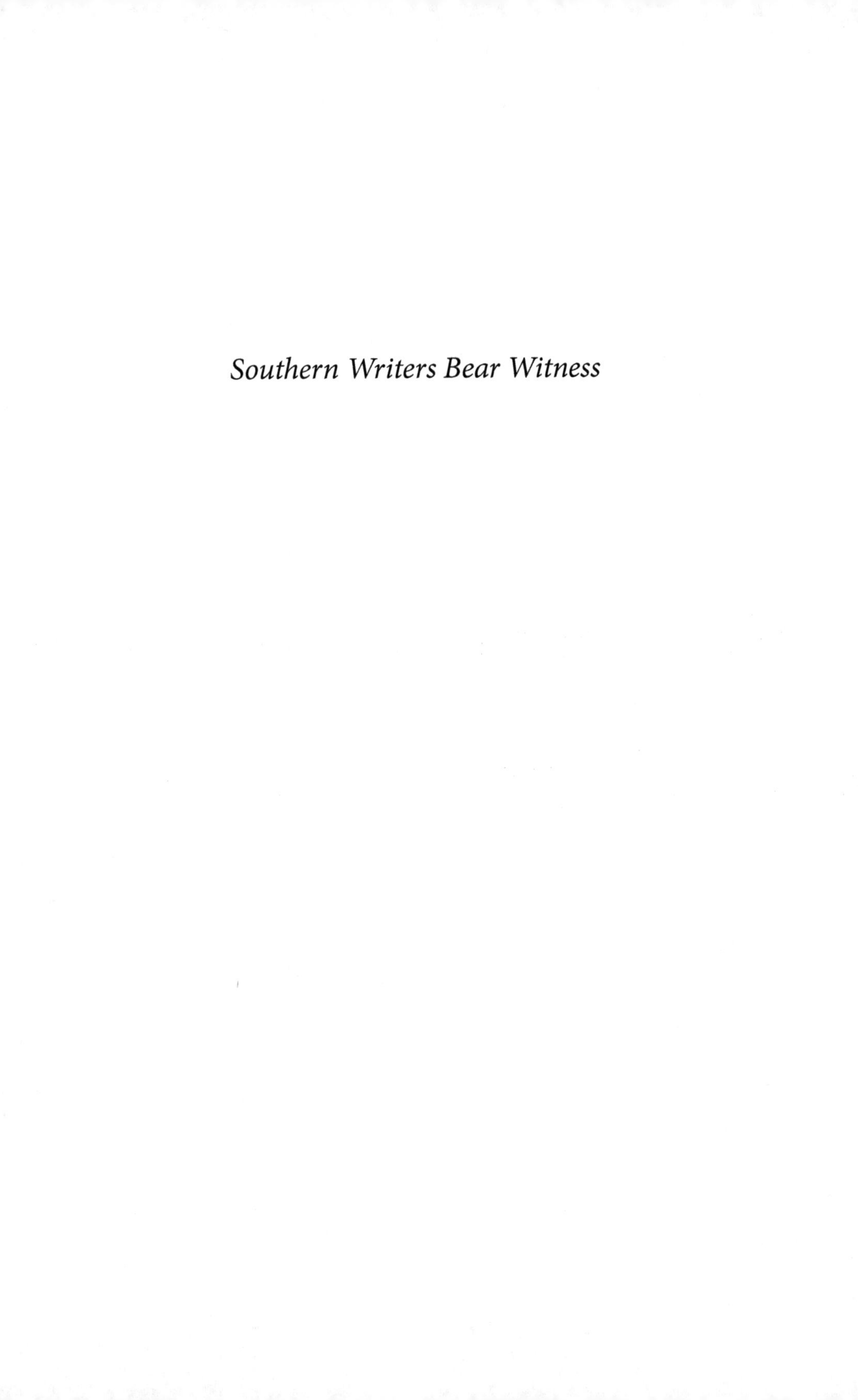

*Southern Writers Bear Witness*

# *Southern Writers Bear Witness*

INTERVIEWS

◆◆◆◆◆◆

*Jan Nordby Gretlund*

FOREWORD BY
*Daniel Cross Turner*

The University of South Carolina Press

Published by the University of South Carolina Press
Columbia, South Carolina 29208

www.sc.edu/uscpress

Manufactured in the United States of America

27 26 25 24 23 22 21 20 19 18
10 9 8 7 6 5 4 3 2 1

Library of Congress Cataloging-in-Publication Data
can be found at http://catalog.loc.gov/

ISBN: 978-1-61117-876-0 (hardcover)
ISBN: 978-1-61117-877-7 (ebook)

For Annie

*Gratefully Remembered*

Ashley Brown
Richard J. Calhoun
Pat Conroy
Shailah Jones
Lewis A. Lawson
Marion Montgomery
Regina Cline O'Connor
C. Vann Woodward
Thomas Daniel Young

I think that if there is any value in hearing writers talk,
it will be in hearing what they can witness to
and not what they can theorize about.

Flannery O'Connor,
*Mystery and Manners*

# CONTENTS

◆ ◆ ◆

## FOREWORD

*Daniel Cross Turner*

◆ ◆ ◆

For decades now, Jan Nordby Gretlund has been a highly prolific and attentive scholar of the literature of the contemporary U.S. South. From his professorial post at the University of Southern Denmark, Gretlund has long offered a unique international vantage on Southern literature and culture. His influence has encouraged us to adjust our sightlines on the region and its literature. No more do we view the South simply as the "lesser" part of the United States, a region forever tangled up in the briar patch of backwardness, aberrance, and ignorance. Thanks in large part to Gretlund's presence, we no longer see the U.S. South in isolation but seek connections between the South and other regions and nations, on a global scale. Because of his keen, long-standing acumen as a Southernist, we might invent a new word for Gretlund and similar international scholars of Southern studies: he's an "*extra*patriate," adding an extra layer of cross-national regional identity on top of his native Danish. Over the course of his extensive career as a Southern *extra*pat, Gretlund has had much to say about Southern literature and has said it memorably.

But Gretlund has proven himself a good listener, too. This is clear in the numerous interviews he has conducted with major Southern writers over the past forty-plus years, now collected here in a single volume. In *Southern Writers Bear Witness,* Gretlund asks telling questions and then generously cedes the floor to permit some of the finest Southern storytellers around to do exactly what they do best: tell about the South. And they do not disappoint, turning phrases and spinning yarns in fine form. Thank goodness Gretlund was there to record every word, so we get to listen in, too.

As the collection's title rightly suggests, this constellation of excellent Southern writers *witness* major issues in our time, including racial segregation, the civil rights movement, gender dynamics, religion, (sub)urbanization, political demagoguery, the ecology, education, and economic hardship. While these matters are often deeply associated with the American South, they are certainly not located exclusively south of the Mason-Dixon. Through these interviews, we come to know the South, inside *and* out. On account of the interviewer's pointed questions, these writers witness to so much of the cultural history behind their work. The interviews, then, are also significant as cultural artifacts, helping us to view literature in its larger contexts.

But the title of this interview collection contains a further meaning. These Southern writers also *witness to* us: they talk not at us but *to* us, engaging with us, clearly aware that there is an interested audience. Throughout this collection, Gretlund's interviews reflect a heightened sense of reciprocity between interviewer and interviewee and between the storytellers and their wider listeners—summoning responsibility in its etymological sense of "responding to." *Southern Writers Bear Witness* initiates a call-and-response between interviewer and subjects and between authors and audience. The interviews collected here are sharp without getting lost in the arcana of academia. They are smart but not showy, striking an informal, conversational chord while at the same time tendering unmatched insights into the workings of life and literature that may well be rooted in a particular region but can also be rerouted to connect with other cultures, other spaces, other times.

There have been previous collections of interviews with a variety of Southern writers, but these typically are dated or concentrate on a specific genre. The majority of interviews with contemporary Southern writers are published individually in journals or on websites, or, if several interviews are published in book form, the collection usually focuses on only a single author. Gretlund's collection of interviews, by contrast, presents something unique and much appreciated in bringing together in one place so many trenchant and distinct Southern authors. *Southern Writers Bear Witness* indeed achieves the interviewer's intention to record "the voices of a literary tradition" and to maintain what is "perhaps the South's most impressive cultural legacy" in tying together fourteen Southern writers across thirty-two interviews. These collected conversations are invaluable as "an archive of the thoughts of fourteen southern writers from the 1970s until today."

Despite Gretlund's disclaimer about viewing "interviews as art" in his preface, the collected interviews present significant information about the authors' lives and work and their region and do so quite *artfully*—in the author's incisive, thoroughgoing questions and in the eloquence, even brilliance of the writers' responses. The interviews reflect an array of "styles," with some writers making good use of compressed, even terse prose in their responses and others reeling out verbose answers so artfully done that these sometimes read like the beginnings to a new novel. It is clear that the interviewees feel comfortable with the interviewer, and the resulting interactions come across not just as smart and insightful but also as relaxed and often humorous. In terms of presenting legitimate, detailed accounts of the author's interactions with these varied writers, the collection is accurate . . . save, perhaps, for the author's second interview with Barry Hannah, who—clearly unimpeded by the restraints of sobriety—provides a gloriously inaccurate interview, finely balanced by the interviewer's polite, if dogged, professionalism and self-deprecating humor. Which I suspect readers will enjoy quite a lot. I know I did. Even if a reader is unfamiliar with a particular author, the interviews supply enough biographical and publishing information so that all the conversations are meaningful. And the interviews repeatedly associate current Southern writers and writing with the big names of Southern literature past: Mark Twain, William Faulkner, and Flannery O'Connor.

In any sort of anthology like this interview collection, certain questions always arise: "But why is this author included, and not that author? Where's [other author]?" Of course, no collection can ever collect everyone, and this book offers an impressive spectrum of writers, all of whom are notable. There are of course many other black Southern writers who would work well in such a collection (for instance, Ernest Gaines, Brenda Marie Osbey, Yusef Komunyakaa, Natasha Trethewey, Jesmyn Ward), as well as Native Southern writers (for instance, LeAnne Howe and Allison Hedge Coke). One might also ask after writers of the Southern working class (for instance, Dorothy Allison, Lee Smith, William Gay, Ann Pancake). But these objections may be tempered by the fact that issues of race, especially black–white dynamics, are central to several of the included interviews, and matters of class upbringing also recur across the selections.

And if there are some good, important authors absent, I doubt anyone can really find fault with any of the particular writers included here—certainly not with the likes of Eudora Welty, Walker Percy, Barry Hannah, and Pat Conroy, who are surrounded by a chorus of quite fine, recognizable voices in the other interviews: Pam Durban, Clyde Edgerton, Percival Everett, Josephine Humphreys, Ron Rash, and Dori Sanders. The possible exception might be Martin Luther King Sr., since he is not a writer per se. However, King's interview is one of the most powerful in the collection and provides excellent context for concerns expressed in the other interviews, such as racial tension and de facto segregation, conflicts between urban and rural life, and the value of religious faith. Perhaps, too, a reader might wish to see a greater range of genres covered (the authors included are almost exclusively prose fiction writers, primarily novelists), drawing from the wealth of contemporary Southern poets, dramatists, comics/graphic narrative writers and illustrators, television writers and screenwriters. However, Gretlund recurrently asks the writers included to compare and contrast their fiction writing to other genres, especially poetry but also drama and film.

These interviews are not overly scholarly; they are more attuned to the feel of a literary journal. The collection follows through commendably, in truth, on O'Connor's advice (cited in the preface) that the main value in interviews with authors lies "in hearing what they can witness to and *not* what they can theorize about." These interviews are important as aesthetic guides, offering crucial advice on how to write deeply and well. These authors present excellent models for aspiring creative writers. The writers included also prove themselves apt readers of their own work, providing signposts for understanding their aesthetics that scholars of Southern literature would do well to mark.

Some current scholars of Southern literature, especially those of us associated with the New Southern Studies, may take umbrage at the more traditional understanding of the South and Southerness implicit in the discussion topics here, such as place, family and kinship, community, ruralness and country life, the presence of the past, the Civil War, religion and the Bible, ancestor worship, foodways, regional humor, moonshining, and the opposition between "us" (Southerners) and "them" ("Yankees"), between South and North, between cultural insiders and outsiders. These interviews align with the Louis Rubin/UNC–Chapel Hill scholarly genealogy that paints the South a certain hue. If the literary tradition the interviews evoke might be deemed by some thinkers to be outmoded or limited in some way, many Southern scholars, Southern writers, and, hell, just Southerners in general have thought it so. Those who were raised, critically speaking, on the other side of the Rubin/Chapel Hill tracks may well grimace and grumble at some of these traditional themes and approaches. But we'll very likely still *read* this book of interviews, precisely for what the included authors witness to, which is well worth the trouble. And if it stirs a critical pot or two out there among the New Southern Studies set, that will get our scholarly debating skills simmering again—we love to see what else we can theorize about.

This book's appeal, however, goes well beyond the Southern lit scholar to reach a general audience of readers of contemporary Southern lit (and contemporary American fiction overall). Moreover, the interviews also integrate a rich range of perhaps unlooked-for topics, including discussions of writerly techniques, aging and healthcare, labor in the South (for example, work in textile mills and connections between slave labor and craftsmanship), sexuality, anti-Ohio sentiment in Southern writing, existentialism, Gullah culture, the legal and financial pressures of the literary market, and many more. Even as we sometimes undergo substantial time warps in the interviews, which span from 1978 to 2015, there is continuity amid change, reinforced by the steadying presence of Gretlund throughout.

This is an insightful, scintillating collection of original interviews with an array of crucial Southern writers over the past four decades. The authors Gretlund has collected are true witnesses, presenting clear-sighted testament in full voice to the continuing cultural value of the contemporary American South and its literature. We should all open this good book and have a long listen.

## ACKNOWLEDGMENTS

◆ ◆ ◆

Several of the interviews herein were first published elsewhere. Permission to reprint interviews appearing in this book is gratefully acknowledged:

Pam Durban, "Lines out across the Gap," *American Studies in Scandinavia* ("A Southern Issue") 38, no. 2 (2004): 104–19.

Kaye Gibbons, "In My Own Style," *South Atlantic Review* 65 (Fall 2000): 132–54.

Barry Hannah, interview, *Contemporary Authors* 110 (1987): 232–36.

Mary Hood, "Fiction Is Like Fire," *American Studies in Scandinavia* ("A Southern Issue") 33, no. 2 (2001): 69–82.

Josephine Humphreys, "The Excitement and the Mystery of the Immediate," *Chattahoochee Review* 22, no. 3 (2001): 33–55.

Madison Jones, interview, *Contemporary Authors,* new revision series 7 (1982): 253–56.

Madison Jones, interview, in Jan Nordby Gretlund, *Madison Jones' Garden of Innocence* (Odense: University Press of Southern Denmark, 2005), 158–83.

Martin Luther King Sr., interview, in Jan Nordby Gretlund, *Frames of Southern Mind* (Odense: Odense University Press, 1998), 117–23.

Walker Percy, "Laying the Ghost of Marcus Aurelius?," *South Carolina Review* 13 (Spring 1981): 3–12.

Walker Percy, "Difficult Times," in *More Conversations with Walker Percy,* ed. Lewis A. Lawson and Victor A. Kramer (Jackson: University Press of Mississippi, 1993), 103–7.

Eudora Welty, "An Interview with Eudora Welty," *Southern Humanities Review* 14 (Summer 1980): 193–208.

Eudora Welty, "Seeing Real Things: An Interview with Eudora Welty," in Jan Nordby Gretlund, *Eudora Welty's Aesthetics of Place* (Columbia: University of South Carolina Press, 1997), 259–72.

# *Autobiography and Fiction*

AN INTERVIEW WITH PAT CONROY

◆◆◆◆◆◆

*Beaufort Inn, November 4, 2015*

Pat Conroy.
*Photograph by Annie Sten, used with permission*

◆◆◆◆◆◆

**Jan Nordby Gretlund** Are you always writing out of biographical territory? How much is really straight fiction—by that I mean purely out of your imagination?

**Pat Conroy** Almost all the fiction is straight autobiography, something that made me feel strange, made me concerned. With me it is almost always autobiographical impulse. In *The Great Santini* it was *one* big question: why did I hate my father?

And I wrote *Prince of Tides* based on another big question:

why did I have to serve so much? Why did I react so much against the plebe system?—Or, why is my sister crazy and was always crazy, and what did my family do to make her crazy?

These are sort of the beginnings and then, you know, I am a collector of stories and a collector of histories. And right now I am frustrated answering your questions, as I have a hundred questions to ask you all [Annie Sten, the interviewer's wife, was present during the interview].

I was educated at a *not* very impressive college, but I wasn't overwhelmed by theory—literary theory. There was nothing I brought to the table that I have to write this way or that way. I tried to figure out myself how to do it, how to get it done, and what felt natural to *me*. Then I have an idea and try to write "a prologue"—sometimes it will take me years, then I usually know what the book is going to be about—where it is going to lead.

**J.G.** You have said that you are trying to explain to yourself what kind of person you are. At seventy, are we there yet?

**P.C.** No! I have no idea. I am old enough to know at seventy, but I'll never know. This is what I thought I was doing when I first started writing:

I tried to explain my own life to myself and the times, what they felt like, what I was thinking, what people did around me, the friends I made, the women I loved, the men I loved. And I tried to write this. You never know if anybody is going to be interested. It did not seem possible, coming from the background and family I did, that I would become a writer. I knew I lacked the academic background and I worried about it, I still worry about it.

But I have read more than anybody I have ever met. You told me about Johannes V. Jensen's sense of place, and I will get the novel, *The King's Fall*, and read it.

**J.G.** Is the sensibility of the narrator always yours—or do you sometimes see the narrator in your fiction as a stranger, maybe even a foreigner?

**P.C.** I am comfortable "doing" the stranger because of the military life we lived. We moved too much. The twenty-three moves before we came to Beaufort were too much for me. I came here not knowing how to meet people, I don't think I'd talked to five girls in my life. I would get to a place, play sports, make friends, play this, play that, and we leave! Most of my brothers and sisters went to four high schools, I was lucky, I went to only three.

I was so needful of *a home* before Beaufort, and Beaufort has no reason to call me a native, I'm *not* a native. They have no reason to accept me or embrace me, but they have! And I have been *moved* by that because I was from nowhere. When New York critics began to refer to me as a

Southern writer, other Southern writers said, "How dare they refer to him as Southern?" I was delighted they would call me something. Delighted they thought I was from somewhere.

It amazed me that other Southern writers raised bristles because I was called a "Southern writer." I was on this panel one time with about five hundred Southern writers, and the question was:

"Do you consider yourself a Southern writer?" And I consider myself "a regional writer," and I told them, "It doesn't seem to be a disgraceful 'thing' to be. How many people can you write for?" When I finished saying this, three or four writers attacked me for saying "I am a Southern writer."

I have moved around a lot, lived for periods in France and Italy. The "Southern writers" talked about goobers, black-eyed beans, and okra pies. They were the most Southern people you ever saw, and one of them I couldn't believe, she wrote stuff about Dixie living and gave me "crap" about being Southern. "You are as Southern as a hound dog," I told her.

I have liked very much being identified with the South, that means a lot of things you connect with the South, including some negative aspects such as homophobia, but that is part of being from a region.

**J.G.** There are some drawbacks, of course.—Is it possible to use material or events that you have only heard about—and things that happened to total strangers?

**P.C.** I filter it in. Once I have a story going and I hear a great story, I slip it in. I can offer an example. In *Prince of Tides* I made my father buy an old gas station, simply because I knew about Happy the Tiger in Columbia. I thought if it doesn't make sense in the book, I will cut it out. I am sorry he had to buy a gas station and give up shrimping, but he ended up owning a tiger and I wanted that. I love that story too much to give it up.—So I will slip in stories such as the story about the white porpoise that swam here in these waters, when I first came. It was magical and unbelievable to me. And the stories about the warfare between families that were going on when I first came to Beaufort, I can show you where these families lived. It was exciting to me.

I had a great teacher, Monsignor Monte, a Jesuit from Washington, D.C., and that was the most intellectual year I had in my life. They were really mental warriors and Monsignor Monte wrote me a letter, he is still alive, for my birthday that somebody handed to me. How lucky can you be with these people who teach you about literature, this great gift was presented to me. If you have kids in your class that have something special going on, it is a glorious thing. I had three great English teachers in a row.

I went to the Citadel. Because I was an English major, all the military guys thought I was gay. But I had these men, who were distinguished in the academic world, teaching me. They loved literature, and they loved teaching it. I was one of five English majors out of a class of four hundred. I loved it. There was nothing I didn't like about being an English major, but I always worried that I didn't have the cultural weight that Walker Percy had, that William Faulkner had, even though he didn't go to college he had bits of culture from his family, and certainly Flannery O'Connor was exposed to culture in Savannah and at Iowa State University.

**J.G.** I did visit with Mrs. Regina Cline O'Connor, when I worked in the manuscript collection in Milledgeville. She was most helpful.

**P.C.** She scared me to death! Her sister-in-law had this dinner party for me. I had asked how I should dress, and she said "casual," meaning something different than a New York woman on Park Avenue. So I go like this, in a T-shirt, to a first Park Avenue mansion and I walk in, and "my God, I have screwed up." Everybody is dressed up, and *I* look like Li'l Abner! So I come out and try to make the best of it with a "how are you doing." One of them had friends from the *New York Times* visiting, and they were talking to me as if I couldn't understand English. Imagine that they behaved as if you couldn't understand Danish. The attitude was "we see a thousand guys like you, and we promise you that you will never hear from us again!"—One of them says, "Isn't it amazing the South can actually produce people that know how to write anything?" And a woman, across from him, says, "It doesn't amaze me as much as anybody in the South can read!" I was just sitting there and my first impulse was to beat both up. But that would just confirm *their* idea of the South. I am younger and insecure and didn't know what to do about it and basically did nothing to take revenge—until years later when I used the scene.

**J.G.** When we talk humorously about "the family," do we mean the ridiculousness of all families?

**P.C.** I think if people could be honest about their family, that is true. Where I found that *I* am rare is that I *can* be honest about my family. I have hurt many of their feelings over the years, and several in my family have not talked to me for some time. The literature I have read, that is the literature that has moved me the most, seems to say that the truth about human life is a "no-go"! They couch it, they may put it in another character, and they may hide it, but it gets across to me.

The mistake I made early, and I made a terrible one with *The Great Santini,* and I knew this. I had read Thomas Wolfe, I knew how his family reacted, and I don't know why I thought mine would be different.

**J.G.** Because you used them as characters in your fiction?

**P.C.** Yes! But my mother did not understand why Mrs. Wolfe was upset. She would just be proud if her son could write a book, any book.—But she said,

"Your book is pure trash!" Her thing was, I gave the book to dad, instead of to her.

**J.G.** And that was a basic mistake?

**P.C.** The power structure of that house!—Mama, I recognize that I loved you too much, and I needed you to be perfect. I needed that when I was growing up. If she were flawed, I chose not to see that.

**J.G.** Most fiction tries to display reality as the writer sees it. Is there enough room for some humor? Is the humorist not to be taken seriously? I am thinking of the long tradition of humor in Southern fiction. What is the balance between humor and realistic drama in your mind?

**P.C.** I think humor is just a part of Southern life, it is what makes Southern life tolerable. I think humor is what got black people through the Depression. Talk about black people, they were hilarious, they were a riot. Comedies are appreciated, literature deals more in utter seriousness, but there is more to life. In the book of life you throw everything into it, and there is humor, great humor, and there is tragedy, if you want, there is that, too. Life has been much harder to live than I thought it would be. I thought I could walk away from mom and dad, and the family, tell a few jokes, and tell a few happy stories. I thought I should be a high school English teacher my whole life and write poetry and meet a great girl. And we would have children, who would grow up in Beaufort. We would all live in Beaufort, except to travel. That was the life I had planned for myself.

**J.G.** And that is pretty close to what happened!

**P.C.** Well, it didn't work out quite how I wanted it to. I didn't plan on marrying "twenty-five" times! I didn't expect to have children and children and children, adopted children, and children from everywhere!

Basically I got to do what I want to do, which is to write. I didn't know it was possible for me with my background to write books—that has been my great surprise in life.

**J.G.** Someone should have made that clear to you much earlier.

**P.C.** Yes!

**J.G.** Dealing with the Marines and military heroes, you are also writing about the image of the American male, maybe even about Hollywood's image of men with "true grit." Is this on purpose? How is the Southern male doing?

**P.C.** The Southern male is the worst example of that! I get a kick out of Red Fedders' talking, he makes the best redneck I have ever seen. And that guy in *The Great Santini,* the guy with tumors to kill tumor, he was scary. He was the kind of kid with his origin in Beaufort. Hollywood loves the lonely, as I found out when I did screenwriting for Robert Redford in *Above the Falls.* The movie was about the newspaper guy in Atlanta who was trying to make the best newspaper in the world. He was, of course, gotten rid of, so there were protest marches. And Hollywood hired me and a guy called Sonny Rawls to write a screenplay. In Hollywood I learned that the hero, the true grit man, John Wayne, Clint Eastwood, et cetera, can *never* ask a question, but he *always* has the answer! If there is a good line given to another character, the lead male actor simply appropriates it. Whether the line is meant for a woman, a child, or a horse makes no difference, *he* wants that line to be written into the screenplay where *he* can say the good line. The lead male actor *wants* the colloquial gestures, as well. He is a man of action but supposedly profound. He is, however, terrified of humor, scared of being funny and not taken seriously as a hero.

The heroic males in Hollywood are all about four feet tall. It seems that God can combine a beautiful head, hair, and face for an actor, but He does not make them tall, at least not in that location. It is His way of assorting human virtues. That kind of farce was just news to me.

At the Citadel I had more of this macho-male crap playing basketball, baseball, and football. Do you know that I had a more military upbringing than Napoleon did? I saw more of these tough guys, and as you can imagine it wasn't for me. I didn't like it, I *hated* it!

Dad was such a tough guy. It was too bad that Robert Duvall was such a midget, dad was at least seven inches taller; but I told dad not to worry, I said, "Just relax, dad, you look really tall on the screen." So I had this father that I did not admire, and I hated him. The hardest part of the film to watch was when he said good-bye to his wife and kids. I used to pray every time he flew:

*"Dear Lord, please blow up his plane!" It is a bad prayer, but I thought it would relieve the pressure on my sisters, brothers, my mother, and me. And it would have been honorable. And it would have been a big funeral, with the planes flying over.—And, he would be gone.—I hated that image of the Southern male from almost the start of my life.*

**J.G.** In my paper at USCB, at the celebration of your seventieth birthday, I talked a little about the aesthetics of place *and* the ethics of place. I thought I should come to "The Point" in Beaufort, where it, for some people, is the point of life to live. But in *The Water Is Wide* a visitor from the North claims that "The Point" is not ethically a good place, but the resident in the novel doesn't want to discuss this and wants the man to leave, but, of course, the visitor had a point.

**P.C.** Oh yes, a great point, it was *the* point about the South. The truth about the South is that from the time of the first slaveship arriving in 1619 until today, what we have done to black people is simply *horrible.* It is *the* stain on the South. When I go up North they have dinner parties for the writer and I never see a black person. And there weren't enough black people at my reading. When I have a signing session there are few black customers, I always notice it. Is it failed integration, lack of education? I think it will take hundreds of years to get rid of the stain of slavery and to forget the loss of *freedom*—that's the word, freedom. From the point of view of people in Rome, the U.S.A. is only a baby; Romans know that historical mistakes are not forgotten or forgiven after just two hundred years.

**J.G.** When you write the truth about anything or anybody, people are offended at times, not just family members, and possibly very angry. And you become a persona non grata, is it worth it?

**P.C.** My sister's first love sued me on the day the celebration began. And she wrote my editor at Doubleday and said I had ousted her from the same celebration, saying she is gay! We still love Kris. We loved her then, she was great for my sister. I am not worried about it. I have not traditionally been antigay. We had a gay marriage in my yard on Wednesday. What I described happened—she was my sister's lover for fifteen years. The fight that she sued me about took place on The Point, I lived on The Point then, it was the night she and Carol told the family that they were lesbians and that they were in love. But the particular point of the fight was that Carol wanted Kris in the family portrait we were sending to my father in Vietnam. And their love should be taken into consideration equal to my love for Barbara, or the love of brothers and sisters and children. It was a huge fight, but when mama and I talked about it, I said she is right! "Even though the Catholic Church does not believe in it?" my wife asked. "They don't believe in anything, they just don't," I told her.

**J.G.** You once mentioned your Aunt Helen and Uncle Ross as the normal South, hunting and fishing et cetera. But would you have become a writer if you had lived the "normal" Southern life.—If there is such a thing?

**P.C.** I am sorry that you asked, but you did. Here is the truth about that:

I thought it was a normal Southern life. Now they are all adult, two of them are dead. One of them was a paranoid schizophrenic. I had no idea that my Uncle Ross was a *bad* alcoholic and made my Aunt Helen miserable.

**J.G.** Maybe you needed this image of "a normal South"?

**P.C.** It may have been in the same way I needed a certain image of "mam." "Mam" would not let me hunt and would not let me fish, because she did not want me to be a redneck; she thought that somehow it would prevent that.

**J.G.** Your recurring statement about your father is "I will never be like him!" Don't you at times recognize him in yourself?

**P.C.** I *am* my father! It is one of the most agonizing things to admit. When my brothers and I sit around and play the game "most like dad"—m.l.d.—it is agonizing for all of us. My brother will command "Pass the salt!" and we will go "m.l.d., m.l.d." Or one of us will rearrange his face so it shows no love whatsoever and go up close to your face:

"m.l.d.!" And there will be no family reunion without that. But I hated dad's temper and have been having to control my own temper my whole life. My poor brothers and I, we all have it. We all have tendencies of dad. My brother Jim is most like dad, he can't help it. He always wins these games, but it kills him. He is rigid, he is dark, and he is all these things. But I feel like I'm more like dad.

**J.G.** You'll always be a better writer than he was, isn't that enough for you—now?

**P.C.** Because he is my father, and I am my father, I can't say that! I recognize him in me. Dad first came to an autograph party in 1973 or '74, this was at the Old New York Book Shop in Atlanta. He is mean, bitter, so mean over his changeover. I take him around and introduce him to everybody. So he comes around the next day and says, "Do you know these people are faggots, and why are you hanging around black people and Jews?" And just like him, I said, "Dad, let me tell you something, if you ever want to come to one of these things again, get used to it, because you are not likely to meet Marine fighter pilots in my crowd. Be prepared for people!"—And dad, to his credit, did! And all of Atlanta loved him, and I said, "relax," and he did. He was a powerful man, and a jerk, a terrible jerk. We have all been afraid we would be just like him.

**J.G.** Tell me about your time in James Dickey's classroom.—Have you written poetry? And who wrote the poems in *Prince of Tides*?

**P.C.** I thought I was going to be a poet. I was a poet in college, and I was a poet in high school, and that was my dream. I wrote the poems in the novel, here is why. I was going to use my sister Carol's poems. But when the novel was about to be published, she withdrew permission. *She* said no, not her publisher. She said, "I don't want my poems published by my brother in any way, shape, or form."

I said to her that "it would be a first for a brother to include his sister's poems in his novel. We will make history." And Carol had some "explosion." So Nan Talese, my publisher, said, "Write the poems!" I argued, "I don't write poems." She said, "I don't care. Do it!" And I said, "When do you have to have them?" And she said, "We have to have them by tomorrow, we are going to press!" So I had to stay up that night and write the poems; I can't help it that I am not a poet.—I wanted to be a poet when I was in James Dickey's class, but I could not be satisfied with what he had. It seems that poets are only thunderstruck about five or six times in their lives. I couldn't be satisfied with that kind of percentage, and also the story had proved too important to me to let the fiction go.

**J.G.** Is there still "a fear of intellect and achievement" in you, in your family, and perhaps in many people?

**P.C.** I just wanted my children to never fear that I would hurt them. I told myself that I would kill myself if I ever beat my children or beat my wife, so I didn't do that. But I didn't know life would be so tough! Your children will make choices about their lovers, husbands, wives—and some of the choices will be wrong; but I would make sure they didn't feel any pressure from me. Nor do I want them to feel they have to outdo me. We didn't put that kind of pressure on them; but now I sometimes think, maybe we should have.

**J.G.** What does the favorite son of the Lowcountry want to write above all?

**P.C.** I am finishing one more book about Charleston, and it is going to include the teachings of Daddy Rabbit of free love. It will also include the Vietnam War, which I am not yet done with, and it will include a lot on the black and white relations. And I also plan to write a novel about Atlanta and the growing *ugly* South; they now tear down old houses to build highrises. It is a nightmare!

# *Lines out across the Gap*

## AN INTERVIEW WITH PAM DURBAN

◆◆◆◆◆◆

*Beaufort, South Carolina, January 23, 2004*

Pam Durban.
*Photograph © Tom Meyer, used with permission*

◆◆◆◆◆◆

**Jan Nordby Gretlund** The father figures are a powerful presence in both the stories of *All Set about with Fever Trees* and in *The Laughing Place,* your first novel, even to the extent that they dwarf out the role of the mother figures. Many writers will not even talk about their parents, but you write about yours all the time.

**Pam Durban** It is one of the central dynamics of my life. The place my father occupied in *my* life was central, as you can tell from my essay called "The Old King." I am thinking of it as a part of a book, for which I have three essays done. "Veterans" is the title of another essay and it is about the Christmas immediately after my mother's death. I tried to go and make Christmas for my father, and both of us failed at it. We tried, but we ended up watching all ten episodes of *Band of Brothers*. It follows a company of parachutists who were dropped into France on D-Day and then fought all the way through.

**J.G.** And this had your father's interest?

**P.D.** He was interested in everything to do with the war. He was in the Pacific as a combat infantry commander, so he was right there in the thick of it. "The Old King" is about his last two years. It was amazing how much he still had inside of him, you couldn't fight him. And you realized what a commander he must have been. He would have fought us every step of the way, if we'd tried to put him into a home. And he would have won, he had that in him.—He called me his "second-in-command."

**J.G.** But in your fiction you are not writing of the family in any idealized sense. Mostly it is father, mother, and daughter, as in *The Laughing Place*. There was a brother in that novel, why does he disappear out of the narrative?

**P.D.** I didn't think I could carry him through. It may have been a mistake, but the book won. It took me a long time to write it, and I just had to give up on him. I cut 150 pages out of that manuscript. It is long, but I *did* cut it. It took me seven years to write. The first time through I had four hundred pages of language, and not much of a story. So the rest of the time was spent finding the story and strengthening the storyline that runs through the book.

I will tell you something funny. My editor at the time, after I had turned in the manuscript at one time, came down. And her idea for what I needed to do in the book was to make Melanie, the father's illegitimate child with his secretary. So "perfect Mel" would be marrying her half-brother. My editor wanted it to be revealed at the wedding, so there would be this big dramatic scene.—It was so depressing to me that this was what they wanted that I could not work on it for several weeks after that.

**J.G.** Just looking at the titles of your books makes it obvious that place is important for you.

**P.D.** Place is really important, and I see that even more now after dismantling my parents' house; the house where I grew up. I took my father's desk, the most beautiful bird's-eye maple desk, to my house and put it in one of the rooms. Of course, it is not the same thing; it doesn't have the same presence there. What matters are things in their places. The place of things is as important as the things themselves, so it is a whole. Memory is built on the unified whole: the recollection of this object, this person in this room, and in this particular light. So to me place is the center of all of that. You come back to it again and again, it is the place that's always there; that's what's important to me about it.

**J.G.** Does place matter wherever you happen to be?

**P.D.** Yes, in fact the novel that I have in my mind now, I've started pieces of it, begins in Ohio and ends up in El Paso, Texas. So the journey between these two places is important, but El Paso is the important place.—That's where my husband is from.—I think it is having grown up the way I did and where I did. Maybe it is Southern that the place is so important. It is the place you came from, it is the place, if you are lucky, where people like you came from for generations. It is a certainty, in a way, and that is why it is so devastating when it changes or falls apart; as it does with the flooding of the valley in Ron Rash's *One Foot in Eden.*

The very same flooding is in *The Laughing Place.* I worked in Seneca, South Carolina, on the newspaper there, when that lake was being built and that is where that image comes from. Lake Jocassee is what the lake is actually called.

**J.G.** I thought the senator behind the creation of that lake sounded a lot like old Strom Thurmond

**P.D.** Yes, he is old Strom.

**J.G.** There is a lot of poetry in your description of the landscape. Have you written any poetry?

**P.D.** I started out as a poet. But I only published in little magazines that don't even exist anymore. But when I went to Iowa to graduate school, I was accepted in both the fiction and the poetry workshops. I decided early on that I needed to focus on one and would rather write fiction.

**J.G.** But as "a failed poet" you are now qualified to write great fiction.

**P.D.** Exactly! [laughing].

**J.G.** In the information you gave me about yourself for the *South Carolina Encyclopedia,* you mention publishing interviews with textile workers [in *Cabbagetown Families, Cabbagetown Food,* 1976]. Do you have a strong social concern?

**P.D.** I wonder what drove me to it.—My mother's family were textile-mill people, that's the more personal concern. But it was what *I did,* I was working at a little social services organization at an old textile-mill village in the middle of downtown Atlanta, a place called Cabbagetown. I had a job there, just working for a nonprofit organization.

My title was communications coordinator, and basically I did this book. I did those interviews to keep from going nuts, because there was nothing much to do really. It was a very, very poor place. You know how those nonprofit units make up all these things you're supposed to be doing; I was supposed to be doing brochures about the organization. Instead I started working with the kids. And I was taking the kids of the neighborhood with me to interview these older women. Some of the kids liked it a lot and were really into it. These were visits with the oldest women in the community, it was a very close-knit community. The oldest women were their grandmothers, or the kids had known them, or had made fun of them all their lives. That's what made it good for them to hear the stories.

**J.G.** Did the old women tell you their life stories?

**P.D.** It was pretty amazing.—I am still proud of that book. It took about a year, and I went back, over and over again, to talk with them. I would just start it and we would go off on something, and I'd listen to that and figure out something else and go back. I pieced it all together so that there was a narrative. Then I went back and read it to them, if they wanted me to; some of them couldn't read.—There's some pretty bitter stuff in there.

**J.G.** Had they ruined their health working in the mill, like Gree's father in *The Laughing Place* [who gets emphysema from breathing cotton dust for forty years]?

**P.D.** If I had stayed there, my next project was to talk with the oldest men about the textile industry. Even though they would not talk about the strike, in 1930, I think it was.

**J.G.** It sounds almost as if you, unaware, were collecting material for future fiction.

**P.D.** I was. That's actually where I began writing. In fact my first "big" publication, the story "This Heat," was based on something from that time and that place. Stanley Lindberg published it in the *Georgia Review* [in1982]. The Cabbagetown book is out of print, but a theater group in Atlanta still performs a play based on it, called *Cabbagetown: Three Women.*

**J.G.** Did you work as a journalist in Atlanta?

**P.D.** I was one of the founding editors of a literary magazine called *Five Points.* I was the fiction editor. But before I had that job, I worked as a journalist for *The Great Speckled Bird,* which was one of the great alternative newspapers of the time. Then some friends of mine started their own newspaper, the *Atlanta Gazette,* and I went to work there [1974–75].

**J.G.** Do you feel that the training in the newspaper world has helped you in your career as fiction writer?

**P.D.** Yes it has.—Although, it is interesting now, that I always know if I have somebody in one of my classes majoring in journalism. They have the hardest time in the fiction class because of the way they are taught. They have all these really mechanical models. I didn't have my training in journalism, I just went to work on a newspaper in Seneca. But now it is a school, and you are taught exactly how to write and think.—But I *do* believe the work has helped me. I learned how to observe and how to think of the questions to ask, even of myself, about a situation.

**J.G.** But you did not have a Kansas City *Star* "style sheet" to guide you?

**P.D.** No I didn't. But I *do* feel my style is getting simpler, more direct, I like that.

**J.G.** In your fiction there is an emphasis on the lingering presence of the past. Is that *your* Southerner coming out?

**P.D.** It probably is. But it is also a function of having lived. I'm sure that for people in other parts of the country, who have grown up in a place where the family has lived for a long time, the past is always still there around you, it is like you're living the past.—Do you know the essay I have on the subject in Eve Shelnutt's book *The Confidence Woman* [1991], called "Layers"?—I wonder what's peculiarly *Southern* about the past in the present.

**J.G.** It is not that the dialogue between past and present is not recognized elsewhere, but Southern writers pick it out and talk about it. They deal not only in "time is" but also in "time was," as you also do in *So Far Back.* In New York they may think more about the present. During the "Reconstruction" occupation, the present may have seemed shabby and the past may well have looked better to defeated Southerners.

**P.D.** Isn't it typical of people everywhere to think of the past as a golden time?

**J.G.** Not necessarily. In many places people can't think of the past as anything but terrible, of how depressing it was, how dirty and poor, how early people died, and how much better it is today. And there is certainly no idea from the past that is worth much today. As Mark Twain said repeatedly, "Old Europe is a dust pile."

**P.D.** Maybe it is just a function of that Southern mythologizing, that denial, that attempt to make the past into something better than it was. I have an essay that I sketched in years ago about sentimentality and Southern memory. It's like the perfumed handkerchief held to your face as you walked the smelly streets of Charleston. Maybe it is a function of denial to glorify the past.

**J.G.** In your fiction you obviously warn against the falsification of the past. What is it we do that is *falsifying?* Aren't we just celebrating our ancestors?

**P.D.** We falsify by only allowing so little of it in. Of course it can't be changed; it can't be healed by apologies or anything else. The only thing that can happen now is that you can look at it and acknowledge that you see it more clearly. And the evidence is there, if you will look at it, the imbalance of it, and the evidence of the injustice of it. But we only see one side of the story as long as we only *have* that one side of it and don't want the reality of the other. We only tell the "white" side of it.

**J.G.** Don't we tell the whole story in museums and history books nowadays?

**P.D.** Now they do more, but not in Charleston. Part of my research for *So Far Back* was to go on every one of those house tours. How is it that they never once mention slaves? It was like those houses grew up out of the ground like flowers and only white people live there.

**J.G.** In Europe, perhaps also in the U.S., many people have the impression that contemporary black Southerners are really depressed about their slave ancestors. Actually, the black people I have met are very proud of what their ancestors contributed to Old South architecture, the craftsmanship that made it all possible. I think that should be mentioned.

**P.D.** Do you know what the beginning of that awakening was for me? Friends I've had from the North think I am being disingenuous when I say, "We didn't think about that when we were growing up." But there was *nothing* that would encourage you, permit you, or lead you to think about that.—I was driving through the bluegrass part of Kentucky, up near Paris, Kentucky, where the thoroughbred farms are; there are miles and miles of intricate stonewalls that run along there. We were with some friends from Louisville, and our friend said, "There's a guy in town who has a business renovating and restoring these walls, and he is a descendant of one of the slaves who built the walls." And it was like it hit me, it was a bolt of lightning!

So now I realize that all these things we claim as our own, all these walls in Charleston, the beautiful ironwork, the houses, the gates, the bricks of the streets, and all of that, which are symbols for us of *our* way of life once, do not belong to us at all.

**J.G.** And the Charleston baby gown in *So Far Back?*

**P.D.** And the baby gown, too.

**J.G.** Did the gown really exist?

**P.D.** It did, yes. I saw it on that pedestal during one visit. I went back later and it was *gone.* And I made an appointment with the textile archivist, who looked at all the garments they had, and they couldn't find it! I don't know if it were in a traveling exhibit, or what happened to the gown, but it *was* there at one time.

**J.G.** Josephine Humphreys talked to me about the racial situation in Charleston and mentioned that in some ways the racial situation is better there today than it was in 1989.

**P.D.** I can't say. I don't live in Charleston. It is very different where I live now, in the upper South [Chapel Hill, North Carolina]. The African Americans who live there don't have the past that they have in the Lowcountry. That past is particular to the Lowcountry.

**J.G.** Down here in Beaufort County, South Carolina, black people are proud of their Gullah dialect, their music, and their cuisine. You don't feel that you meet with people that have been deprived of their identity.

**P.D.** No, you don't. I think their identity has remained intact in time and place; perhaps because they were isolated on the islands. They know who they are. They know their origin, history, and culture.

**J.G.** The Lowcountry would not be what it is without the four hundred years of black and white cohabitation.

**P.D.** We go shrimping every year down on Jekyll Island with friends of ours from Ohio. One time on a beach where everybody goes to shrimp, there were two men, who had this wonderful elaborate set-up for their shrimping, one of the guys was black and one was white; I think they were military friends. I was just talking with them about shrimping, and when I was done, my friend from Ohio said, "*That* never happens in Ohio!"

**J.G.** Don't you think that if the Ohioans are around long enough, they will imitate even that?

**P.D.** Yeah, I think so. Yeah [laughing], I *do.*

**J.G.** Barry Hannah said, "Drop the bomb on Ohio." And Walker Percy claimed that if you found yourself in Disney World, wondering why you were there, you would be standing next to people from Ohio. And Josephine Humphreys writes funny things about people from Ohio looking for the shortest way to the sea.

**P.D.** She does, I've noticed that. Ohio comes in for that kind of ridicule.

**J.G.** I wonder if it is really a deep-seated historical prejudice. There seems to be an overload of monuments to dead Ohioans in the southern Civil War battlefield parks.

**P.D.** I guess that's right. But I don't even know how much the War matters anymore. I guess it means a lot to some people, and maybe it lingers in the stories people tell.

**J.G.** Talking about monuments to the dead, it struck me that throughout your fiction, you are preoccupied with aging! Most people do not like to think of the spotting and clotting, but you seem determined to constantly face the fact that we are falling apart.

**P.D.** That seems to me to be one of the central facts of life, isn't it? Why do I write about it? I guess that is what I see in people. I fear it. But I would say that I'm more preoccupied with death or dying than with the process that leads you there.

**J.G.** I'm not thinking of just the physical disintegration, but also the fact that we disappear even as a memory.

**P.D.** What I realize now, having just lost my parents, and seeing my son grow up, is that people are *not* going to remember you. My son will probably pass on things to his children about us, but how much he will pass on about his grandparents I don't know, and so they will be forgotten. When I'm gone, and when my brother and sister are gone, they'll be forgotten.

**J.G.** And so, according to Katherine Anne Porter, their lives might never have been, if they were *not* recorded.

**P.D.** Right. And there are millions of people to whom that happen. My husband is a photographer, and he likes to ask antique stores if they have old photographs. And he comes upon whole collections of photos of people nobody knows who are any longer. They have clearly been discarded by someone. And those people are gone from the earth.

**J.G.** In Europe we tend to think of the South as a place where names, births, and deaths of ancestors are remembered. But maybe this is no longer true?

**P.D.** We just opened my father's safety-deposit box. And in it were all these documents, some from my mother, where her mother was applying for membership in the United Daughters of the Confederacy. There was the whole account of who Joseph Palmer was, where he was born, and what qualified my grandmother to be taken into the UDC. Maybe it is a generational thing, for all those people knew their people a long way back.

**J.G.** But you didn't know about this old application before the safe was opened?

**P.D.** I knew vaguely but did not remember his names. I couldn't tell you where he is buried. So maybe it is passing now.—But you would think that in old Europe people would celebrate the memory of ancestors; but maybe the detailed memory is a function of *not* being old?

**J.G.** Europeans often see the attention paid to your Civil War, as being out of proportion and as a result of your brief history

**P.D.** And we are young enough to think that it is important to remember all of that and to trace back your family history. Look at the obsession that people in this country have with finding out if their family came over on the Mayflower.

**J.G.** That *is* funny. I find, by the way, that you can be a most humorous writer but that you do not allow yourself to be so very often. Mostly your fiction is serious and fully focused.

**P.D.** This was one of the things I intended to get across in "The Old King," by saying, "You can laugh at this." It *is* a serious topic, but it did strike me as funny, a lot of it, and I thought I got that across. I was really pleased with that essay in part because of that. I mean I was able not to write it as this mournfully sad piece.

**J.G.** You did that with nonfiction, which is difficult. Whereas you would think it would be easier to sport with "serious" topics in fiction. But you haven't done much with rollicking humor in your fiction.

**P.D.** Yeah. And it is funny because I think *in person* people think of me as having a great sense of humor. Maybe as I get more comfortable with myself as a writer, and more confident, I'm going to do it.

**J.G.** But not everybody wants to be Mark Twain.

**P.D.** No. True, and I don't. But I still appreciate humor. You know who does that really well is Tobias Wolff. He writes very droll humor.

**J.G.** Some writers, like Clyde Edgerton, will sell their souls for a good anecdote. Also when it was not exactly what the reader was hoping for.

**P.D.** I know. See I think it can go too far in that direction, too. And that's my worry.

**J.G.** But Faulkner was very funny sometimes and Miss Welty.

**P.D.** And Flannery O'Connor!

**J.G.** Oh, above all! In my irreligious country the readers do not pay much attention to her religious aim, but O'Connor was funny and is well known there.

**P.D.** Just her descriptions, and her timing!

**J.G.** As a point of departure for your narrative, you often use a diary or old family letters, as if you try to bring out the present by constantly relating it to the past. Is this a favorite strategy?

**P.D.** It must be. In terms of the essays I am writing now, there's one thing I am thinking forward to:

in my parents' attic I found a suitcase with their letters back and forth during World War II. And I'm shaping in my mind another essay for this collection about those letters and their lives together.

**J.G.** Why do you turn that material into nonfiction? Do you feel uneasy using it in fiction?

**P.D.** No, I did that before with my father's actual diary, a whole narrative, that he kept throughout the war ["Notes toward an Understanding of My Father's Novel," 1983]. Most of it is tedious: the first day we are on the ship; the second day we are on the ship . . . but I can edit it and make it into a real narrative. There are some really amazing parts to it:

the first day in combat; the first dead man he saw; the first. . . .

**J.G.** I've noticed that you stress other senses than just sight, especially the olfactory sense. It is obvious, of course, in your description in *So Far Back* of the Charleston of 1837.

**P.D.** It struck me one day, when I was walking around down there, doing research for the novel. Sometimes you'll just catch a whiff. It is either the paper mill and the wind blowing the wrong way or the pulp that smells or just the smells that come up from those grates in the sidewalks. I just catch a whiff and I realize this city really stinks. And in antebellum time it really had to with the damp rotting wood and their privies.

The story I'm finishing now is about a child, an adopted child. I was reading back over it just the other day, and a lot of it has to do with smell, the smell of his mother, the smell of his sister, and of things he remembers.

**J.G.** You do not devote much space to old-time religion. If religion is brought in, it is to be ridiculed, as in the section of the mother getting *saved* in *The Laughing Place,* which reads as a hilarious short story.

**P.D.** Yes. I don't know why, exactly. I think that above all is an adopted attitude. I was brought up Catholic, and it is very serious to me. I consider lots of things in organized religion really destructive, but I don't consider spirituality a joke at all. It is some inner sense of a larger meaning, within what one's life exists. I am not cynical about religion. Even now I would like to be able to go to church, because it is important to me. But I want to sit there with one of these little cards that a person who is deaf or blind will come and hand to you in a store. I want to be able to hand that to the people who want you to join and to bring a casserole, to hand them a card saying, "I am a contemplative, may I please come to your church to take communion and *not* have to bring a casserole?" [laughing]. Religion *is* very serious to me, but I don't know how to write about it. When my father was dying, it meant a lot to all of us, especially that the priest was able to come and it certainly meant a lot to my father. He had been a Catholic all his life; it meant a lot to him for the priest to come to hear his confession and to give him communion.

My mother was a Presbyterian. So when they got married, which was a long while back, she literally, she often told, had to sign us away. She relinquished any kind of influence over our religious upbringing. That was the law of the Church for a Catholic to marry a non-Catholic. They had to sign a paper saying that their children would be raised Catholic and *not* Protestant. That sounds medieval [laughing].

**J.G.** In your fiction there are women whose identity resides in the dishes they make. So if you hear the name "Catherine Henderson," you will expect "Squash Casserole." Is it still true that Southern women make their identity in this way?

**P.D.** I don't know, but food *is* a major theme in the South. When my mother was dying, in the morning word would go out that she liked custard or that she liked that fruit salad from Publix, and by afternoon there would be ten custards there, or ten fruit salads. All her friends had brought them. It was because of the connections she had made over time with people all came back to her then, people really took care of her.—Her life with my father was tough, he was a difficult man, *impossible,* you can tell. But my mother had friends, she played bridge all the time, she was a great bridge player, and that was her life.—My father had not made such connections. Men don't do that, and he was very lonely. I took care of him for the last two years of his life. He didn't have much in terms of other people.

**J.G.** I have always been interested in Southern stoicism. If I see it in your fiction, it is in your women characters. Are Southern women "stoics"?

**P.D.** Yes. Definitely, that is one of the archetypes: optimistic, fierce, and determined. They do what is needed, always have, and always will. My mother was that way when she was dying. I had never quite seen that part of her before. She said, "I have liver cancer and my doctor and I have decided we are not going to do anything. You know that I had a good life. It is in God's hands." Even if she had not had religion, she would have been strong. And everybody who took care of her said that. I have never seen anybody as brave as she was.

**J.G.** In your first novel Melody Givens is given beauty with grace and confidence, whereas Annie Vess has to struggle to gain hers. Does so much still depend on beauty criteria in the South?

**P.D.** I think so. If you look around you [in Beaufort County], there are women around here who are sixty and still look thirty. I don't know why, but it is true that that remains acute.

**J.G.** In Europe we also celebrate beauty, but in itself it doesn't give you a standing in society. Melody seems to live off her beauty, and being "Miss Sun Fun," "Miss Vaucluse County," and, my favorite, "Miss Rural Electrification."

**P.D.** [laughing] My cousin was Miss South Carolina one year, and she had some trouble with the description of Mel. "Miss Rural Electrification," see that's funny, so I have a sense of humor!

**J.G.** There are romantic scenes in your fiction, men and women are attracted to each other, and presumably have sex. Do you feel it would cheapen your work if you were to describe sexual encounters?

**P.D.** With some of my classes, it is funny, I used to have a contest, I would say, "Write the best sex scene." And they try to write one, and it is really hard to do, it is almost impossible. You either go to a sort of romantic lushness or to some kind of clinical description, which is not good either. I just never found a way to do it.

**J.G.** But you describe the animal attraction of some men, such as Canady in *The Laughing Place,* very well.

**P.D.** That is again what you take from your life and other places and bring into fiction. When I met my now husband and we had started dating, we went to his cousin's wedding, and she married somebody like that. He was one of the breathtakingly handsome men, and he knew. He was going around at this reception talking to women and holding their hand. But he was really taking their pulse to see what he was doing to them. It was pretty terrible and he actually turned out to be. . . .

**J.G.** I kept expecting Canady, the handsome man, to get a hard time. But he never quite does.

**P.D.** But he does! When he shows up to get his baby, he doesn't even know that the baby needs a sweater! That's another funny scene.

**J.G.** What we have been talking about today has really been about reality and fiction. And I am tempted to conclude that there isn't much difference. Everything you write has at least a basis in reality.

**P.D.** Yes, those are the things that draw me, I don't know why, those are the things I see; but it is invented around. And as Chekhov always said, "I can't write about what I don't know!"

**J.G.** But you do more than report reality in the way you use your art existentially to overcome the alienation you write about. You use the power of words not only to soothe but to try to bridge the gap between you and reality. In your fiction your characters share obvious feelings of being alienated, but through art they try to overcome their problem.

**P.D.** Yes, that's true, and they try to make connections where they can. They throw these lines out across that emptiness, that loneliness, or that alienation.

# *Interview with Clyde Edgerton*

◆◆◆◆◆◆

*Jackson, Mississippi, March 26, 1996*

Clyde Edgerton.
*Photograph by Stephanie Cara Trott, used with permission*

◆◆◆◆◆◆

*This interview took place when Edgerton was Eudora Welty Writer in Residence at Millsaps College.*

**Jan Nordby Gretlund** The last thing I did was to go back and see Dannye Powell's interview with you.[1] She said you were one of the difficult ones to interview, you didn't volunteer very much.

I was wondering what year was it exactly that you were flying in the Far East?

C.E. That was from October 1970 to August 1971.

J.G. The reason that I ask that is that when I read you it seems obvious to me as a critic, who has read all your books, that Vietnam and the foreign experience, even North Carolina boy leaving the country, seem totally absent in the fiction. Is it too serious, too painful, to write about?

C.E. I have one, maybe two . . . do you remember a short story called "Search and Rescue"?

J.G. I did not see many of the short stories, mainly because they have not been collected.

C.E. What I have written about in *The Floatplane Notebooks* [1988] I wanted that to be about . . . well, there's *Raney* [1985], in that I had the black-white experience—Charles Shepherd and Johnny Dobbs; when I was in the Air Force I had a good friend, named Johnny Hobbes, as a matter of fact. He was from the North and had never been south. I had just begun a transformation out of my own cultural racism into asking questions, and he and I met and became good friends. I took that with me from my Vietnam experience.

In *The Floatplane Notebooks* I knew I wanted to write about family history, my boyhood, and Vietnam. I wanted to write about certain nice experiences I had to tell. In fact the first novel I tried to write was a novel about flying airplanes in wartime, and it just died. So, in *The Floatplane Notebooks* I had, I think, about ninety pages of Vietnam material. A good deal of it dialogue between pilots on whether or not the war should be fought. At one point I had Mark on a rescuing mission and he sees Meredith getting beheaded.

J.G. As in James Dickey's poem "The Performance"?

C.E. Yes—so I had all that going on and as I revised, I threw all that out. The main thing I kept was the scene where Mark is looking down at a person walking on the road. I had a memory of the first time I had seen from above a person walking along the Ho Chi Minh Trail and I knew that was the core of what I had to write about in *The Floatplane Notebooks.* As I saw that, the other stuff had to go. I ended up just putting it in the end, hoping for an effect. What was left was the sense of loss.

J.G. I read *The Floatplane Notebooks* and it has been some time, but I looked at it just before I came down to Jackson and remember their looking down at the graveyard, but I do not recall the Vietnam pages.

C.E. They are not there! I threw all of that out, because it did not work well. It was mainly polemics about the war, which I wrote for myself. But the core of it was the humanity versus the machinery of those bombs, and that ended up being in the book. However, I knew that one of these two boys would be wounded or killed, I did not know who, until I was writing it. The wound and the loss at home were what I wanted to write about, rather than the experience itself.

Then when I was working on *In Memory of Junior* [1992], I had a scene in which the father of the boy called Morgan hints that there is a story that his wife fell in love with him partly because of one of his "war stories." Well, that story used to be in the novel, and that story is called "Search and Rescue," which I removed because it was too heavy.[2] It was not so much about war, but it was about the experience on the ground in villages outside of war.

**J.G.** You have told me about material you have taken out of two novels. Are you saving that, and mulling it over?

**C.E.** I could end up writing about it.—It seems to me that some kind of distance is often needed for material, whether it is in time, or psychological, or just a matter of revising, it is a kind of distance needed. It took me ten to twelve years after the war to be able to write about it.

There is another short story called "Venom," of which there are three rewrites.[3] Do you remember the scene in *In Memory of Junior* when the airplane crashes, it's upside down, and they are hanging in their seatbelts? That started out as a short story in which two Vietnam veterans were flying, a former ground soldier and a pilot. The pilot felt guilty about not having fought on the ground, and they crashed, and one of them dies. It is a dark story with Vietnam connections.

The two stories mentioned had a true background story in common: a pilot was on the ground set in Laos and I was flying above him in charge of his rescue. The cloud cover meant there was no way to get down to him; we could talk to each other over the radio, and before I left to go back to base, short of fuel, I heard him being killed. He was shouting into his earphone as he was being shot. That's what I needed to write about. That was a part of that story called "Venom," and then in the novel *In Memory of Junior* I tried a reworking of that story; but the reworking came out and became a second short story. But in the meantime the scene—the hanging upside down in a crashed airplane—was rewritten and used for different purposes. It was used to show Morgan, the boy in *In Memory of Junior,* finally using storytelling in a relationship, having earned and learned that.

I had an airplane, "Annabelle." A friend of mine Tim McLaurin,[4] whose name you may recognize, wanted me to fly him from Durham to Wilmington to get four rattlesnakes. I decided not to do that. But I thought:

wouldn't it be interesting if Tim and I were hanging upside down by our seat belts in a crashed airplane about to catch fire with rattlesnakes loose in the cockpit. And that became a short story with a Vietnam connection. Then a few months later (in January 1991) I crashed my airplane, a little Piper Supercruiser, ground-looped it tail over head and hung there from the seat belt, upside down. There were no snakes, there was no fire; it was lucky nothing happened.[5]

**J.G.** It is interesting that you pick these novels, they are the ones I consider your two most serious efforts as a novelist. I have thought of *The Floatplane Notebooks* as being in a class by itself. It is also the novel that appears to have connections to other Southern fiction. I am thinking of the "Vine" passage and the burial of the blown-off leg; it is simply great Faulknerian humor. And my students think of *In Memory of Junior* as a serious book. It is, of course, very amusing, but it is also a serious book about aging, gender, and race.

**C.E.** Yes, I think it is a serious book. It is interesting that I used the airplane crash. It is the only real incident that I recall using more than once. An incident that was somehow translated and used again. *The Floatplane Notebooks* took much longer to write than *In Memory of Junior.* Writing it was a more complex job than *Junior.* I worked on it off and on for eleven years. Embedded in it was the first short story I wrote. After that story and a few others, I wrote *Raney* and went back to *Floatplane Notebooks,* then I wrote *Walking across Egypt* [1987] and went back to *Floatplane Notebooks* again. I worked on it from 1977 to 1988, eleven years, taking out three or four years for the other two novels. I had problems with it.

I found that I could not write an omniscient book with me as author, I just couldn't make it work. Then I decided to find some thread from 1850 to 1977–88 and, of course, my thread was a ninety-nine-year-old widow. And there is a real graveyard that our family came to and there is an old wisteria vine. Then I realized I could just have that wisteria vine cover the entire history of the family. So one day I let the vine talk. I remember I read the first paragraph and I felt like I had stumbled onto something. So I started out to write the whole book like that, for about sixty-eight pages. It didn't work. Then I had a student named Bliss, and I thought I have to write about a character named Bliss, and the obvious came to me:

I'll have her marry into this family. As soon as she started talking I realized that she was from *outside* the family. Before I had been writing almost incestuously and had no perspective, because they were all like each other in their ways. It was like orange goldfish looking at each other trying to describe the color orange.

I realized that Bliss had to talk, but *she* had no way of telling other stories. And I had eighty pages from the vine's perspective. Then it finally came to me, I had read *As I Lay Dying* a long time ago, and I was going to have all these points of view. It was what I had to do to tell the story that I wanted told. And additionally, in order to have these older and dead people tell their stories, I had to be in the graveyard, so I decided on the vine, blue moons, and all that. That's how it came about.

**J.G.** It is a very good idea.—When I read through the novel again, I came upon a lynching that reads almost like a short story, a Faulknerian lynching.

**C.E.** The one about the black woman and the white man and the father? That used to be a short story. I changed it and put it in there. The lynching . . . I needed something dark before the Vietnam stuff. I also needed to deal with race; there was no ready-made way to deal with it.

**J.G.** Europeans often think that race is the only Southern topic. British colleagues, who have their own problems in this area, tend to focus entirely on race. I don't see the same focus on race in new fiction by black or white Southerners.

**C.E.** Do you know Randall Kenan? He is very young and has two books. His best book is *Let the Dead Bury Their Dead* [1992]. In the title story he has written footnotes and all kinds of paraphernalia about family history and race, which when I looked at it, I said, "This is excellent!'

**J.G.** It seems to me that we, in the 1990s, have reached some psychological saturation point where few Southern writers want to even mention integration and rights. As if nobody wants to read about race, and nobody wants to deal with it. Publishers do not want it. Black people want to write about trouble in the black community, trouble between men and women, yes, but not trouble between blacks and whites!—But I see some progress in Josephine Humphreys' novels and in your novel *Killer Diller* [1991], with the individualizing of black characters. Ben is not like any other black man in fiction, and he is not stereotypical. This is perhaps not progress in any political sense, but it is important if it reflects a changing psychology in the South.

**C.E.** It may be an attempt to relax. But I agree, in my life, starting in the early '50s, living in a racist community and family, at least racist in language, I was invisibly taught superiority. One of the interesting questions to me in Southern writers of the 1990s is the variances. You will find variation in the racism from family to family. My family mostly used the word "nigger" in an indirect teaching of superiority. The classic problem Southerners of my generation had was in going to college they came to have new points of view; in my case it was at Chapel Hill. They meet and have relationships with black persons and the white person goes "wait a minute"— something was drastically wrong! And they go back home and the vocabulary of that old racism is still used among the people you love. So there is a tremendous tension. And you would sense that if you were black and if you were new, and then you would probably hate these people.

I just learned an interesting lesson with *Redeye: A Western* [1995]. I read about the Mountain Meadows Massacre [1857] in researching Mormonism. I knew little about Mormons. I read about how they massacred in a most outlandishly cruel way a group of people, mostly Christians probably, from Arkansas, and I found myself *hating* Mormons. I was able to use the resulting energy in propelling my plot. I didn't know what would happen when I saw a Mormon. I was so outraged.—But before I toured, I read John Egerton's book *Speak Now against the Day* [1994]. The title is a quote from Faulkner. The book is a history of the civil rights movement before 1954 in the South. Egerton carefully chronicles lynchings that I had never read about, so that suddenly in my general hatred of Mormons I saw a black person's general hatred of white people. The description of the lynchings touched me just like the terrible massacre I had discovered. But then I met some Mormons and found they didn't seem evil, yet still. . . .

So prejudice came to me in a new way, but their main problem back home remained. I see that somehow, it is hard to disengage the history of Southern culture from your own history, of course I have a few friends who happen to be black; the guy in the Air Force, he and I talk to each other and we kid each other. In fact, the first relationship I had with a black woman in an all-black setting, a government program, and she wanted the next program to be a "*why* you're not." So we got on with a kind of racist humor, which, if you read it, is *not* humorous. But it was fun at the time. If I had my connections to black people, I am blind to the track of their culture. But when I read the paper, it does seem that there is a new separation. A lot of it is coming from a new strength, which is that the voices are heard more in the media now.

**J.G.** Many black people have the advantage of living in traditional families with rather conservative values. This is obvious when you see black Americans heading to church on Sunday mornings, when they dress and behave much like most families did in the 1950s.

**C.E.** No doubt about it; in fact, I wrote a review of a book by Bebe Moore Campbell[6] in which I said that in three hundred years there will be a group of anthropologists studying a group from the 1900s called the "Cornbread Eaters."—As a group they were composed of subgroups of dark people and white people. What they had in common was food, music, certain language and religious practices, extended families, dogs, chickens, and in many cases a lack of political or economic power. They ate cornbread made from just corn meal, salt, and water. Among these people one difference was in the color of the skin, but they had plenty of cultural material in common.

I had a good question from a tenth-grade student, and this happened more than once. She asked if my novel *Walking across Egypt* [1987] is about black people or white people. And I said, "Why'd you ask?" And she said, "Well, she cooks all this food my grandma cooks."—But sometimes it seems to be a gulf that is coming back. And of course when you throw power and white privilege into the mix, things can get ugly.

**J.G.** You bring the old uncle, Grove McCord, back to the family, *In Memory of Junior,* and he is, of course, of the old school. He has grown up with segregation, and he is a racist. But he is not a disagreeable character. The reader gets to know him and begins to like him. Morgan, the young man in the novel, has problems accepting his Uncle Grove, because of the way he thinks about black people.

**C.E.** It reflects pretty much my own problems, later in life, with my own uncle, whom that character was based on, in certain ways. I had several uncles, but the uncle in *Junior* is based on, lived in Florida and was clearly a racist. I idolized him, in part because of the way he treated me; he treated me in some ways like an adult. He looked at me and talked to me, and was telling me stories as if I were alone in the room, and this was when I was ten years old. It takes a certain kind of heart to do that. Yet this same man was a racist in all the traditional, nonviolent ways of my people. And I really can't accurately say "nonviolent" given the history of turned heads. There are family stories about my uncle that romanticized his traveling around with a black guy, who was his help and rode with him on cross country trips and all that. I have been with him and heard his language and I love him as my uncle. One of the things I thought about, after I began writing *Raney,* is—wouldn't it be neat if people could actually find a fictional character with whom they disagree politically but yet have to *like* as a person.

**J.G.** There are some things about black-and-white relationships in the South that go further back than civil rights battles. I see this again and again when I live here among blacks and whites who have known each other and lived together for generations. They clearly share knowledge and experience, for better and worse, that no Yankee or foreigner could ever hope to fully understand. Is Southern fiction in a period in the 1990s where male writers are reacting to the almost fanatical pressure of correctness on gender issues by going back to a male-oriented world, a Hemingway country of men without women? Are the men, in the tradition of Twain, reacting against being "civilized," as in Barry Hannah's *Never Die* [1991] and Cormac McCarthy's two novels of the trilogy, by going west, sitting around the campfire with the horses, or just anywhere away from the domestic situation? Bumpy of your novel *Redeye* has a hard time because he is not "civilized," as "the west denudes men of manners."

C.E. The source of *Redeye,* I was writing about a fellow who I saw chewing tobacco in a strange way on a beach one time. I wrote a chapter that was taken out; it is a separate story now. This fellow chewing tobacco had a family, and I am interested in his family, because I am interested in the way he chews tobacco. Then I overhear a conversation about someone who "won't let their children go next door because the family over there eats out all the time." Then I find out that the family next door ran an embalming service, in a kitchen. So, I say, I want to write about that, but it died on me.

Then I visited Mesa Verde, I was visiting some friends and took my daughter out to Mesa Verde. When I saw the Cliff Palace I was swept away, I just couldn't get over it. So I went to the museum there and bought a biography of a cowboy. He and his brothers lost their ranch because they were obsessed with the cliff dwellings. They lived at the base of the mesa, had never been up top, and they stumbled in there and found hundreds of cliff dwellings from an early civilization, the Anasazi, dating from around 1100, all of the dwellings intact, nobody had been there in there for a long time. I knew I wanted to write about it, so I just moved my tobacco-chewing character back a hundred years, moved him and his family over several states, and put him beside an archeologist and made him a fictional rancher who discovered some cliff dwellings.

I read all these stories about the Native Americans. I took five hundred pages of notes, dividing them into categories:

language, horses, land, clothing, on and on. I had all the notes from the most fascinating stories and then I came upon the Mormons. So I had to get that in there somehow. I mixed all that up, and I knew that I had to have a familiarity with the West. And when I saw the West I was amazed, and my feeling was that a woman would be more likely to talk about that than a man—she would notice with the kind of amazement I experienced. So I had Star travel west to try to communicate the vastness, the power, and the magnitude; even though she overdoes it, she was still able to do that and that is the purpose of her being there. My mother was born in 1904, so I've listened to older people talking a lot. I've got a feel for gender differences back in those times. I was thinking in more personal terms of how Star would be proper and how she would be enjoying her trip west.

**J.G.** You could see that story as a sort of walking in the footsteps of Mark Twain—he could have been out there at that time. This is high comedy except for the presence of the sinister Pittman, the cynical cowboy who doesn't speak and disappears with the dog Redeye. He or a similar character, I am sure, is bound to pop up in another book. But apart from him this book seems to be less controversial. People like Roy Blount, Lewis Grizzard, and Dave Barry who wrote humorous fiction for the newspaper, and in the antebellum South there were also numerous humorists, but Mark Twain wrote humor meant to last. He outlived the southwestern humorists by being didactic and concerned about humanity. I feel that *In Memory of Junior* there is that concern, but I feel, that except for the rage against the Mormons, you sometimes sold your soul for a laugh in *Redeye.* There is more American sitcom action in that novel than in your other novels. This is, of course, criticism. I am saying, "This is wonderfully hilarious, and so what?" The reader might ask, does this in any way refer to my situation?

**C.E.** Sometimes I think my soul for a laugh could be a worthy trade. The hilarity I look for—and in this particular book there were at least two things on the serious side, the Cobb Pittman character helped me direct my rage. He was just perfect for me to channel my rage into. Of course, he was also guilty, he was there and was part of the massacre. So guilt and rage I was able to connect with him.—The other serious question I was dealing with, of course to a certain extent it depends upon the reader, and I am at great advantage as a reader of what I just wrote. The last scene—because of the very questions you asked me, I had all kinds of trouble in deciding how to end that book. Because I did have this hilarity and I did have this dead seriousness.

The second dead-serious matter for me in the writing of the book was about faith and fathers. Hiram [son of Bishop Thorpe who led the Mormons in the massacre] and Bumpy have a conversation about this at the end of the book; they're sitting at a campfire, and Bumpy helps Hiram smoke, Hiram's got his hands tied behind him. Bumpy asks him did he believe in what happened at the Mountain Meadows Massacre, and Hiram says yes he does. Indirectly, they discuss the problem of believing what your father believed, only *because* your father believed it, and the whole business of having a faith is handed to you. In this case it is the Mormon faith, which in some ways is not unlike the fundamentalist Protestantism I grew up with. The son of the Mormon priest wavering and the issue of faith make up a serious part of the book, and then you have the hilarity.

At one time I had the book end much more seriously with the father and faith theme. But it stood out. So I moved it back and camouflaged the seriousness a little bit. That is the serious matter I was thinking about, as I ended the book: faith and fathers. Also there was the father–son relationship between the Englishmen, who in real life were Swedish. His real name was Gustaf Nordenskiöld [1868–95]. Oh, you've got to read about him! He was at Denver and had tuberculosis. His father Adolf Nordenskiöld,[7] a famous polar explorer and scientist in Sweden, was sending Gustaf around the world, and Gustaf found out about the cliff dwellings and got obsessed with them.[8] His is a small book of letters to his father. It is wonderful. His relationship with his father was interesting.[9]

**J.G.** One of the things that I have noticed, especially with some Southern women writers, is that they were so successful with their first novel that they keep slipping into their comfortable initiation voice. It is so convincing, so funny at the same time, and it sounds *really* true,—but they keep doing it in book after book. You did it, of course, in *Raney,* but you have not repeated the use of that voice. What I sometimes miss in some of your fellow writers is a negative capability, where they not only look at their grandmothers from their youthful perspective but actually try *to become* the grandmothers. What does it mean to be *her* and to live *her* life.—Now, if we turn this around and see it from the writer's point of view: do you feel that moving your fiction back in time and out of North Carolina, as in *Redeye,* makes it harder to answer questions like "Is this a Southern book, set in the West?" or "Where is Clyde Edgerton in all this?" or "Why doesn't he go into the menacing killer's mind?"

**C.E.** I am not sure of how conscious I was of this, but he gave me an outlet and also gave me an owner of a dog. I stumbled on his bulldog; bulldogs are bred to hang into the noses of bulls, and I didn't know that until I started on this book. Somebody told me about a dog that would do that and I said, "I can use that, it is great, I can use a dog" and then matched him up with Cobb Pittman. Early on I realized that he was guilty of participating in the Mountain Meadows Massacre and that later he was going to feel guilt, and I wanted to kill him off. If I had been truly honest with the reader on the first page, I may have had him remember his source of guilt, although I am not sure how much he did remember. His predicament and his committing suicide were reasons for me not to get deeper into his character. It was a new kind of technique for me, I hadn't written from a killer's point of view before.

About this question of doing the same thing over and over, well, the best for me is to have some new technical problem for each book, even if I have to almost devise it, to keep it interesting. I could have written this from a blameless point of view, but it would have been deadly boring. So point of view is what I find more and more fascinating, and more difficult, and more interesting. Each book presents its problems just like a different child, but in each one I have had something, even the present tense in *Killer Diller,* some new technique to make the book. My question is "what can I do" to make a book even more omniscient, which is something I want to do. I've got a story which needs to be told and, of course, the point is you've got to be mastering the story or it wouldn't work at all.—I like to have a new technical problem and sometimes, if I run out, I have to come up with one.

J.G. I found Jimmy Knight, of *In Memory of Junior* [1992], to be a most convincing character. He voices opinions that are prejudiced, hopelessly conservative, and out of an old political tradition. You don't sell him short. He comes across as a full human being, and he is not ridiculous in that sense. *Some* of us would reject most of his opinions. [Edgerton laughing] But he is so convincing, so delightfully politically incorrect, that you listen to his point of view. I am thinking of his attack on the feminists at Duke, who spend their time killing off dead white men, on lesbians, who want the human race to *peter out,* and on people who think sea turtles are more endangered than those who catch them, and add the poor white attack on book learning in general, which *is* in an old Southern tradition.

C.E. Jimmy Knight came out of nowhere. He came from an overheard conversation. Of course, if you are on the coast of North Carolina, you'll understand the seriousness of some of the environmental laws which keep you from trapping—they declare these turtles an endangered species. I overheard a conversation, two guys sitting beside me in the afternoon, they'd been drinking and they were talking about this endangered species. I just sat there, and listened, it was like discovering gold. I went away, and wrote down much of the conversation, and then transplanted it to the endangered species part in the book. I later separated them, but at the time I still had the feminists, the abstractionists, and all. Any vocal, narrow point of view automatically sets itself up for satire.

J.G. And the satire is not in there to entertain or for hilarity. You are out there in a rather didactic way, saying here is something that deserves ridicule. Are you saying, "How can people have opinions like that?"

C.E. No, I'll tell you what I think. We are talking about the deconstruction of a story. At Duke they got all these people, Stanley Fish and all these deconstructionists. In North Carolina you've got a lot of people who really do not like that a lot, we're ruled by people who are very conservative and who do *not* like that type of criticism. Finally I started reading some of it, because I found it fascinating. It was recreational reading.—In many ways it is exciting, it is fun, it is interesting, it is something fresh, and it is something different. So when I first started reading any criticism at all, I became interested in certain aspects of this whole deconstructionist perspective that I thought were healthy. When I say "certain aspects" I mean I also felt that certain aspects were extreme and unhelpful. But in general, it was "fresh air," but I had friends who would say, "You listen, this is heresy!" So I was sort of in the middle and could see it both ways and be playful with it. I was just enough removed to have this character buy into it in a good way. But personally I don't have enough knowledge to have strong feelings about specifics of theoretical deconstruction.

**J.G.** I sometimes feel provoked when so-called literary critics publish entire books on the criticism of others without referring to any creative literature whatsoever, thereby trying to make criticism into a philosophy of life, a cult, or a religion. For me the purpose of criticism is, above all else, to help facilitate the distribution and reading of literature.

**C.E.** Did you read the piece on Willa Cather in *The New Yorker* by Joan Acocella from November 1995?[10] Willa Cather had an experience at Mesa Verde. It was similar to the experience of the ranchers who discovered the cliff dwellings, and to what I experienced. She stumbled onto this thing and wrote Tom Outland's story, which is the middle part of *The Professor's House* [1925]. Her story was based on the same people I was writing about. I didn't know about this until I had researched it very thoroughly, and then I read her piece. And the reason I mention that piece on Cather is that in a very commonsensical way it reflected the opinion you have, in writing about her critics in this century. It is a delightful piece trying to overcome some of the narrowness of critics criticizing critics' criticism.

Let me ask you a question, is this true: in America feminist critics are interested in what women wrote, in France feminist critics would be more interested in what's written from a woman's point of view—more of a gender point of view? The reason I ask is, I've often thought, given that some of my characters, as in *Raney,* have a woman's point of view, that this would be interesting to feminists, if for no other reason than it is a feminine point of view written by a male, but nobody has commented on this.

**J.G.** I would have thought that *Raney* would have been an obvious subject and a fine target for feminist criticism. In the climate of rather monomaniacal women studies, I am surprised to hear you have not been grilled and roasted for presumptuously insisting on seeing life in Listre, North Carolina, from a young woman's point of view.—Talking about women, let me bring up

Flannery O'Connor's name, because the Southern grotesque obviously lives in your fiction, as well. Have you studied O'Connor's fiction?

C.E. Yeah. My wife Susan—when we were married in '75—she *knew,* she had read Faulkner, Flannery O'Connor, and Eudora Welty, and I hadn't. I grew up on Hemingway, I was reading Mark Twain, and Crane, and those people. I didn't know that much about Southern literature even though it was all around me. I had majored in education, *not* creative writing. I wasn't from a reading family. I had read Flannery O'Connor in college, and it didn't make much sense to me. But then I started, and I read everything, and by the time I started writing I got ahold of *The Habit of Being.*[11]—When did *The Habit of Being* come out? I started writing about '77–'78, I think, it was about that time.

J.G. It came in February '79.—I remember because Sally Fitzgerald, the editor, sent me a copy. I had located some O'Connor correspondence.

C.E. If you had a copy of my copy of *The Habit of Being,* you'd see that all the whites and all the note pages in the back and all in front are full of notes, because she talks a lot about writing stories in her letters. And it struck me, not unlike *Understanding Fiction* struck me, and the *Paris Review* interviews:

"Writers at Work." These are at least three sources of nonfiction I remember reading. The whole talk of the mechanics of writing was fascinating to me. So I read a good bit of what O'Connor had to say about stories and I read and reread her stories. I never quite got the Grace; and the religious implications never hit home with me. What *hit home* with me—I said somewhere, "If I could have written the first two-thirds of 'Good Country People' and had that last piece to go, I would be in Heaven." That's my favorite of her stories, for the humor and, what I got to come back to, how she handled the omniscient point of view she uses.

J.G. When did you read Hemingway?

C.E. I read Hemingway from the time I was in college on,—I read everything. Whenever I try to write like Hemingway, it is a terrible failure.

J.G. Well, you have that same precision in language.

C.E. I appreciate that. In that "style sheet" of the *Kansas City Star:* accuracy, clarity, and conciseness were the gospel for the newspaper reporters, I've never forgotten that.—My early tests of Faulkner did not do anything for me, I couldn't read it. So when I was in college, I remember "The Bear" pulling me very strongly because of the dogs, woods, and hunting. But then I read a book by a guy named David Minter[12]—in that book he had, more or less, "a translation" of *Absalom, Absalom!*—that prepared me when I read that novel. In the meantime I found a few of the action short stories, like "Death Drag," "Turn About," which I really liked, and that got me into reading more. Then I went ahead with *Absalom, Absalom!* and saw what I was confronted with, and then I read Faulkner. This was just after I started writing fiction.

**J.G.** Unlike O'Connor you were not afraid of reading Faulkner when you were writing?

**C.E.** I know she talked about not wanting to be stalled on the railroad track in her car with the Dixie Limited headed her way—something like that. If I had read Faulkner before I started writing, I would have been more intimidated. But I also started writing under the influence of Eudora Welty's stories, her early stories. Those were so powerful to me, in fact on May 14, 1978, I saw her read "Why I Live at the P.O." on TV. Six months before that, I had been in several readers' theater productions of that story. I almost had it memorized, my wife had it memorized, she had been a character, but until then I had never heard, nor had I seen Eudora Welty. But I turned on the TV and *there she was* on PBS. And I said, "Tomorrow morning, when I wake up [May 15, 1978], I will start writing fiction seriously." Before that I had written only one short story. It was a consequence of that language, that story, that angle that I wanted to *do* what she had *done.* So I started. But when I read Faulkner, I realized that this was a whole different kind of ballgame. I wasn't tempted to do anything like it, although some of the short stories, "That Evening Sun" and other stories, may have had some influence, but I try not to be conscious of it.

**J.G.** You do what Faulkner did in that you choose *your* postage stamp of land, concentrate on the people there, and see all sorts of universal aspects in their lives. Now with the setting of *Redeye* in the West, it appears that you have found Listre, North Carolina, rather confining. Although you do, of course, send Miss Star out West *from* Listre.

**C.E.** My obsession was with the story of the ranchers' obsession with the cliff dwellings. That got me out there and once I got out there and started reading about the West, I had to anchor myself first of all, because I had so many great stories. So on a wall I drew a map, the map which is now at the beginning of *Redeye,* to create a place to have these people. I said to myself, I have five hundred pages of interesting stories, I could almost just put them in the book. The book has got to be about the relationships between these people. So I forced myself to make the book about relationships between people, which is what I have been doing in all my books.

It may be that once I started talking about the family it became more like what I had written before. My problem was in writing the Southern books, I did not have to think to pick the detail that would put the reader in the right place. In *this* book, set in the West, I had all this research to do. I had to avoid two things:

I didn't want the reader to say, "Ah ha, this guy is *not* from the West! You can tell by the details!" Nor did I want someone to say, "This is a book which has been overresearched, and this stuck-in western stuff he found somewhere." My challenge was to concentrate on the relationships and let them develop. The only thing different about *Redeye* was that the setting came from books, rather than from my own experience.

**J.G.** One of my interests since the early 1960s has been to observe the increasing focus on the badly adjusted, ill-at-ease individual in the Southern novel, from Walker Percy's *The Moviegoer* and William Styron's *Nat Turner* and on. It is a development that could be called "existential." You don't seem to want to focus on somebody with the malaise.

**C.E.** I remember my early reading as I started wanting to be a writer. I liked *Nat Turner* a lot, but I have not been able to connect with Percy. But I only read *The Moviegoer.* My wife loves *The Moviegoer,* I have friends who love *The Moviegoer,* but. . . .

**J.G.** You might prefer Percy's *Lancelot.*

**C.E.** That's the one I want to read.

**J.G.** What I am thinking of is this movement away from a broad focus on the family and the community to seeing the very same, but entirely through the mind of one troubled character, *not* an entertaining and funny person but somebody with problems.

**C.E.** If I had been a good student at Chapel Hill, I would have become interested, I think, in philosophy or the reading of literature, before I started writing. But nothing intellectual interested me, other than Emerson and Thoreau when I was in high school. I moved from the Transcendentalists into Hemingway, into reading fiction, and to being fascinated with stories. So I never had the background to get into stories that someone like Walker Percy wrote.

**J.G.** But my point is that everybody, even you, has personal problems, but you choose not to write much about these problems.

**C.E.** They are kind of somewhere else, I am not sure why.—Do you know Bob Richardson, who wrote *The Mind on Fire* about Emerson?[13] I just met him and he had read *Redeye,* and he said that the Emerson Society was really up in arms because I made Emerson a Mormon, although he didn't know it.—He was just kidding.

**J.G.** There is, of course, the tradition in the South that Emerson intellectually somehow is the enemy; because he is moving toward the total abstraction that Southerners fear.

C.E. In high school I read as much of Emerson as I could. I was fascinated, but I didn't get it, not enough to make any kind of judgment; I didn't even know what the word "abstract" meant. I was fascinated with many of his sentences, you know, "if the stars should appear one night in a thousand years, how would men believe and adore,"[14] those kind of statements. And several essays, "The Divinity School Address" and "Self-Reliance" and "The American Scholar" set me on fire.

J.G. In *Walking across Egypt* it is, of course, hilarious that everybody, even the most unlikely to, has guns under their pillows, if they have pillows. Is this a part of a satire on the Southern culture of violent self-protection?

C.E. I can tell you exactly where that came from. I was driving away from my old house one time on a dirt road and there was a neighbor walking along the road and she had on a sweat suit. I pulled over and said, "How are you doing?" Called her name. She said, "Fine." We talked a bit, and she showed me this pistol she was carrying in this Kleenex, and she said, "I'm just out taking my walk, ain't nobody gonna jump out of the woods and get me." And I drove off and I said, "I have to use that!"—It was hilarious, the dichotomy, the collision of this weapon with this little lady walking along in a soft sweat suit. And there she was, covering up that gun with a Kleenex. The danger is in making it too ridiculous, but I couldn't give that up. It is like the floatplane with the aluminum lawn chair bolted down in there. I saw a floatplane just like that at a lake near Raleigh, North Carolina. I wrote about it in a short story. I later put it in *The Floatplane Notebooks*. I thought to myself, "That is just ridiculous, you couldn't make that up."—Did you ever read *Teller in the Tale* by Louis Rubin?[15] It is about the personality of the writer telling the story. I just got that, it's fascinating, I've been trying to understand the omniscient point of view a little better, and Rubin suggested that I read that.

J.G. Are you thinking about the omniscient point of view in connection with what you are writing now? Do you know already what you want to use it on? Or, don't you like to talk about what you are doing right now?

C.E. Sure, I don't mind. I am writing about a 1950s intersection in North Carolina. I am going back in time, in that the story comes from when I was six or seven years old and an intersection where my father and an uncle ran a grocery store. It was a very classic little intersection, with our grocery store, another store, a grill and a service station, and two old variety stores. It is gone now, but I dreamt about it. I can't write a clichéd story about an old intersection, but I wanted to revisit all of that, and I have the relationship between a boy and a mother to focus on. It is a short story in the new crime issue of the new *Oxford American*,[16] and it is pulled from several portions of my own history. Maybe I have 160 pages and I have introduced a character not unlike Cobb Pittman (from *Redeye*) into the middle of this little community in the 1950s, although he has changed, we don't know how he is going to behave.

**J.G.** The characters develop as you write.—Do you have a working title for it?

**C.E.** One title that I have thought about and mentioned to my editor is "UnChristian" with a capital C.[17]

**J.G.** I did, of course, read the interview with Susan Ketchin in *The Christ—Haunted Landscape.*[18] And found that some of my questions have been asked before.

**C.E.** She is, by the way, teaching that book here in Jackson at Millsaps College; we are sharing the Eudora Welty Chair.

**J.G.** What a great idea, to teach the fiction *and* the context.—Many Southern writers have a success with a first novel that it took them a long time to write. They work at the craftsmanship, poetry, technique, and so on. And then they are "red-hot." And somebody, an agent or a publisher, will say to the writer, "Your name is 'hot,' so why don't you hurry up and write another one?" So we might have a first novel that the writer worked on for ten years and then the next one that the writer worked on for ten months, perhaps.

Nevertheless, readers hope that number two will be even better than the first novel, which is unrealistic when you think about it. It will not happen often.—When we consider your publishing schedule, from 1985 until today (with new novels in 1985, 1987, 1988, 1991, 1992), do you feel there was pressure on you to follow up quickly with a new book? Would you have taken more time if you could do it over?

**C.E.** As it turned out the first three books were written while I was *not* making a living as a writer. I was making a living teaching education courses. And I took plenty of time on those. Now I guess there's a pressure to write faster. I try not to. I don't think I have succumbed to that. One way I prevented succumbing to that is to do a one-book contract when I need money. Last time I did a two-book contract, which helped relax me for a while. But it might become a problem of money, though it would be blasphemous for that to happen, and it hasn't happened. I can perceive writing faster with no pressure about schedule or about topic, which is wonderful. My publishers keep their hands off, so it has been easy to do. It is more important for me to take a job and write slowly than *not* to take a job and write quickly.

**J.G.** You would also have to experience living some in order to have something to write about, wouldn't you? Ralph Ellison never thought he had lived enough or gathered quite enough experience to publish the second novel.—But the danger for you and other novelists is that you spend much time being lionized and are paid more for a couple of appearances than for a book. Think of how much Faulkner would *not* have written, because he would not have had to, if he had received the kind of honoraria novelists receive today for readings, once they have a few books out.

**C.E.** Oh, it is killing.—I didn't do any speaking engagements last year, partly for that very reason. Somehow the readings bring on a depression, a clinical depression, as a consequence of touring. So for *The Floatplane Notebooks,* I cancelled the tour. Of course, for *Raney* nobody arranged a thing. With *Walking across Egypt* there was a bit of a tour, not much. Then the preparations for *Floatplane Notebooks* were launched. The publisher was expecting great things, they printed sixty thousand copies, planned a big tour, but I had begun experiencing what I thought was mononucleosis. I asked the doctors, and it was a depression. So when I started the tour, I couldn't do it, I had to say no.

So from *Killer Diller* and with the next two books there's been some contention between my agent, my publisher, and me, because we all have different purposes. At a point I said, "I will not tour, unless it is in my contract, I will tour only this many cities." Whereas my publisher, this is a New York publisher, was saying you need to tour. It was those people putting pressure on me, and I said "I'll not do it. I will do only so many cities." But then my editor convinced me, I think I was convinced, that it *does* make a difference in the number of books that are sold. I didn't realize, for example, that when I didn't go to the West Coast—there were no reviews from there! Whereas with the last two books, I have been going to the West Coast, and was reviewed. I thought this time that *Redeye* being a western would make a difference, but it didn't. So now Penguin is doing the paperback and they called me up two months ago and said we should go to eight cities. Now it is down to three cities on the West Coast. What has happened to me is, I could now stop writing and do lectures, readings, and "performances" and make a living, but for me, it is too taxing, I can't handle it physically. I can see very well, however, why a writer will become enamored with this new light that is thrust upon him, and unless there is an obsession with *writing fiction alone in the morning,* he will head for the spotlight.

**J.G.** Do you miss manual jobs, physical jobs, like flying, anything that is not immediately related to writing?

**C.E.** My wife, daughter, mother, and aunts bought me a Bobcat, which is a little bulldozer, a funny vehicle to have; a manual kind of thing with four big wheels and a cage and a shovel up front that you can use. Once I crashed my aircraft, they decided it'd be a better idea to give me something else, to keep me on the ground.

**J.G.** What are you doing with your Bobcat?

**C.E.** Oh, we live there on ten acres, so there's plenty to do.

**J.G.** As I read your fiction, it is full of poetry. Did you ever publish any poetry?

**C.E.** Yes, I did. I sent some stories to George Core at the *Sewanee Review* and some poems. He wrote me back and said, "I am not a fiction writer, I am an editor. You are not a poet, you are a fiction writer."

**J.G.** Yes, he has a way with words. But maybe he is wrong, he has been wrong before.—You focus on the generation gap in *Walking across Egypt* with Mattie Rigsbee and Wesley Benfield and continue with the same characters eight years later in *Killer Diller,* and they have become some of your most convincing characters. I feel I know Mattie, personally, she was in my family, too.

In a way this is an essential part of the family theme that you return to in your fiction: "If you do not have a family, create one!"

**C.E.** My parents' experience had been exactly that of their grandparents, in many ways. The physical environment and social norms, cultural and religious norms, were what had happened to their parents and grandparents and great-grandparents. What happened to me? It turned out I went away to college, to Chapel Hill, and the resulting gap is in many ways interesting to me.

**J.G.** Did your family leave records, or were they all stories and anecdotes?

**C.E.** Those were stories.—My mother's favorite sisters were all in their early forties or late thirties when I was born, the three of them. So I grew up, in many ways, with the undivided attention of these three women with one child. This was the norm for me. I heard a lot of their talking and certainly felt their values, which in many ways were somewhat differing among them, but there was attention on me. Then the "gap" came, when I left home. When I came back and could see that I could still get along with them, visit with them, and talk to them, it helped me write. Most of the absorption of stories was unconscious as I grew up. The origin of the fiction would be little stories told about somebody, on occasion I would make one up. A good amount of talk, in the first several novels especially, grew out of family stories, family talk.

**J.G.** Can you hide behind family stories? Or do you go in, as Faulkner advises, and steal the shirt off your grandmother and expose her? Can you make the leap that makes you *her,* and do you tell us what she was really thinking? We know what they always say at every family reunion about her, we know they tell the same anecdotes, but what was she feeling?

**C.E.** Do you know, it is true what Robert Penn Warren said, and my mother actually said, as well:

"Fiction is made of stories about made-up characters." And usually I am able to differentiate. Once I get going, a character really does come to resemble, say, my mother, the *character* comes to resemble her. If I want to get into somebody's head, then I am getting into that *character's* head. And I can be confident that what I am thinking that character is thinking and by definition *is* that character, and I don't have to worry about using my grandmother, or mother, as models anymore. Once I get started they will get me going, so I don't have to think about that too much.

I never worry about what any of my relatives have ever thought about anything. I did have an uncle who committed suicide. In *Raney* an uncle also commits suicide. So I was worried that my mother would feel I was infringing on her privacy, as the uncle was her brother, but because the character in the book was so different from the real uncle she did not feel threatened. Thank goodness! Although the fact of the suicide would've threatened many people; they would have taken the literature literally. So I try to go back, over and over, in my teaching to "fiction is made up stories about made up characters." I realize that I am involved in all my experiences. Another thing I use a lot is Faulkner's "fiction comes from observation, experience, and imagination." And in fact if I *believe* it comes from observation, experience, and imagination, and if I *believe* fiction is a made-up story about made-up characters and *say* that to myself, it releases me from worries about who is thinking what.

**J.G.** What was your main object in *Killer Diller?* Was it the attack on the phony college?

**C.E.** I had just moved to downtown Durham. I had finished three novels, and it wasn't clear what the next novel would be. I walked down to the front porch of an old house where I was living and across the street was a diet house, there was an empty lot, and then there was a halfway house. Across the street from the halfway house was a Baptist church. And I immediately thought about Wesley [Benfield], whom I had left somewhat unfinished at the end of *Walking across Egypt.* I had asked the police about the halfway house, if it were dangerous, they said check with the zoning commission, I called the zoning commission about the status of the halfway house, and they said, we have more problems with the diet house than we do with the halfway house. The setting—the diet house, the halfway house, and the Baptist church was so rich to me, because I had just resigned from a teaching position, and there was a good deal of animosity toward the administration. I saw that I could change the church into a university, a Baptist university, put Wesley in the halfway house, and have him fall in love with somebody in the diet house. The setting was so rich that I began to write, not knowing what would happen. That is my only novel that has not been generated out of situation and character but out of setting, out of place. So I started to see what would happen, I knew who would have to be in it. But at the same time another experiment of mine, which was personal, was my reading the Bible for the first time, front to back. Growing up as a southern Baptist we pitched a little, and picked our New Testament scriptures.

**J.G.** Is this when the contradictions in the Bible begin to come into your fiction? The idea sticks with you from about then.

**C.E.** It does. I had another character read through the Bible, on his own, in *The Bible Salesman.* But Wesley was the first one to start reading. It was interesting to me to start reading, personally, and then have him beside me reading also. So my reactions could be exaggerated in him and he could do whatever he wanted to—and he wanted to preach. His fascination with *blues music* reflected my own, so I was projecting somewhat into Wesley, number one; number two, I was dealing with *the age issue* with Mattie; and *the love affair* was fun.

**J.G.** Do you appreciate heavy women?

**C.E.** Wesley did have a little weird thing about Phoebe's ounces, didn't he. Another thing, I had an evangelist named Markham Thorpe in the novel in all the early drafts. He came from a sighting of an evangelist in the mountains a couple of years before that. He was an associate of Wesley's, but he never worked. He didn't fit and wouldn't come alive, he was neither conservative nor liberal. So I had to take Markham Thorpe out of the book.

In the meantime I had a character who was "mentally retarded," as we said back in the '50s and '60s. I worked in a camp and was this fellow's counselor. I had always wanted to write about it. So I said, "I'll put him in the book," and I thought I will just start the book with him and see what happens. I immediately saw the connection which was that the halfway house people helped the handicapped children. So I started with Jules Vernon Jackson, based on a fellow I knew, and put him throughout the book and completely changed the character of the book. So there were all kinds of things going on, but my animosity toward administrators was too strong in my last draft, so Louis Rubin, warning me, said, "Look, you are way too sarcastic, you have to cut it back." If I were a reader, I might say the author has a problem with these people that is getting into the story, but I had a lot of fun satirizing that whole administrative bit.

**J.G.** You actually have fewer comments on religion in this novel, although you do go back to the subject at the very end. But you have just as many comments on the social scene, and race is one of the topics:

Ben's racism, Phoebe's prejudice, and Shanita's all-out black prejudice against white people is refreshing. We do not often see it portrayed in a novel by a white writer. The first time I read it I felt it was written for the movies, and I still do *not* think this is one of the best novels to teach. Do you use it?

C.E. I don't use it, you know, I don't use my stuff any when I teach. There are two things that cross my mind about what you said. Number one is that I recorded them all, I recorded the first seven on cassette tapes—I didn't record *Lunch at the Piccadilly*—and people who listen to them say that *Killer Diller* is by far the best to listen to. It is an abridged version. A woman filmmaker fell in love with the book, wanted to make a movie of it and spent several years trying to get it made. She was attracted to it, and it is the only one I thought would sell really well. When I'd finished writing it and read through it, I said, "This will sell." Of course, it has not!

J.G. It did become a movie, didn't that help sales?

C.E. It may have, the movie went straight to DVD, more or less. I think it is a better movie than *Walking across Egypt.* I enjoyed the movie, and I had a bit part in it. I was one on the board of trustees which was written into the script, and I got to meet all these young people. And the music was a push, too. I am a fan of blues music, and I wanted Wesley to be obsessed with that stuff.

## NOTES

◆ ◆ ◆

1. Dannye Romine Powell, *Parting the Curtains: Interviews with Southern Writers* (Winston-Salem, N.C.: John F. Blair, 1994), 82–91.
2. "Search and Rescue," *Southern Review* 30 (Summer 1994): 452–61.
3. "Venom," *Southern Exposure* 19 (Fall 1991): 37–42.
4. Tim McLaurin published the novel *The Great Snake Show* in 1997. He died in 2002.
5. For a longer version of this incident, see Edgerton's *Solo: My Adventures in the Air* (Chapel Hill, NC: Algonquin, 2005), 260–64.
6. "Medicine for Broken Souls," a review of *Your Blues Ain't Like Mine, New York Times Book Review,* Sept. 20, 1992, 13.
7. Adolf Erik Nordenskiöld (1832–1901).
8. Gustaf Erik Nordenskiöld, *The Cliff Dwellers of Mesa Verde, Southwestern Colorado: Their Pottery and Implements* (1893; reprint, Glorieta, NM: Rio Grande Press, 1979).
9. *The Letters of Gustaf Nordenskiöld* (Mesa Verde National Park, CO: Mesa Verde Museum Association, 1991).

10. Joan Acocella, "Cather and the Academy," "Life and Letters," *New Yorker,* Nov. 27, 1995.

11. Flannery O'Connor, *The Habit of Being: The Letters of ——*, ed. Sally Fitzgerald (New York: Farrar, Straus & Giroux, 1979).

12. David Minter, *William Faulkner: His Life and Work* (Baltimore, Md.: Johns Hopkins University Press, 1980), 152–60.

13. Robert D. Richardson, *Emerson: The Mind on Fire* (Berkeley: University of California Press, 1995).

14. Ralph Waldo Emerson, *Nature* (Boston: J. Munroe & Co., 1836), ch. 1, 1.

15. Louis D. Rubin Jr., *Teller in the Tale* (Seattle: University of Washington Press, 1968).

16. "sendmetotheelectricchair," *Oxford American* (Spring 1996): 42–45.

17. The novel's title became *Where Trouble Sleeps* (Chapel Hill, NC: Algonquin, 1997).

18. Susan Ketchin, *The Christ-Haunted Landscape: Faith and Doubt in Southern Fiction* (Jackson: University Press of Mississippi, 1994), 352–70.

# *Interview with Clyde Edgerton*

⬩⬩⬩⬩⬩⬩

*Wilmington, North Carolina, September 29, 2010*

J.G. In *Where Trouble Sleeps* [1997] Jack Umstead listens to Roy Acuff, but Umstead is still a suspicious character and turns out to be all bad. And in *The Bible Salesman,* Clearwater, who is a criminal, has once played with Roy Acuff. And Acuff is mentioned again in *The Night Train.* What did the venerable Grand Ol' Opry star do to deserve such treatment by a fiction-writing banjo player?

C.E. He happened to be, and you, of course, have uncovered something that I didn't realize that I did, which is a mark of a close reading, he was a favorite singer of my father's. My father had two favorite singers, Ernest Tubb and Roy Acuff, and my memories from the early '50s are of listening to these people and of my father being interested in them. He was not a musician—he was interested in baseball and hunting. He was a quiet man and not observably passionate about much; the fact that he liked these two singers stands out. He died when I was thirty-six, so when I remember him and I get in the area of music, I will latch on to those people. I am sure that explains why. On "Will the Circle Be Unbroken," Roy Acuff, as an older man, is heard on that album, chastising the musicians. I met Acuff just before he died, when I was touring the Grand Ol' Opry.

J.G. Jack Umstead, in *Where Trouble Sleeps,* is suspect for not having any family, any responsibilities, and any relatives, or, if he does, for not staying with them. Does this attitude to strangers still exist in today's South?

C.E. When you mention "Is it true in the South?" I immediately have to distinguish, as a consequence of living in Wilmington, between here, where there are more and more people from the North, and twenty, thirty miles away. If I am in rural North Carolina, and there is much rural Carolina left, the answer is a resounding "yes!"—less so in urban areas in the South, probably, where peculiarities are less noticed. But not having any family would be a peculiarity, very much so.—Both my parents grew up in large families on a farm and they were poor, relatively speaking, but I think about *the harmony* that was necessary for survival. This harmony would reduce chances of children leaving home. So harmony, manners, and a sense of family loyalty mattered—but at a breaking point it was no stronger than in any other family. For example, in later years *this* harmonious close family squabbled over the family farm. But originally the family loyalty presupposed the presence of everybody.

J.G. Why do *you* want to kill off Jack Umstead, the "gypsy man," so badly? His not having a family, or any responsibility, hardly seems enough of a justification. He *is* killed off by the author, isn't he?

C.E. You are discovering secrets that should not be told. This was part of a short story that was written before the novel. It was named for Roy Acuff's "The Great Speckled Bird."[1] It was a consequence of Flannery O'Connor killing off the old lady in her story "A Good Man Is Hard to Find." I wanted to even that up. I wanted the old lady to kill off a bad man, a misfit. So I evened up that score and felt good about it, and it came to me that it would be a good ending.

J.G. *Where Trouble Sleeps* shows the social differences in the town of Listre as of 1950, and you start the book with a map of the blinker-light area. The blinking light registers the heartbeat of the town, but also every blink is a second gone in the life of the town. And you end the book with a map of the stoplights at Hunter's Grove in 2000. To what extent is the end of the blinker light also the end of life as you knew it in Listre?

C.E. It does demonstrate an end to something—that's a wonderful question, something I think about—I almost forgot, I wrote a movie script for that book. Nothing has been done with it; but I had six months, and I wrote the script. The blinker light, of course, is gone, but there are about ten stop lights to take its place, and the road is six lanes rather than two, so we have this sense of movement, of urbanization. My intention when I started the book and drew the two maps was to write a book which covered fifty years. I was going to have the young man grow up, but I never got past two weeks! But when deciding whether or not to take out the map, I decided to let it stay, just because of that old contrast for anyone who wants to study it carefully. It is a fictionalized blinker light of the community I grew up in.

In fact, that book started with my memory of seeing scenes from my childhood, before I was six, several scenes: my mother killing my cat, Inky, with a baseball bat, because she had to, he had been run over, and the grocery store, it is more biographical probably than most of the others. The mule and truck collision was a story I heard as I was writing the novel. It was one of the most difficult scenes to write, a learning experience. It *was* one of the funniest stories I ever heard, but the first time I wrote it, for me it was not funny. I had to have somebody telling it, but the second time I wrote it, it was still not funny, not as funny as it had been to me. I couldn't quite understand why, so I had to continue manipulating. I got a third character to interrupt the person who is telling it and I finally milked it for the humor that it was worth, but I was never quite satisfied with it. It is one of those things you pull from real life in ways that really don't work. Critics and readers, like you, would probably pull those things out. For *In Memory of Junior* I had a twelve-page transcript of my uncle talking and I transplanted it with a fictional character into the book, and my editor, Shannon Ravenel, said, "what are you doing, this is horrible, it just goes on and on!" As a reader I was the nephew of this person and was enamored with his every word, I idolized him. I had to go back and cut to finally get it down to something that was not reflective of my own personal obsession.

**J.G.** The title of the novel indicates that there is "trouble," but it "sleeps."

**C.E.** The dog was named "Trouble," and he slept inside when he knew it would rain. Where he slept determined whether or not the robber would be able to rob the Blaine sisters' store.

**J.G.** It does seem to be very autobiographical. You could call it Stephen's initiation story and look at what he is being initiated into. One of the things Stephen's mother wants her son to have is a fighting spirit, so that he will defend himself, which seems reasonable enough. But it seems to be part of an attack on the American love for "a fighting spirit," when associated with 600,000 who died as a tribute "to the fighting spirit of the American people."

**C.E.** At about the time I wrote the novel, I was in a cab in California and the cab driver says, "Where are you from in the South?" I said, "I'm from North Carolina." He said, "That Civil War was something, wasn't it?" And I said, "Yes." He said, "Do you know much about the Civil War?" "Not a lot, I know that about 600,000 people died." He paused and said, "I think that's a great tribute to the fighting spirit of the American people." And my mouth dropped open, and I didn't know how to respond. Consequently, I put it into the book.

**J.G.** Otherwise Stephen's thinking is deeply influenced by the ever-present Baptist religion. He knows he will go to hell if he does not accept Jesus. But what can you expect in a town where grown-ups believe that Jesus has arrived to collect the minister's "discretionary fund." This is, of course, satire, but do you feel that the pervasive religious brainwashing of children is harmful?

**C.E.** I had a sociologist argue that it is helpful, because it gives you something to turn against. And as a child, if you have nothing to turn against, what do you grow up to be? I just remembered there's a play of it opening at the Barter Theater in Abingdon, Virginia, on October 9 [2010], by Catherine Bush, a playwright who has adapted it for the stage. I am interested in seeing how that works out, and *that* scene is in there. It is very reflective of a kind of conflict within any youth. I owned a shotgun when I was twelve years old, it was the norm; when I think about that now, I cringe.

**J.G.** Are any of your children boys?

**C.E.** I have two.

**J.G.** Are they going to have shotguns when they are twelve?

**C.E.** One is seven and one is five. We've shot a BB gun. I have friends who will have them shooting, but they will *not* have shotguns when they are twelve.—My mother was very protective and very religious, but she did push me off the back porch to fight that next-door neighbor, one time. Her meek Christianity combined with a certain aggressiveness, which reflected the way she parented.

**J.G.** The results of the love of violence and the good faith come together in Stephen's fine reading of what exactly Abraham was going to do to Isaac. It is a hilarious and popular passage, I use it when I talk about Southern humor.

**C.E.** I completely forgot about reading that passage. I got to start reading it again, in fact there is a writers' week coming up in November, and I want to go back to *Where Trouble Sleeps* and read some. If I were touring outside the South and I mentioned Abraham and Isaac, the audience would have no idea what was coming, but in the South, as soon as I say Abraham and Isaac, people start laughing because of their familiarity with that story.

**J.G.** Like Shakespeare, who was said to be unable to resist a pun, you have a hard time resisting a good joke or anecdote, such as the Rosalind Russell story or the leg/head loss war story, but they do not actually fit in, do they?

**C.E.** No, they don't. There is no way I could go before a literary committee and do anything other than say, "I throw myself on the mercy of the court." They were a couple of jokes that I had heard and had to publicize. It was like with *Raney,* my first book, I had just written a song which nobody would buy. I couldn't win any contests with the song, so I had to put it in the book. I wouldn't do it now, I did all the verses of "This World Is Not My Home"—it is about kamikaze chickens. Now I would put it in a little piece, but when I wrote *Raney* I put it in the novel.

**J.G.** To end this part on *Where Trouble Sleeps* I have to say, it is very un-Southern of you not to tell us what finally happened to Terry's finger! We never hear the end of the story about his chopped-off finger, you leave it dangling. We learn that he was brought to the hospital; but we do not hear whether his finger was put back on or if he lost it.

**C.E.** I am surprised I didn't cover that. I should have. It was so strong in my mind, I think, from the autobiographical fact that my neighbor did almost lose a finger but had it sewed back. I was not there when it happened, but I looked at his thumb many times and saw the scar. It was attached back. I am surprised that *I* didn't notice it, and it is hard to believe my editors didn't spot that.

**J.G.** In *Lunch at the Piccadilly* [2003] there is serious criticism of how we treat the elderly. It is criticism aimed at Medicare and Medicaid from page one. Are the homes for the elderly and the daycare centers nothing but business and exploitation?

**C.E.** In any endeavor in which we try to care for those who are less fortunate, there are mixed consequences. And, as always, the room in the human heart which embraces greed goes to work. There clearly are people who are taking advantage of precious human lives. There are also genuine efforts in old-age homes, for sure, and in nursing homes, often by fundamentalist Christians. As a person who is not a fundamentalist, it is easy to jump on and satirize, but there is also a constancy in care for the poor among religious people which makes you pause and think about how humane they are.

I did jump on Medicare for what happened to me, leading up to this book, were, of course, three years with an elderly aunt who had no one to care for her, except for me. So I got to see the inside of all this, I had to do the Medicare forms, the kind of things that any bureaucracy puts you through, something to be satirized. I remember having fun with that and not knowing where to put it, in the beginning. There is a play from 2008,[2] and a full musical now of *Lunch at the Piccadilly*, a new production. It is opening at the Festival Stage of Winston-Salem in February 2011. We staged it in Fayetteville last spring, but we are still working on it. It is really a lot of fun. Mike Craver of the Original Red Clay Ramblers, a Southern band, did the music; he sometimes performs with me and The Rank Strangers.

But I am wandering from your question. I have a feeling, for what it is worth, that in two hundred years when we look at ourselves as a society, we will see our treatment of older people today to be not unlike people turning a blind eye to the victims of yellow fever in the nineteenth century.

**J.G.** In the present U.S. debate about Medicare, it has greatly surprised the Danes of the welfare state that the very people who would really benefit most from having comprehensive coverage are dead set against the idea. Why are people without any money out there demonstrating against Obama's attempt to get the poor some kind of social security?

**C.E.** I agree with you. The people who are behind that are people with money who don't need it. In many cases they are very conservative millionaires who want the government out of everything, so they can get more for themselves. They are finding successful media outlets and personalities to push their agenda.

J.G. When their "home health care" runs out, are the rather old victims left without therapy of any kind?—Are they cheated out of their money?

C.E. Yes, it happens. We have to ask ourselves, can we go back to the family model? In the reconstructed unreconstructed South, any agrarian place, as in Japan or other places, the family stays and takes care of their old people, and the old people serve a function in many cases. The lengthening of lives, the way people are kept alive far longer than they used to be, complicates matters. Whose responsibility are they?

J.G. Your notion of setting up nursing homes in the generally vacant churches is, of course, ingenious. What could be more natural for good Christians than to help needy old people, so nursing homes and churches would be synonymous? How has your idea of creating "Nurches" been received? Has it been picked up by any of the TV evangelists?

C.E. Not yet!—The play brings it to life. If we get the ending right, where there will be an established nurse, advocating nurches, in a way that will be attractive to a certain brand of theologians, *maybe* we will be heard. The play and the musical, in particular, differ somewhat from the novel.

J.G. Is Christianity in America, in the new millennium, "more watered down than at any time in history. Watered down by Americans"? If so, isn't that a positive thing?

C.E. This is a very conservative person speaking, Mr. Clarence Rhodes, the fundamentalist administrator; his point of view is "we are getting soft." My point of view is, yes, we could do with "softness" in many ways, but then I get disturbed personally by other things. There are certainly matters about which we could be less wishy-washy. But this has been true throughout history and will be.

J.G. What do you think of the warring Christian denominations and their fundamentalism? Is it possible to even be a Christian and not be Pentecostal, Methodist, Baptist, Presbyterian, et cetera? "You sick redneck . . . You Unitarian," as Miss Emily McPherson accuses Mr. L. Ray Flowers of being, as if it were the worst person she could think of.

C.E. Any denomination goes from conservative to being liberal. The Baptists have conservatives in the Southern Baptist Convention, and then you have what is called the Collaborative Baptist Fellowship, which is more moderate. I started attending a church, after not attending any church for many years, it was an interesting experience. But there is a gentleman named Brian McLaren, and I interviewed him. It is the only interview I've ever done. The preacher where I went to church and I went to Maryland to interview McLaren because even though he is a pastor and preacher, he worries about the term "Christian," and "Christianity" makes him very nervous. Even though he is enamored of the teachings of Jesus, as was Thomas Jefferson, who did his own Bible, as was Tolstoy, who did his own Bible, leaving out the miracles, et cetera. So there is an emerging set of beliefs about the Bible, it is loyal to the Bible in a sense, but intellectually it downplays Plato and the Greek, perhaps Persian, dualism. The whole idea of having hell and salvation is thrown aside, in its place is what is called "The Kingdom of God," which relates to our conversation about caring for the old and the poor. That's a simplified version of what it is, but it is now being done in an intellectual and a more scholastic way than it was ever done before, and of course people are very angry at Brian McLaren. I just happened upon a book that he wrote, *A New Kind of Christianity*,[3] and read it. Something I wouldn't have done five years ago, simply because of the word "Christianity," but it is something I'm more interested in now.

**J.G.** Is it fair to say, "It seems like church members often have a desperate need to be *un*aware of the local needs of the local wrecks of local women stacked along the local grim halls of local nursing homes"? And is it fair to say, "It's a free country—unless you're old and in the way" or to say, "if the old stay very still, the young will not know they are here." It reads like anger as a result of personal experience.

**C.E.** Yes. It is a desperate kind of play. A human reaction is to become angry when you are involved and to avoid it when you are not pushed into it with your own relatives. I don't visit nursing homes very much, but I am conscious of them, and I'm beginning to try to do music there, to do something. It is the old guilt versus purpose, humanity versus egoism, which, of course, I like to play with in fiction.

**J.G.** But you don't want to end up in a nursing home.

**C.E.** No!

**J.G.** It seems that with old age gender issues are suddenly unimportant—at least for the people at Rosehaven. Is that the effect of aging?

**C.E.** This was a funny plot problem that I had to solve. There needed to be something extraordinary about the aunt and the nephew, and her having lost a child was something I made up to cause a certain attraction to him. So much is pulled from biography because it is there and useful. It is a tool. I love Faulkner's experience, observation, and imagination, and you pull from each one of those three. It is always useful for me in teaching literature to talk about each reader having a different set of experiences, observations, and imagination, so each piece of fiction will be different as a consequence.

My having two aunts who were childless at my mother's age and their care for me manipulated me into creating Aunt Lil with a strong need to feel for Carl in *Lunch at the Piccadilly.*

**J.G.** You do not emphasize gender issues the way many fine women writers do, such as Pam Durban, Kaye Gibbons, Mary Hood, and Josephine Humphreys. They often seem preoccupied with that topic, but you don't give it much space.

**C.E.** I think the gender issues are there in everyday life for me, because I have a twenty-eight-year-old daughter. Of course, she didn't begin to talk about her perceptions of gender issues until maybe eight or nine years ago. Now she is aware of them in everyday life, as a consequence of her growing up *not* being aware of gender issues. It is much like racism, which doesn't translate automatically to that issue being on top of the story, or even within it.—I am always aware of anything that is "political." You are right, the topic of gender among older people, in general, is not an issue for me.—The gender problem kind of solves itself, as women live longer. After a while there are not that many men there.

**J.G.** We, especially relatives, don't even want to look at old people in a home. L. Ray asks if it would be better if old people were left under a tree or eaten, as they were thousands of years ago. It is funny and yet serious enough.

There are many times that I have to laugh out loud when I read your fiction. Mark Twain is the only other one that makes me laugh so much. Has Twain influenced you? I see his photo here in your office. I see him in certain short characterizations:

Mrs. Talbert evaluating people by their shoes, Mrs. Cochran's swearing, and Mrs. Parson's being saved. And certainly Twain is there in all the didacticism of the book, as represented by L. Ray's thinking. You are trying, the way Mark Twain did, to make us change our thinking by constantly lambasting your readers.

**C.E.** That makes my year! That's a great compliment for any reader to see that and understand. It is a compliment because of my reverence for Mark Twain. I do fear becoming as bitter as he did. It is tempting, the more you know, the more bitter you are. But I know much less about him than I want to. What I know about is the *sheer* delight in reading the fiction, mainly *Huckleberry Finn* and a few of the others, I haven't read a lot, but most of the fiction. He has been there in a lot of ways, when I was writing my western, *Redeye,* I had to find out how people talked in 1888 in the West, and I go into *Roughing It,* and there is a chapter on western dialects. It was as if he came in and said, "Let me help you out." And I read that and used it. In *Letters from the Earth* his observations of the human condition, the combination of humor with his biting satire saves it for me and makes it delightful. Twain is a guiding light. I found that he had been incensed with the Mountain Meadow Massacre himself and wrote about the Mormons in ways that were quite angry.—Mark Twain is a spiritual godfather, subconsciously I may be trying to write like him.

**J.G.** The whole idea of flying, the peace of it, but also the misgivings about being up in the air, is of course the ordinary situation of a pilot. But in *Solo: My Adventures in the Air* [2005] you move quickly from the peace of mind that you have when you fly to a preoccupation with the execution that you witnessed "indirectly" over the radio.—Have you been able to keep your early fascination with flying after the Southeast Asian experience?

**C.E.** Yes, I think they are separated out. The physical fascination with flying is related to that small amount of fear that accompanies you and makes the experience exhilarating. I see it that way, but I don't love it enough to be doing it every week, like I was in the '80s and '90s. Also, my wife is opposed to it, she thinks it is dangerous. And because I am busy with other things there is not time enough to do it, so I hesitate when I say that the fascination is still there, but the idea of the fascination *is* still there. It is a great high, a great adrenaline rush, a great experience to go up, and a great view in the late afternoon with the sun setting. There is the tactile experience, the nostalgic idea of flying the old airplane in which *you* are doing everything. And to touch down on a grass runway with those big wheels, it is for me an enticing physical experience.—When I think of the physical sensation, I think of a roller coaster. I think the fear makes it exhilarating; you move a bit toward something that's not available, which is death. It is hard to explain, but the exhilaration is still there.

**J.G.** It seems to me that when you describe the lessons in flying that you are also giving lessons in living. You even bring up piano lessons.

**C.E.** It has to do with me and feedback, which is, of course, different from in writing and teaching. With flying you see your mistakes immediately, in terms of airspeed and altitude, and at the piano you hear your mistakes immediately. If you are writing a book you may find mistakes *years* later.

**J.G.** *Solo* has a serious message, and it comes fairly early, you write, "I didn't want to be a serious warrior" and "a funny warrior is no less responsible." Is it possible to be a funny warrior?

**C.E.** I think it is possible, and I probably was, but what I feel guilty about is being involved in that war. This is nothing new. There is a spectrum of guilt that people feel after any given war. For me supporting Barry Goldwater in '64 and supporting George McGovern in '72 says it all. That's the story of the political background. It is a coming to view government at its worst and a beginning to understand having been a part of *imperialism* at its worst. And looking back on it, I realize that some of it had to do with my enthusiasm with flying. Being a warrior is a serious business, you kill people. We can have a conversation right here going in eight different directions about all aspects of that. My experience in Vietnam has followed me around until I wrote *Solo,* perhaps less so since I wrote the book. It was difficult to say what I wanted to say. And when I got to it, it was still not conclusive, but more like asking questions. That's how I ended the book.—If I could do it over, as many older people say, I would not have been a part of that war.

**J.G.** But at the time you were convinced you were fighting Communism?

**C.E.** Yes, I was.

**J.G.** Several passages in *Solo* are not in your usual style, they are hard to read. I think they reflect the contortions of your soul when you think of the time.

**C.E.** I think you are exactly right. It is hard for me to talk about and to think about. At worst, and this just occurred to me thinking about why it is so difficult, at worst I can consider myself a war criminal. At best, I can consider myself somebody with a somewhat blind eye, who was naïve and drawn into crimes. And then you ask, "Who did that?" "Who pulled you in?" And you can ask how much *I* had to be *pulled in,* with my fascination with flying. I probably never did, and probably never will, get the words right about that whole experience.

**J.G.** You make a good effort. But it is obvious, when you write about the blues band and the importance and the explication of poetry, that when you talk about the war, you need to talk about something else at the same time. Otherwise it gets intolerable for you and the reader. You obviously also realize how hard it is to achieve some depth in your memoir by just recording what happened, day by day.

**C.E.** Let me tell you about an editorial decision I made, with the help of my editor. When I was writing the early drafts of *Solo,* I would combine something that happened with how I felt about it *then,* with how I feel about it *now.* Consequently, the action was slowed down in a way I didn't like, but I knew I had to talk about feelings, so my editor and I decided I would write the action, and then in the end of the book more or less how I felt about it. That was a general decision that was made; again it was one of those sacrifices you make, and there are places earlier on in the book where I could have been more reflective.

**J.G.** You are on the verge of reflection when you write of the death of friends, but after about two pages you let it go. But there is also the letter home, although I didn't quite believe that you had written a letter home on "why are we in Vietnam." Was this a literary trick in order to say what you needed to say?

C.E. That *was* my letter—verbatim. As a writer it was kind of a gift, I guess, but it was there, I found it, picked it up.

J.G. When you fly combat reconnaissance, emotions are important.

You mention that flying could make you feel "invincible," but another reaction was to feel "indifferent." Wouldn't it be necessary sometimes to work up an emotional numbness, in order to be able to do what you had orders to do?

C.E. You mean to do actual combat flying? I was fortunate in that I didn't have to bomb people. I was marking targets for other people to bomb, I had the smoke rockets, and I would mark a target and give the clear for the bombers to fly in. This was usually in areas where there were no villages. This was in Laos, and it was all military. So there were ways in which I could talk myself into indifference, unconsciously. I didn't have to worry about "I am killing somebody, personally." I was, of course, part of a machine that was killing people, and you can extend that to the "somebody" who was planning tactics as a part of the machine that was doing the killing. You can drive yourself crazy trying to delineate your guilt. I was not enjoying the thrill of it. I rationalized: "I'm doing what I'm doing to protect my buddies back in South Vietnam. If I don't do this then the chances are higher that they will be killed." Why we were over there is another complicated question, which volumes have been written about. But because I was not directly involved the way a combat soldier might be, I did not have the nightmares I would have had otherwise.

J.G. You had the nightmare of actually hearing a friend being killed.

C.E. It was not a friend, but it was a guy I actually heard die. I'm assuming I did, I heard him being shot at, that was clear. I could hear the shots and hear him screaming, and that was nightmarish.

J.G. Towards the end of *Solo* you are clearly without any illusions about the war. Did you have any illusions before you went?

C.E. Sure, in 1962 I go into the ROTC and there is no war going. I want to be a pilot and I want to be a part of that force which made the world free for democracy in World War II. There might have been some questions about Korea, but Korea didn't really count, it was World War II, it was Hitler, it was what I grew up with, the G.I. movies, and everything else, I was going to be a part of that—that victory! And in the meantime I would do something that I had seen on TV, which was to fly a supersonic aircraft. So it was like a big party I was going into in '62. By 1966, when I'm getting out, there is something going on over there, but I am twenty-two years old, why would I weigh down my mind with anything about the war? What am I going to think about from twenty-two to twenty-seven? Unless I am extraordinary, unless I am John Keats or Stephen Crane, and I am not, so I did not worry about it.

**J.G.** *Solo* does not read like a book that your publisher was begging you to write. It reads more like a book you wanted to write and needed to write.

**C.E.** It is, it is something I needed to write. I'm glad I did.—I just got notice that *Solo* is out of print, which is okay—that and *Redeye* are the only ones that are out of print, that I know of.

**J.G.** Were you doing a Hemingway thing with *Solo,* thinking, "If I can write it, maybe I can get rid of it"?

**C.E.** It made a difference in my writing. It was my third experience in flying. The first was the Air Force, the second was "Annabelle," the plane I bought and flew for two years, the old PA12, and the third experience in flying was writing that book. Reliving and trying to put into words what had happened. Writing nonfiction is not that interesting to me, I had to worry about things and look up facts and so forth.—I have only flown once or twice since I finished the book. I wrote an article about flying for *Garden & Gun* magazine, in their first issue [April 2007].

**J.G.** What is the relationship between writing the lyrics of songs and writing fiction? You seem to be able to write the songs even if there are no problems to write about, as in the country song "Ain't Got No Problems." Do you sing your songs "The Safety Patrol Song," "Baloney, Bacon and Beer," or "Fat from Shame" when you perform with your band?

**C.E.** We do, we still perform. We are "The Rank Strangers." Now it is mostly just two of us, more than the whole band. The word "rank" is used to mean "extreme" in an old country song: "everybody I met / seemed to be a rank stranger," that means very much a stranger.[4] It is a less used definition of "rank," than the normal word "rank," but it is funny, and we can play on it either way.—Mike Craver and I have done a musical of *The Bible Salesman,* a one-hour reader's theater musical.[5]

**J.G.** Henry in *The Bible Salesman*, in his yellow socks, in shoes that are too big, and with an imagined heart disease, has, of course, walked straight out of Flannery O'Connor's "Good Country People" (the story that made such an impression on you in college) and into your novel. But your goal is quite different from O'Connor's, isn't it?

**C.E.** It *is. I don't get her!* I *love* her fiction, and I love those yellow socks, and I love the way she looks at something and describes it. I love her writing. But the whole business, about Grace and God and Catholicism, escapes me.

J.G. O'Connor wanted to save our souls! Whereas you seem more interested in pointing out the many inconsistencies in readings of the Bible:

"What in the world"; sex and religion; two stories about the creation of the world in Genesis, with differing orders of creation; and the American translation of the Bible.

C.E. I think in doing that, seeing the inconsistencies, I have come to appreciate rather than degrade the Bible. I now see the Bible as a library rather than as a constitution. McLaren makes a good point: if we look at the Bible as a constitution, it is not any fun. If we see the Bible as a library, it is an amazing collection of stories. It is about everything, and it was written by people who love to tell stories.

It is a fascinating document. It is how it was used in my early life that causes me to write books wrestling with it. And I have come to the place, sounding like this, via McLaren, even though he and I part paths talking about the afterlife and things like that. On the other hand, it is so refreshing to read someone who sees the Bible as a library and is serious about it.

J.G. When we mention the Bible, we usually mean the King James version of it; but you bring in "the American translation" of it. What Bible is that?

C.E. In the 1920s and '30s some scholars in Chicago translated the Bible. Of course, it was not the first translation, but it was a serious translation in which Hebrew was seriously looked at, more so than in the King James translation.

As I understand it, there was a nod to the Hebrew texts in the King James version, but only a nod, most of it was from the Greek, as translated from the Hebrew. So these scholars attempted to look at the original. I have a cousin who is interested in all this, he is more of a scholar, and when I talked with him I was finding, as an example, one that I honed [*sic*] in on: "I will dwell in the house of the LORD forever" in the King James version, and in the Hebrew text it reads: "I will live in the house of the Lord to an old age." Not only is this not quite the same thing, the difference is *infinity.* And for me, as a true believing teenager, to read the difference there was shocking. In my view now, it opens it up so much; it becomes refreshing and interesting. It is much easier to read for somebody who does not believe in everlasting life.

J.G. John Grammer argues that you are asking the same question as O'Connor: "What must one do to be saved?"[6]—But I am not sure that this is your purpose.

C.E. What is it to be saved? That's a preliminary question that must be asked and answered. And Flannery O'Connor would answer that question quite differently from the way I would.—Two writers, William Gay and Tom

Franklin, called me up five years or so ago and said, "We are doing a tribute book, an anthology, to Flannery O'Connor, would you write a tribute story to Flannery O'Connor?" I said, "Yes" and hung up the phone, and then I thought, "A tribute story," what does that mean? But I decided not to call them back, thinking I'm going to do what I want to do, and what I wanted to do, I knew immediately. And this is the background:

O'Connor has written an essay, "Writing Short Stories,"[7] which you are probably familiar with, about her writing "Good Country People," she is really writing about symbolism and the wooden leg, et cetera, and how she did not know where the story was going as she wrote it. "Good Country People" is my favorite story of hers, and I love the first two paragraphs. If I were a teacher, I would say, "You got to get rid of those," because she did not know where she was going. But she saved them, and I think they belong there. But, if one night I had written to the point just before the Bible salesman and Hulga go to the barn and I then had gone to bed, it would have been one of the happiest nights of my life, knowing that I would get to get up and find out what happens next. Because I would love to have written that story, I decided that I would write a story with a Bible salesman; it is not going to be her Bible salesman but *a* Bible salesman.

What I could do is to have my Bible salesman meet her Bible salesman. And the Misfit also interests me, so I want to put a criminal like the Misfit in my short story. Once I finished the short story, I kept in touch with William Gay and Tom Franklin, and when I realized they were not going to print the book right away I sent the story out and *Southern Review* picked it up [see note 1]. When I finished the story and started to work on another novel, I thought, "Oh, wait a minute, there's a novel there!" Then I had the problem of writing the novel, which was a noticeable problem. I had two stories, I had Henry's upbringing and I had his few weeks on the road in 1950 with Clearwater, so I ended up starting with him on the road and going back, and again on the road and going back. I was again having a character reading the Bible through from start to finish, seeing what his response would be. His naiveté in selling Bibles, and then, of course, the contrast is that he is actually *selling* Bibles that he has gotten for free. In the short story the Bible salesman is very unethical, he is quite bad, so these two guys are both criminals. As soon as I started writing the novel I realized that to have tension and suspense throughout, I couldn't have them that much alike. I had to have an innocent character. What was left over, I enjoyed that clipping in that front page very much and I didn't want to make him too clean altogether and I kept it just to give him some warm color so I kept the Bible-sniffing scene in; but it was fun.

**J.G.** Your novel says it is okay to have premarital sex and to masturbate (if you ask forgiveness and mean it) and to question Jesus' behavior when he curses moneylenders or curses a fig tree and drinks wine and God's behavior when he kills his enemies and punishes the snake that "hadn't had a chance." Your main character *sells* Bibles that he got for free to distribute. How is your reputation among Southern fundamentalists?—Do you receive threatening phone calls late at night?

**C.E.** I have had fundamentalists walk out of one or two readings. I can number on one hand the people who have responded negatively. They generally do not, they usually keep quiet, but I do get some negative responses.

**J.G.** When Uncle Jack takes his family to Swan Island to see the Electra all lit up, the band, and a movie, they are evicted as "white trash," and a social theme is introduced. Although the social milieu is sensed throughout, it is not in focus for very long. Why did you choose *not* to develop the class issue?

**C.E.** That is a great question. The Northerners reviewing this book, of course, say, "It doesn't have any race in it." I was faulted for writing about the '50s and the South and not writing about race relations. The novel was structurally complicated and I wanted to show *Henry,* because it was about him and because it had a lot to do with his stealing, his being fooled, and his coming to see the light. The theme did not warm itself up to a lot of social-class business. There was that one opportunity, and it reflects where I live now, and I was going to make it a nonfictional island. There is a little museum on the island, which shows a place called Lumina, which was a dance hall. Up into the 1940s there was no way to get over to the island except by a trolley car. The Lumina was an experiment with electricity, so it had amazing lights. It showed films in the surf at night. After a big fire the place was finally torn down in the '70s. There was, if you study it, the whole Jim Crow business of African Americans doing all the work there, dressed in white. It was a very class-conscious place. It was the upper end, even into the 1950s. When my family and I went to the beach, we went to the blue-collar beach, which was Carolina Beach, twenty miles to the south. Wrightsville Beach was sort of a white-collar beach.

**J.G.** I think there is a link between the topic of the true faith and belonging to the right class. It is brought out when we hear that Uncle Jack's family from Strickland County do not know Jesus, because they are "common." And, of course, Henry is finally able to bring Marleen to the Deluxe Olympia Hotel without pretending to be working there. It is the end of his quest, but was it finally a spiritual quest?

**C.E.** For John Grammer, who wrote a piece in terms of salvation, the author's purpose is in Uncle Jack's dog's Bible, Trixie's Bible, which says "there is no magic" and "no one can see into the future"; in many ways *that* defines Thomas Jefferson's theology, when he rewrote the New Testament. Uncle Jack's sarcastic view of the Church is there, but in the end, in the honeymoon, in the "sentimental" part of the book, there are sliced apples, redfish, and white bread—that is a kind of ceremony between *them* and marriage. And the most that they can even speak about, spiritualize, is a shadow which theoretically, once you've brought the sun, goes to infinity. Looking at it from a purposeful point of view in terms of religion, his Aunt Dorie is quite the fundamentalist, although she is a *loving* fundamentalist, and Uncle Jack is not, which causes them to split up. So we have Henry making moves toward Uncle Jack, and that is the "message," maybe that is a kind of salvation.

**J.G.** In this community of people who are convinced they will be swept up into heaven and spared the fires of hell, Uncle Jack is a refreshingly realistic presence. He knows what Henry will need to know (and sends him condoms). I know you had an uncle like that, you told me about him. Initiation stories are always read as if they were autobiographical, even if the perspective is changed. Are you out in a personal crusade in going from Exodus, to Genesis, back to Exodus, and again to Genesis, in order to end with Revelation? I see, of course, the early period of first impressions and the following period of striking out on one's own. But why jumble the narrative?

**C.E.** To tell the story you might sacrifice point of view or chronology, et cetera, to get it right. The question might be: how do you lose less in telling your story; for example, there were complaints about the early drafts—this is hard to talk about without talking about the early journey of the composition of the book—there were about fifteen messages back and forth early, it was way too much. This book changed a lot.

One of my choices was to start in 1930 when Henry was born. I could start there and have a flash forward. In which case no one could complain about flashbacks [laughing], and I have a *big* problem with flashbacks with my students. As soon as you start in 1950 and go back, then you've set up the fact of flashbacks. For me the energy and the emphasis had to be when he meets Clearwater, so I had to start with that. Then Henry's story, his being naively involved in a crime and what that meant, needed the backdrop of his upbringing.

Before I was ever published, I had a story about a teenager drinking a beer and what a traumatic experience that was:

he thought he was denying himself eternal life in Heaven. But that was in the story and a Northern critic said to me, "What's the big deal?" Well, the big deal was *eternal life,* that's what the big deal was. So I felt the need to have some narrative support to enlighten what Henry is going through. Not only reading the Bible the first time, not only experiencing sex for the first time, not only being involved in crime, which he is going to realize. It was the last resort in composing the book to do whatever it was doing, most effectively. I didn't feel comfortable with the structure.

J.G. You obviously still don't. I think it works. The years 1937–51 and the jumbled way they come into the narrative, reflect the idea of your personal relationship with the story. I think there *is* something achieved by going back and forth in time. If you had told this story using a straight time line, it would not have been nearly as effective. We need the perspective that is added with the time shifts.

Clearwater is not Copeland; but I recognized the name Copeland, with Grandma Copeland as that of the sinister character in *Redeye.*

C.E. When I am doing the names the last time, I try consciously sometimes to put together kinships that no one would ever discover—except somebody who has read all the novels.

J.G. It is my impression in that first, really great, chapter of *The Night Train* [2011] that your emphasis is on rhythm, in the spectacular names, in the music, and in your fiction. Then in the opening of chapter 2, Larry Lime [cp. "The Third Man"] is even trying for synesthesia. The sense of a place—its education, racism, and social distribution—is clear from the start, also in the movie theaters, where the showing of *The Birds* and the lunch counter sit-ins pinpoint the time as the early 1960s [1963]. What is of primary interest on the first twenty-five pages is the detailing of the racial situation. Is *The Night Train* primarily about *the effects* of radically segregating a town, so nobody doubts who is serving whom?

C.E. Yes.—And add to that the effect that separation has in friendship denied between a white boy and a black boy; in my head *that* goes with what the book is about. Professors always ask me, "what's it about?" An answer to that question, though the answer could change during revision, always helped me decide what goes, what stays.

J.G. You mention that "Starke people didn't dwell on the Civil War." Isn't that unusual for Southerners?

C.E. It is unusual for a certain class of Southerners, it is unusual for the middle and upper classes. I would have five classes rather than three:

I would have the upper class, middle upper, middle class, lower middle class, and lower—I think the latter two are less likely to worry about the Civil War or talk about it at any point. The upper class is very wrapped up in all that, the middle class less so. The reason I say that is because I consider myself from the lower middle class—and in my "autobiography," knowledge of Civil War history was not a big deal. Sherman was a big deal, but Lee and Grant.

**J.G.** But there was hatred of Sherman?

**C.E.** Oh yes, that was thorough in my family, and with stories about him. But the War wasn't eulogized, it was not talked about a lot, there weren't pictures and reminiscences. We had great stories about hurting the Yankees; "Yankee" was, of course, a bad word—but there was less hatred than I *feel* there was in the upper classes.

**J.G.** Do you still cherish the idea of the Atlanta Braves beating the Yankees in baseball? Not that it will happen all that often.

**C.E.** Later on, yeah. But for me it was the Brooklyn Dodgers and the Yankees. And everybody in the family was for the Yankees because the Dodgers had black people on the team. I remember during the late '50s and early '60s the concern of my uncles and father about the Dodgers having black people on their team and the Yankees didn't. So there was no question of whom to pull for.

**J.G.** Even though they were called the Yankees?

**C.E.** Yes—that is the irony and the strength of racism. It is amazing, when you think about it. You would pull for the Yankees because they had no black players on the team. That I was against the mainstream, pulling for the Dodgers now helps me embrace my younger self.

**J.G.** Both the Bissetts were born during the War, and your well-known topic of age is always present, even Billy Graham is mentioned, but in this novel the topic of age is clearly dwarfed by race issues. But when Flash's mother has a stroke, the topic of caring for the elderly forces itself into the plot and takes away some of the built-up tension in the racial-*music* theme.

**C.E.** I understand exactly what you are saying and you will understand exactly what I am saying when I talk about the reasons for that.—It is fascinating to me that you come up with that, here is the evolution of what happened. I played in such a band in 1963, all white, I came in late while the band was learning the James Brown music. The kid who was running the band, tall, lanky Dennis Hobby, wanted to sing and act like James Brown. I didn't know much about James Brown. I knew about Ray Charles, though. So I came on board, as the piano player, I learn these songs, *then* I hear James Brown.[8] We perform that album and the lead singer, who plays no instrument, falls down on his knees, and he is singing the song "Please, Please." We had a lot of fun together, and the rest of us played a trick on him one night at the Castaway Club, a redneck nightclub. He is down on his knees saying "please, please," and we are supposed to fall in with the basic rhythm, so that he can stand up and keep singing, but we just stand there. So he rolls his eyes up at us from down there on the floor and plaintively sings "please, please," and we just stand there. I have always wanted to write about that. We finally came with the song. That scene never got into the novel, but when I started to write the novel I had a bunch of old men in their 60s remembering their days in the band. I wrote for a year or so with the center of energy *not* in the novel; I threw all that away and I started over—with the time of the novel being 1963.

As it grows I have my villain, Flash is my villain, he is the racist. Immediately I saw an ending, which I've discarded, the clichéd ending of something bad happening to the black people. I said, "I am not going to buy that kind of book, so I'm not going to write that ending." Flash, as with all my bad people, had something endearing about him. I had one other thing left over from about three novels, and that is a conversation among old people about cremation, and I knew Flash's mother would be the one to have that conversation, so she has to be in the book.

Here is the trick, the problem, the concern, or the fact: in 2001 my mother died, and I had a lot left over, unwritten, about that experience. I know no shame when it comes to how to use what's happened in my life, so I had to write about her death. And, of course, it is not directly related to racism, but then I made a mistake, I wanted to make Flash human in a way that most people do not think about when it comes to racial attitudes—or most people who read novels. Tom Robinson, the black man in *To Kill a Mockingbird,* was one dimensional, when I saw the movie recently, because I was supposed to do a screenplay, I saw that. So I found myself with a mission with this Flash guy, and I took the death of my mother and transplanted it into the story. Now, Flash is a racist, so even though we get on to the topic of old people, the purpose is to make Flash human through his experience of the death of his closest relative.

**J.G.** I think that the built-up concentration on the racial situation is undercut by the women talking about how to take care of their patient.

**C.E.** It has been cut way back. My Yankee editor did not like Flash's mother, at all. She was in there, all right. You have lingering problems about what was a much bigger problem. All that stuff was cut way, way back, which is not to say that it can't be cut more, because I do get one more shot at it. [The manuscript had not found its very final version at the time of the interview].

**J.G.** Is the goal to make people think you are writing about their families—not somebody else's?

**C.E.** The goal is to make my readers think I am writing about a family that is—or was—alive!

**J.G.** Did black people in North Carolina actually tune in to the country music show?

**C.E.** No, they probably did not. But television being the novelty that it was in this community, and if nothing else was available, then *maybe* they did. TV was new, we got ours in 1954, because it was "new"! I was ten years old, and I had been going to the neighbors to watch. Because it was new, we would watch anything. There was only one thing on you could get. Ten thirty to midnight there were three shows a night: ABC, CBS, and NBC.

**J.G.** Bobby Lee Reese, who becomes the emcee on the *Country Music Jamboree,* is from Ballard College in Summerlin, the same college as in *Killer Diller*—you really do have a grudge against a certain college, not necessarily of that name, don't you?

**C.E.** [laughing].

**J.G.** It is interesting the way you identify with Baby Mercy collecting her material from her family in the backwoods of East Tennessee, and later with Aunt Marzie's storytelling. Faulkner said that as a writer you might have to steal the nightshirt off you grandmother if necessary for veracity. Do you feel sometimes that you are doing that? Is the secret that you tell the same *family* stories over and over?

**C.E.** Yes.—Yes, very much, especially with the death of Flash's mother. When my mother died, I was taking care of her. I kept journals, my diaries, throughout the period of her death from a stroke, detailed journals, which I obsessed over in earlier drafts, and which were clearly undercutting the story, *even* finally to me. But at the time the details were not undercutting enough to take out. I was stealing my mother's and my own stories. So that the novel in the end becomes, I hope, about more than race.

**J.G.** Is there so much emphasis on the setting, both place and time, and food, that we lose touch with the characters? Does Larry Lime develop, even though he is out of so much of the manuscript?

**C.E.** That's a good point. From working on other books I was conscious of what I was doing, putting in, and taking out.—You know, a lot of it has to do with what is going on in a writer's life. I am against the present resegregation of the South, and I am working with politicians on the school board in Wilmington, North Carolina, who are fighting that [isolating black children within supposedly integrated schools]. I am well aware of it happening, not only in the private schools but now also in the public schools. The word is "neighborhood schools," so where you have black neighborhoods, you have pockets of poverty, and the schools are 90 percent low-income schools, and mostly African American. We have that here, and politicians are finding covert racism very much in their favor in their efforts to push the "neighborhood school" concept.

Being in the middle of all that, and being aware of it, as I was writing that book, some of that feels like a *need-to-say.* It can pull a writer away from plot, character development, et cetera. Even though I start the book with him, I am less concerned with Larry Lime's character development than I am with Dwayne, the other young character. His character actually has some kind of growth and movement that Larry Lime's does not.—The book is more about Dwayne than about Larry Lime, in my view.

**J.G.** We begin to see music as the means by which the races can meet and get along. But we never see it defiantly carried out in their everyday racially segregated world in *Night Train.*—You can claim the drive-in movie incident as a frustrated attempt, but the reader wants Larry and Dwayne to play music together, in public, even if that would be stopped, too.—Even if they are not allowed to play basketball together.—But you never give the reader that moment of rebellion.

**C.E.** I had to make that decision. In your favor, it could have happened, but it did not happen in my experience. I went back and did some research about '67–'68, and it happened then, and I *do* remember even in '62 or so, a black-white nightclub called the Stallion Club, just outside Durham, North Carolina. I never went to it, but white people went to it and black people, it was popular. In the *late* '60s there was much more of that, and there would have been an opportunity for black and white to play together. It was very tempting to have Larry go on TV, he could have played drums or piano; I could have had him come in. If I had responded to the need for cliché in my head, that would have been your expected ending.—*But* the "movement" happened when Dwayne made the decision to play "Night Train" on TV; for me that was the climax and what the book is about. To bring them *together,* I think, would have detracted from that. But I think I am reacting also to a hunger—and against movies like "Mississippi Burning" [December 1988], which I didn't see, but you have the expected ending where all the white people are "racists" and all the black people are "victims."

**J.G.** And the FBI are the heroes, in this Hollywood falsification of history, which made a lot of money.[9]—The irony is that Dwayne accepts Fats Domino and Little Richard and their music, but he can't get himself to ask Larry Lime to play with them. Wouldn't Larry think of this later on?

**C.E.** That's part of the theme of the holding apart, which is very specific to 1963. Larry Lime would probably not think that he would have the opportunity; instead he has internalized racism. He would not even see it as possible; it would be something that was inconceivable.—In '68, yes, I can see that if the book were placed in '68, I could have had them perform together on stage.

**J.G.** Wouldn't the balcony in the movie theater be reserved for blacks every evening? And wouldn't Dwayne's sudden appearance up there have created attention?

**C.E.** There were black people up there when he went up with the chicken. He comes up there as a white person, he has the right to be anywhere he wants to, at any time. Nobody would question that.—I am not sure quite how that worked in all theaters, I don't remember sitting in the balcony.

**J.G.** Walker Percy wrote about the balcony in his Greenville, Mississippi, theater, when he was a young man in the 1930s. The balcony of the Grand on Main Street "had the biggest rats in Greenville."[10] Much of *Night Train* reads as a memoir from your boyhood with many unresolved issues, many things not done, I get the sense in this novel that you don't want to go any further than what you actually remember.

Why is jazz much more dangerous racially than country music? The Thelonious Monk music has places that are crooked or "off" and strange notes and rhythms, which today is an ideal in music and fiction. Could you have used Monk's ideas in the fiction here?

**C.E.** Thelonious Monk and his work came relatively late into the story, as a consequence of my reading his biography, which was new. I was to review it for *Garden & Gun,* and I was going to just scan it, but I couldn't stop reading. It is about twenty-five chapters with about a hundred footnotes per chapter, and it has been about fifteen years in the making. I had a kind of love affair with one of his songs, the song "Blue Monk"[11] from back in the '70s, and I have played that song all of my life.—That painting by the way [pointing to the wall] is Monk, I did it from a photograph, blew it up.

**J.G.** "Blue Monk," it should be on the cover of *Night Train!*

**C.E.** I sent my publisher that cover with "Night Train" written in red and another suggestion.

**J.G.** Why was it daring of Dwayne to do a cover version of James Brown with dance steps and all, when Pat Boone did a cover version of Little Richard?

**C.E.** The difference is that Pat Boone's cover of Little Richard is very "white." It has no bent notes, it has no flatted thirds or fifths and sevens, whereas Dwayne's version of James Brown is very "black," it is like Brown's "Night Train."

Let me play a thirty-second recording of Igor Stravinsky and James Brown together. It comes from an interview with the music director of the San Francisco Symphony, his name is Michael Tilson Thomas.[12] He had a marvelous interview with James Brown, the director was enamored of James Brown in '62–63. When he heard Brown the first time, he, the classical music scholar, was so reminded of Stravinsky in the rhythms that he had to pull up on the side of the road. And when he told James Brown, "I just had to pull up on the side of the road, I was so excited," James Brown said, "Yeah, you did the right thing." [We listen to some James Brown music on top of Stravinsky's, which brings out the similar rhythm and phrasing]. *That's* what Dwayne wanted to do.

**J.G.** It is hard to imagine that an all-white version of James Brown would get so much attention today, maybe it shows how far we have come. I did look for a Dwayne and Larry chapter at the end but didn't get it.

**C.E.** No doubt there were places, as in churches, among Pentecostals, where blacks and whites were playing music together, but otherwise it would be difficult. About the basketball, and the fact that my father asked me not to, he had a store much like the store in the novel. Larry Lime was based on a guy named Larry Lime, and I hope I will find him through the book and hope he is not upset. We never sat on the wall or any of that, but we kidded together and we played basketball together, secretly. In real life he brought his whole team to our community and we broke in the back of an old gymnasium, an old gym which is in a lot of my fiction, and we played one Saturday morning. We only had five guys and he had about eight guys and we played basketball, and they would line up their substitutes, and when one of them got tired he would go to the end of the line and the front one would come in and play. We would have to keep our five players going the whole game. I don't remember, but we probably did lose. But it was the consequence of a kind of a bet, we were kidding each other about who had the best basketball team. That kidding, the little bit of bantering that we had, was as far as our friendship ever got. We did play a one-on-one game in my backyard and my father told me to ask him to leave, and there was just that one time. Those autobiographical facts have a strong import for a writer like me. But in fiction I see myself as always translating.

## NOTES

◆ ◆ ◆

1. "The Great Speckled Bird," *Southern Review,* 43, no. 1 (Winter 2007): 182–96.
2. The play, with some of the songs from the novel, was first staged in Fayetteville, North Carolina, in March 2006.
3. (New York: HarperOne, 2010).
4. Traditional bluegrass lyrics, recorded by Mark Bishop, Kitty Wells, The Stanley Brothers, and Ricky Skaggs, among others.

5. Available from Sapsucker Music # 2328.

6. John Grammer, "Clyde Edgerton: *The Bible Salesman*," in *Still in Print: The Southern Novel Today*, ed. Jan Nordby Gretlund ( Columbia: University of South Carolina Press, 2010), 174–88, 184.

7. Flannery O'Connor, "Writing Short Stories," in *Mystery and Manners*, ed. Sally Fitzgerald and Robert Fitzgerald (New York: Farrar, Straus & Giroux, 1969), 87–106, esp. 98–102.

8. James Brown, 1933–2006. His "Night Train" from 1963 can be heard on YouTube.

9. Paul M. Gaston, "After Jim Crow: Civil Rights as Civil Wrongs," in *The Southern State of Mind*, ed. Jan Nordby Gretlund (Columbia, University of South Carolina Press, 1999), 36–48.

10. Walker Percy, "Cinematographic Souvenir of Greenville," *Delta Review* (Winter 1963–64): 25.

11. Recorded in 1958.

12. Music Director of the San Francisco Symphony since 1995; from 2006, host of the series *Keeping Score*, on PBS.

# *Percival Everett*

◆◆◆◆◆◆

*Odense, Denmark, March 13–14, 2013*

Percival Everett. This and all other photographs by Jan Nordby Gretlund unless otherwise stated.

◆◆◆◆◆◆

**Jan Nordby Gretlund** There is usually *a cause* in your fiction, often it is a struggle against various types of prejudice, but when I read your novel *Assumption* [2011], where the cause is homosexuality, I felt uneasy. I sensed that the immediate impression does not reveal the depth of the novel.—Later I realized that you were sitting somewhere feeling good about having fooled me into believing in the main character.

**Percival Everett** [laughing] I wasn't misleading you. I put in clues all the way.

**J.G.** Sure. At the end of the novel everything was obvious even to me. I suppose someone could write an essay, maybe a whole critical book, distinguishing between your western fiction and your antiprejudice fiction. But finally there would not be much difference. *God's Country* [1994] is a hilarious novel set in the West which reveals all sorts of things about our idea of the Old West. When you bring in a black man as the best tracker, he seems to be outside the mythical West, and out of place, *but he is not.* It is also a novel about interracial relations, and it becomes obvious to the reader why you wrote it. But in *Assumption* humorous racial indignation is toned down, and you are dead serious in calling attention to the scourge of methadone addiction in the West.

**J.G.** Everybody talks about *Erasure* [2001] as a great novel, but which one is your own favorite?

**P.E.** I don't have a favorite.

**J.G.** Is it like the rock star who always prefers his latest recording?

**P.E.** As I get older, I am a better writer. I see all sorts of things I might do differently—that might make it a better-crafted novel. But it would not necessarily make it a better work of art.

I don't want to make *art* some ideally crafted novel; that is a moving target anyway. That's why we have craft shops *and* museums. If your writing doesn't change and you think you have mastered the craft, you might as well stop working, because then there is no art available to you.

**J.G.** There were some writers, Ernest Hemingway for an example, who start out having this wonderfully simple style and then it gets more and more baroque. When Hemingway got older, he tried with some success to go back to the *Kansas City Stars* "style sheet" and he gave us *The Old Man and the Sea.* The style, anybody's style, will change, but it does not necessarily get better from novel to novel.

**P.E.** The style gets more dense. What is interesting is the experiment. A failed novel is not by definition a bad novel. In fact, sometimes a failed experiment teaches me more than anything else. I see all of my novels in a dialogue with each other, all except for *Suder* [1983].

**J.G.** I think that *Suder,* your first novel, is a great novel. It is funny and offers the valuable information that not all black men can play baseball. So that novel is in dialogue with *Erasure* in which Thelonious Monk Ellison enjoys mathematics and Mahler's music but can't dance or play basketball.

There is an overload of negative facts that happen to Thelonious:

his brother comes out of the closet, his mother has Alzheimer's, his sister is shot, and he finds that he has a sister he did not know about, et cetera How much can happen to a guy?

**P.E.** Well, over a number of years, a lot.—But it is a lot for one novel, isn't it?

**J.G.** Can you understand why *Erasure,* at least for now, is the most popular of your novels?

**P.E.** Yes, I see how *Erasure* enters into the discourse, in some ways sadly, about race and literature, because that's what it is about.—But I keep seeing, and I didn't know it, my novel *Glyph* [1999] on lots of syllabi.

**J.G.** That is because it makes fun of what some people still call comparative literature.—Is there some meaning in the French word "erasure" which is not there in the English word "erasure"?

**P.E.** In fact the French don't even use the word "erasure" as the title of the novel. They call it "effacement" which means a wiping out. Originally the title of the novel was not just the word *Erasure,* it was *Erasure* crossed out *with a giant capital X.* But the publishers could not bring themselves to cross it out. But it does change the meaning of the title when it is in fact the erasure that has been erased.

**J.G.** That situation parallels Rauschenberg's erasure of de Kooning's famous drawing and Rauschenberg's sale of the erasure, as referred to in your novel.

**P.E.** That is the parallel.

**J.G.** When I was reading *A History of the African-American People: Proposed by Strom Thurmond* [2004], I had the impression that your coauthor, named James Kincaid, might well be an invention of yours. Does he really exist at the University of Southern California?

**P.E.** Oh yes! We wrote this together, and he is so funny.

**J.G.** Did he write the letters in the book from a Martin Snell, supposedly at the publishing house called Simon & Schuster, Inc.

**P.E.** Yes! He is actually a Victorianist.

**J.G.** Was Senator Strom Thurmond actually in on that venture in any way?

**P.E.** Oh, no!

**J.G.** Was it a totally fictional idea that the senator would ask Kincaid and you to write a history of the African American people?

**P.E.** I woke up one morning and had the idea to actually write the history Strom Thurmond would write, but I did not even consider having him as a character in the book.—Then my friend Jim heard the title and asked if we could work on it together. That became our trying to get the project going.

**J.G.** So you never at any time talked with any of the senator's aides about it—or just heard from them?

P.E. No.

**J.G.** Were you afraid the senator would try to stop the book if he knew it was coming out?

**P.E.** He might have had some such desire.

**J.G.** You still have as "proposed by Strom Thurmond" and "told to" on the title page of the book, which implies the senator's presence. Were you not afraid of being sued?

**P.E.** Well, he was a public figure.

**J.G.** Weren't the publishers worried?

**P.E.** They always check everything with their lawyers, and they were not concerned. I used the real Ted Turner and Jane Fonda as characters in the same way in *I Am Not Sidney Poitier* [2009].

**J.G.** And someone called Percival Everett is Not Sidney Poitier's teacher in that same novel.

**P.E.** What we had to get around that was a rather strange disclaimer written to the publishers as front matter, starting:

"All characters depicted in this novel are completely fictitious, regardless of similarities to any extant parties and regardless of shared names."

**J.G.** The readers and my students see the point in the identity game. The passages situated in the lawyer's house in Washington reveal the common identity prejudice, through the air-conditioning tracts.—This is where Flannery O'Connor comes in with her immortal observation "For the deaf you have to shout and for the almost blind you have to paint large and startling pictures" [*Mystery & Manners,* p. 34].

When I read *A History of the African-American People,* I was interested in what you did with Strom Thurmond, because I had just written an essay on Nikky Finney's poem "Dancing with Strom." I was surprised to see the senator looking pretty good, especially compared to the publishing people, who *do* look pretty bad, whereas the senator makes sense, most of the time.

**P.E.** Strom was pretty bad, but he was a politician, and to be successful as a politician you have in some way to get someone *to like you,* and sometimes it is people you are being bad to, and he was remarkable at that. His career was a good lesson in and about intelligence. In many ways he was not a very bright man, but in other ways he was brilliant!

**J.G.** He had honed people skills.

**P.E.** Yes, people skills, and he was not a dummy. He was not without a very complicated sense of fairness. He would offer reading lessons to anyone black or white on Sundays in his house. He was teaching people to read, and they came!

**J.G.** He knew the value of literacy but also that you could get too much of it.

**P.E.** Yes, it was one of those rare paradoxes: yes, you should be educated, but don't let too much information ruin your life.

J.G. In your novel you have Thurmond talk about the infamous murder of a black man who was dragged to death in Texas, hauled by a pickup truck. The senator says the whole South was blamed, but had it happened in New England, all of that region would not have been blamed, only the particular place where it actually happened. Is he right?

P.E. Well, I made that up. He never said that. It is the American propensity for scapegoating regions. It is the same thing that happened when the game animals were killed in Wyoming in the early '80s. Fuel was poured down into coyote dens and lit. The entire state of Wyoming was indicted for this horrible deed. There was a play about it.

J.G. Is that sad event related to your novel *Wounded* [2005]?

P.E. That was the initial inspiration for the novel—but had something like that happened in Central Park, New York State as a whole would *not* have been indicted for cruelty to animals.

◆ ◆ ◆

P.E. *Sinn und Bedeutung* and Gottlob Frege's puzzle have become a huge part of my thinking about fiction.

J.G. I noted that you went into German with the title of the poems in *Abstraktion und Einfühlung* [2008]. But the new novel is not called *Sinn und Bedeutung.*

P.E. It was called that at one time, but now its full title is *Percival Everett by Virgil Russell* [2013].

J.G. So you are still focusing on sense and meaning. Is there any real change in German from *Sinn* to *Bedeutung?* I mean, does that *mean* something?

P.E. Sense in reference is what Frege is referring to. The discussion of this led to Bertrand Russell and Alfred North Whitehead's famed *Principia Mathematica* [3 vols., 1910–13].—The title of my novel refers to the poet Virgil and the philosopher Russell. Virgil, the poet, is Dante's Virgil to me, he leads Dante through the levels of Hell in *The Divine Comedy.*

J.G. You are very productive! You must write all the time, considering the number of pages you have published . . . when do you have time to read philosophy?

P.E. I'm always reading. I can't write unless I am reading.

J.G. What fascinates you about Bertrand Russell?

P.E. Many things! One was his presence as a public intellectual; he was comfortable with it and uncompromising. Russell was a man with great integrity. He even took care of Wittgenstein—even though he was such trouble—and recognized Wittgenstein's brilliance without having it reflect on himself; it is remarkable. Russell was a great logician and with Whitehead he published *Principia Mathematica,* which is all formalized logic, *but it is very literary!*

**J.G.** Was Bertrand Russell trying to make it easier for us to understand?

**P.E.** I don't think he was trying to make it easier.—He was trying to make it clear! That is one thing I appreciate about Russell. He wasn't writing for a lay audience, and it is all very dense, but it is so thoroughly beautiful.

**J.G.** Is this interest something you inherited from your father? I mean the habit of reading philosophical texts.—Most people who set out to write fiction would probably *not* go to logic and philosophy to learn about style and beautiful writing.

**P.E.** I started reading philosophy as a student, and I felt comfortable with it. I write fiction because my main interest is how language works. I don't think of myself as a natural storyteller.

**J.G.** Well, you could have fooled me.

**P.E.** I am a puzzle former.

**J.G.** So if water all of a sudden is running down the mountain and into a native reservation, you want to know why? This is, of course, from your novel *Watershed* [1996]. Was that based on an actual event in the West?

**P.E.** No! But it is not unlike what happened in eastern Washington State at a nuclear plant. For years they made nuclear weapons out there, and also in Colorado, at Rocky Flats, outside of Boulder.

**J.G.** So they ruined the water—polluted it!

**P.E.** In Washington State there is a high incident rate for cancer.

**J.G.** They produce such great wines, but I will think twice now about drinking wine from Washington State. But I will go and enjoy reading Bertrand Russell's great English in his *History of Western Philosophy.*

**P.E.** Russell had such great artistry and integrity, his ego never seems to be on display.

**J.G.** For me it is a treat to go with you into the West in *Wounded* [2005], in *Walk Me to the Distance* [1985], and in *Assumption,* your latest novel. But these novels are rarely funny; they are mostly dead serious.

**P.E.** But I also admit to being Mark Twain's illegitimate offspring. I believe that the best way into any serious matter is usually comedy.

**J.G.** In *Assumption* the serious matter is that almost anybody we meet is a meth victim. It is difficult to find a character in the whole novel to identify with.

**P.E.** My concern in this novel was not so much to get a story but to exploit the expectations with which people come to the novel. The novelist is combing for what is interesting, even when you do not have, as I do not have, lots of experience with current fiction; we *all* know *all the moves* in a western.

**J.G.** We think.

**P.E.** And we know how it is going to end—we think.

**J.G.** You certainly fooled me.

**P.E.** It is an investigation into the nature of narrative, which shows language as a deceiver in memory, on family relations, and on neighbors. I was trying to play with the whole notion that comes out of reality: the current of the interview with the neighbors of a mass killer. They always say, invariably, "He was such a nice man," "He was a great neighbor," and "He surprised all of us." They *never* say, "Oh, we knew he would kill everybody!"

**J.G.** I think one of the most successful scenes was when he goes to town to try to interview two hookers—or ladies of the night—they came alive and were very convincing characters. It was harder, as a reader, to relate to the drug addicts and victims. There was little or nothing positive about them, they are just the walking dead.

◆◆◆

**J.G.** Talking about popularity, *you* are becoming more popular in the South every day.

**P.E.** Am I? I don't know about it.

**J.G.** I know South Carolina is anxious to claim you as a South Carolinian, and good essays on your fiction are published as far south as Mississippi.—What more do you want?

**P.E.** I never think in regions. I think that people from all over, especially in academia, end up in universities everywhere.

**J.G.** But you can go through the university catalogues and see what is being taught all over. In the 1960s I was in Ft. Gordon and in Ft. Knox and at UVA., and today I see great positive changes all over the South. Among others there is much more emphasis on African American literature in the regular university courses.

**P.E.** Now professors come from everywhere. And in the 1960s there was no body of black students. Now there is no difference in what is being taught in the South and in the North.

**J.G.** That is what I call progress.—I read the criticism, and often it is obvious that people in the South know more about the interracial situation. Not about what is going on in the ghettoes in the northern cities, of course, but about the rapidly integrating South. I can see why somebody like Nikky Finney would be awarded the National Book Award for Poetry. It is well deserved.

**P.E.** Yes, that *is* great!

**J.G.** And Dori Sanders is successful with her cookbook, and her portrait was on a gigantic billboard by Interstate 77 in South Carolina. The last time I met her, she was on Hilton Head for a literacy campaign. Nobody is poor and deprived of education on Hilton Head, but she was there to raise money to support literacy in other areas.

And now I am looking forward to reading a book I just saw advertised by a Percival Everett supposedly titled *I Am Not Reading a Percival Everett Novel; Ghostwritten by Oprah Winfrey.*

# *In My Own Style*

## AN INTERVIEW WITH KAYE GIBBONS

◆◆◆◆◆◆

*Raleigh, North Carolina, June 18, 1996*

Kaye Gibbons

◆◆◆◆◆◆

**Jan Nordby Gretlund** When Trudy goes to New York in *A Cure for Dreams* [1991], she likes "everything about it except for the noise, the dirt, and the people." Is this a rejection of the North, or is it of the city?

**Kay Gibbons** I think it is of the city. You can also look at it positively as an embracing of the South, where there is no noise to speak of; the dirt is out in the country, where it is supposed to be, and the people are not obnoxious.

**J.G.** Although most Southerners now live in cities, like this Raleigh-Durham-Chapel Hill area, you still situate your plots in the country.

**K.G.** I do, because I'm so connected to it. Yesterday, I went to visit my brother, who still lives out in the country, and I wanted to stay. And the reason I bought this house is because it looks out on property that does look like the country. It looks like we're in the woods, facing the house, although we're right in the middle of the city. I prefer the conveniences of the city, but I think another reason I placed all the stories in the country is that there is so much quiet drama there. You don't expect anything to be going on, and you have to look very closely underneath the surfaces to see where all the action is.

**J.G.** You certainly do that in *A Virtuous Woman* [1989], where all the action is over when you begin, except in the mind of one character.

**K.G.** That's right.

**J.G.** It is characteristic of contemporary Southern fiction that we hear little of the secret lives of mall developers and aerobics instructors.

**K.G.** I think we are in such a process that Southern writers who are my age and up are caught up in this change of having one foot caught in the past with farm life and one foot in the mall developments. So we are in a great copse right now. I think that my children will probably write the urban novel; I tend *not* to read the books that are little urban Southern stories.

**J.G.** Walker Percy used New Orleans as a setting, as Josephine Humphreys has used Charleston. There is nothing wrong in using a city with history and atmosphere, is there?

**K.G.** Right! But there is something so tawdry about the change that is going on in the South right now. I don't even enjoy being around it, so I don't want to write about it. I don't see anything spiritual there, and what I always have to find is a spiritual place to set a book.

**J.G.** Would you be more inclined to write social criticism if you described the life of people in the city?

**K.G.** I tend to be much more of an Agrarian and a New Critic than I am a Marxist-socialist. I don't write in order to make political comments on rural or urban life. I just don't find spirituality in big cities that I want to read about.—Right now I am reading James Lee Burke's Robicheaux mysteries. They are set in the bayou outside New Orleans, and I am fine with that. He can make little trips to the city, but he always comes back home to his fishing dock.

**J.G.** But wherever you place the fiction, it is always with an emphasis on the mother–daughter relationships.

**K.G.** It is.

**J.G.** What happened to the rest of the family?

**K.G.** I think, because my mother died when I was ten, I have so few memories of her that I'm always in a book trying to recreate a personal history of a mother-and-daughter relationship. In each book I experimented with what would be ideal, and I finally found it in *A Cure for Dreams*. That's my favorite book! It is because I recreated an ideal situation with those three women living in the house together.

**J.G.** And the ideal situation excludes men?

**K.G.** Well, except for my husband, I will say that's true.

**J.G.** I was disappointed with *A Cure for Dreams*, I felt it read as feminist politics.

**K.G.** I was going through a bad marriage at the time, I think I vented a lot of my spleen on the men in that book, and I regret it.

**J.G.** But isn't this exclusion of men a fact also in *Charms for the Easy Life* [1993]. Think of the young woman who has no emotional reaction on seeing her father dead.—Is it true that men do not have good relationships with their children?

**K.G.** There is a lot being made right now around Father's Day over fathers. Are fathers better now than they used to be? And the answer is: yes, of course they are. They hug the children, they take them to school. But I still feel that the burden of raising children is on women. And I try to do some honor to that in the books.

The Civil War book I'm working on right now breaks every rule I ever had. It won't be coming out for a year. It's about a mother and a son, basically. She has four daughters, but right now their personalities are not developed and they're petty and trifling. She is very close to her son, but he turns out to be the one who ruins her during the War, because he is a never-do-well.

**J.G.** What happened to the manuscript you called "Eagle Avenue"?

**K.G.** Oh that turned into *Charms for the Easy Life* [1993]. I cut out all the Eagle Avenue stuff and kept the charms for the easy life.

**J.G.** An interesting trend is reflected in your choice of material for your new book. Madison Jones has just finished a Civil War manuscript [*Nashville 1864*], and Josephine Humphreys is working on 1870 material for her next book [*Nowhere Else on Earth*].

**K.G.** And I didn't know about their books.

**J.G.** What is the attraction of going back to the Civil War?

**K.G.** There's not a great deal in modern life to write about, unless someone is writing genre fiction, mysteries, et cetera. There's not been enough distance. Mark Twain said, "There has to be a distance between the subject matter and the time of writing." And I think we all have had time enough to reflect on the War now and on its repercussions on integration in the early 1960s. So we do have some time distance, and we can write about it.

**J.G.** Is going back, then, a way of focusing on problems that are still with us?

**K.G.** Yes. The action has already taken place, but the ramifications are still here. And, for myself, I'm very interested in how people lived without air conditioning, washing machines, and other modern conveniences. So I love the detailed research of daily minutiae. I found all I do every day is write about what the children were learning at school during the War and how the woman ordered the clothes that she didn't make from the general store. I'm getting nowhere quickly, but I'm filling out pages at a remarkable rate. Some time I will have to have a plot.

**J.G.** I'm a bit wary when writers talk of the speed with which they write a book. I feel that it is a danger for the writer that initial success calls for an immediate follow-up. Is there time enough between books to write well?

**K.G.** Louis Rubin always says, "Writers aren't waiting for their wells to fill up." My Civil War book has taken three years now. That's one good thing about the effect of money. If you don't fill, your family still isn't going to starve.

**J.G.** Is there a pressure from publisher or agent to publish before you are ready?

**K.G.** Sometimes publishers and agents don't realize that some of their writers have families and are not living for these books. Some editors will say, "Are you working today?" And I say, "No, it is graduation at school." Or, "Louise has an ear infection, so I'm not going to get much done today."

**J.G.** My favorite book of yours is *A Virtuous Woman* [1989]. It is very good, especially for a second novel. Did you work on it even before you finished *Ellen Foster*?

**K.G.** When I started a book after *Ellen Foster* [1987], it was about a man who owned a fruit stand out in the country, and he turned into the farmer in *A Virtuous Woman*. It is a completely different book.

**J.G.** There are many bad second novels by Southern writers, but yours does not belong in that category. How did you get the breathing space to do *A Virtuous Woman* so well?

**K.G.** I was sure that reviewers were going to be gunning for me, and I was paranoid when *A Virtuous Woman* came out. In fact, I was hospitalized when the book came out. And Louis Rubin called and read me the *New York Times* review of it. I didn't go on a book tour, because I was manic at the time. I think I got it done by finally divorcing myself from the first book. Now I think of every book as the first book I've ever written. As I get older, I'm more aware that reviewers are more and more picky. I used to get a lot of leeway for being twenty-seven years old, quirky and cute, and I don't get that any more. So I'll have to work.

**J.G.** Are you still labeled "another Southern voice," or do you feel that with five novels this is behind you?

**K.G.** Yes. I don't feel that any longer. In the South people still speak of me as a Southern writer, but outside the South I am as American as John Updike, Jane Smiley, or Anne Tyler. I'm compared a lot to Anne Tyler.—I gave up on her after *The Accidental Tourist.*

It is hard to think of myself as a regional writer when the books are in so many languages, and I travel so much. At home I do not think of myself as a Southern writer. But my themes are Southern.

**J.G.** On the other hand, Southern writer or not, all your material and entire background are right here.

**K.G.** Willie Morris said, "All my tools are here." And since I'm here, all the tools are here, and that's what I use. But it is hard to think of myself as a regional writer when the books are in so many languages, and I travel so much. At home I don't think of myself as a Southern writer. But my themes are Southern. They used to be in bookstores under Southern literature, and now they've moved out onto the regular fiction shelves. And I was glad to see that happen.

**J.G.** Are your books also selling well in the Northeast and the West?

**K.G.** Yes. The South is the strongest. But the paperback printing of *Sights Unseen* [1995] is, I think, 750,000. That's a lot, and they will sell them. They certainly won't sell them all in the South. I do more touring outside the South than inside the South, a lot more.

**J.G.** Isn't it a danger for a creative artist that it is easier, and probably better paid, to give readings?

**K.G.** I get more for doing a speech than a lot of writers I know get for doing a book. That's because I don't want to do but two or three a year. They're draining! John Updike said they were "soulsuckers," and they do suck souls, if you do them well. You can go to one drunk, or not show up, be a prima donna, or wing it. But to do one well is really draining. You don't get anything done the day before, you know. And you got to travel.

**J.G.** Do some novelists reach the point where the touring, the being lionized, and the readings get in the way of the art?

**K.G.** I used to do everything I was asked to do. Then I realized I wasn't writing and wasn't looking after my children.

**J.G.** You mentioned that race problems are not yet behind us. Do they ever appear in your fiction after *Ellen Foster*?

**K.G.** In *Ellen Foster* the race issue was between two children. Then on the last page Ellen Foster moves it out into society. In the other books the racial issues are brought out inside the household. And it is how the domestic help is treated. In *Sights* when one woman is called "a nigger," she's defended by all the members of the family. With Miss Welty, I believe that the writer should not crusade. I never set out to crusade, but I would like to teach small lessons through stories.

**J.G.** Maybe we should add another question today: must the critic crusade? I think we need an essay on that topic.

**K.G.** Yes. I do, too. I'm a little tired of that.

**J.G.** For many pages of *Charms for the Easy Life* I thought I was reading about a black family. Does that surprise you?

**K.G.** No. I get letters from people who have read *Ellen Foster* all the way through and think she is black. Ain't that pitiful?

**J.G.** I find it hard to believe.

**K.G.** Yeah. But in the South, more so than in any other place in the world, black people and white people grew up so close together, grew up on the same farms together, that we have the same foodways and folkways. We do share a lot of the same beliefs, and certainly the same religious background.—I guess it doesn't surprise me at all that people would become confused by race in the books.

**J.G.** Did your family worship regularly?

**K.G.** They didn't. But I went with my aunts and uncles, and I paid attention and listened. Then in college [at the University of North Carolina] I read Cotton Mather's sermons and Roger William's sermons. It was phenomenally fascinating. Then I went on to Cardinal Newman's essays.

**J.G.** As in most fiction by your contemporaries, religion does not seem to be a very powerful force in the lives of your characters.

**K.G.** No, it is not a powerful force in my last books. In the Civil War book, which so far is called "Seasons of My Discontent," the woman is sixty-nine years old, and she is an Episcopalian. I am Episcopalian, but my childhood religion was Baptist, and when I have questions about matters of faith, I have to call the priest at the church and ask him, "What would she have thought of this?" or "What would she have done then?" So I have to do research on my own religion. In some ways it was always a comedy that I just have not written about. [The novel became *On the Occasion of My Last Afternoon* (1998).]

**J.G.** Your protagonists try to create a universe where they can rely on their own selves and do without the help of others. Your passages on this have an autobiographical flavor.

**K.G.** Oh, they do. I was left to myself from age 10 to 11. So I had to do everything and pay the bills. My father drank all the time. And my husband says that I still put down pieces of tape on the stage for people to stand on, make them stand there, and do what I please. So I think I got a lot of willpower. When you do this for a living, you have to have a lot of willpower.

**J.G.** Are you looking for your characters to live through their various initiations and realize the same type of willpower?

**K.G.** I think with that, I was strongly influenced by William Blake's *The Book of Thel,* she is in the world of innocence and moves into the world of experience and has to go running back because she can't stand it. I read that right before I wrote *Ellen Foster.*

**J.G.** Some of your technical innovations in *Ellen Foster* call attention to themselves.

**K.G.** Those were very important to me. I bet I know what they are. I will just make it easy for you: I don't use commas or quotation marks, because I wanted to see if I could make the voice gradations and the changes so obvious without them—that they were unnecessary. I really made a conscious choice. The publisher did not sell serial rights to magazines because of that. One magazine wanted me to go back in and put in commas and quotation marks, but I wasn't going to do it. I thought no intelligent reader needed those symbols to read it.

I just read the book on audio tape, out loud, and I had a difficult time reading it aloud because I didn't have the visual cues. I could have used some then, but I never regretted it.—I'd just read *Ulysses,* too, and that had a very strong influence. I did *Ellen Foster* in six weeks, that's a fact, I didn't labor over that book. But I was drained by it. When I finished it, I went and threw up.

**J.G.** Was it ever suggested to you that *Ellen Foster* is really a short story?—Do you ever write short stories?

**K.G.** No, I can't! I don't know how! This bothers me greatly, because I would really like to write short stories and publish in *The New Yorker.* That would be really comfortable if I could do that. The problem is I don't know how to write one. I wrote one, one time, about a midget doctor that was perfectly horrible. He treats a woman who is in shock because she found a snake in a purse in the women's room in a chicken restaurant. Is this some story! I published it in a small review, and Fred Chappell gave it an award, but I think he was feeling particularly kind at the time. I couldn't believe it. Then the award made people notice it, and I was so embarrassed. I have not written one since. This was in 1988. Don't go taking it up! I'm not going to tell you where it was.

When I think about short stories, they always become chapters in a novel. It is probably best, since I figure I don't know how to write them or to leave them alone. I keep Katherine Anne Porter's short stories over on that table. So when I can't sleep in the middle of the night, I'll come down here and read the Miranda stories until I go to sleep. I'm trying to model the voice of the Civil War book after the Miranda stories. My narrator is sixty-nine, but right now I'm doing the book in diary form. When I put it in novel form, she will start with her childhood and work forward. It will have the same structure as *A Cure for Dreams.*

J.G. Your vocabulary and language are impressive in both conversation and fiction. Your style is poetic and even Old Testament-like, as in the "resting under a pecan tree" passage in *A Virtuous Woman.*

K.G. The Bible, the King James version, had a tremendous effect on me. *Southern Living* magazine, the other year, did a piece about twenty writers and asked what the most influential books were. Almost everybody mentioned the King James Bible.

J.G. *Ellen Foster* seems technically and structurally to be a perfect book. Is there anything you would like to go back and change, if you could?

K.G. No, there's nothing I would change, I don't think. I did have her saying "my own self" too much. But there is nothing I would change.

J.G. I noticed that in your first novels you don't use dialogue very much. Why not?

K.G. I think it took me a while to develop an ear for it. I never took writing. I never had any formal training, so I had to learn on my own. The Civil War book is almost devoid of dialogue. I know that a New York editor will go crazy with it. There's internal dialogue. The woman remembers conversations. In *A Virtuous Woman* there is not a lot of dialogue.

The thing that's really different about *A Virtuous Woman* and *Ellen Foster* and any of the other books, including the one that's coming out, is that I did not have a single note while I wrote them. After *A Virtuous Woman* I started reading the Works Progress Administration notes and transcripts from 1929 and during the Depression. I started collecting language, archaic Southern expressions. For menopause a woman would say "when nature left me"; for sundown she would say "the pink of the evening." It is difficult to get the right expressions for the Civil War book. Every time I want a character to say "okay"—I can't do that. They must say something else. I can't say "tomorrow," I have to say "on the morrow" or put a hyphen between "to" and "morrow." All I had when I worked on the first two books was myself, my brain, and my typewriter. I think that's why they are so poetic and less dependent on idioms to get meanings across.

J.G. *Ellen Foster* is a dramatic and graphically violent book, but there is little violence in your other novels.

K.G. When I studied Southern literature with Louis Rubin, he would give to each graduate student a theme that we each had to follow all semester and report on. I noticed a *boy* always picked "violence." I always picked "language." But it was always "violence in Faulkner" or "Faulkner and violence." I guess it was not a part of my experience growing up, and it is certainly not now. I feel very distant from it. It is something that doesn't get included.—I used to feel a need to look at all the qualities of Southern literature and check them off in the books. In the Civil War book I hit everything. I got it all: honor, glory, memory, place, religion, race, and violence. It is all there.

One characteristic of Southern literature that has been important historically, and which I still try to work into the books, is the sense of honor. One of the things that Ellen Foster strives to do is to be an honorable person, not chivalric, but she wants to live as an honorable person.

Speaking of things chivalric, did you see my knighthood [on the wall]? I got it in March, but the official knighting [to "Chevalier de France"] is in Paris in October. I'm going to buy something hot to wear! I was nominated by Catherine Berge. She is a documentary filmmaker, who has done some work on Miss Welty.

J.G. Your house is full of framed photos by Miss Welty. Did you read her fiction in detail?

K.G. Yes. My favorite piece is the essay on the midwife Ida M'Toy. And there are the stories "Death of a Traveling Salesman," and "Moon Lake,"—also for the humor.

J.G. Does the humor in your own fiction come natural to you? Is that the way you are?

K.G. It is.—In the movies I prefer comedies to dramas. I know that I don't sound very funny right now, but if somebody said, "what do you like about yourself?"then I think it is the humor. My husband and I laugh every day. We do something, say something, and it is usually a commentary on the outside world. We see ourselves as sitting in here looking out.

J.G. There is, of course, the tradition of Southwestern humor, as continued by Charles Portis, Lewis Grizzard, and Roy Blount, where the object seems to be to entertain. But there is also the humor of Welty, Faulkner, and O'Connor.

K.G. In Flannery O'Connor the humor is so thoroughly integrated. It always bothered me that I went to a Flannery O'Connor conference and nobody talked about her humor! They just see her as such a Catholic writer, but she is very funny. It is one of my favorite scenes in literature when that woman gets on the bus in "Everything That Rises Must Converge" and sees the matching clothes of a black lady. It is extremely funny. And Mr. Shiftlet in "The Life You Save May Be Your Own" is funny. They are tragic, but they are funny, too.

My father was a very tragic man, but he was notorious for his sense of humor. So we grew up laughing at things. He was a tragic folk hero, talented in so many ways. He was a photographer in World War II. He was on the *Hornet,* an aircraft carrier. In fact, he took the photograph used on the cover of *A Cure for Dreams.* It was not my idea to fold the picture the way it is, but I like it that way. He was talented but just ruined by alcohol.

**J.G.** Is it enough to entertain, or do you feel there should be a message behind the humor?

**K.G.** I want more than anything to communicate the message of self-reliance and to dispel the myth of the fainting Southern female.

**J.G.** Is the fainting belle still with us?

**K.G.** Oh yes! They live in all these houses. They do manage to play tennis, but they don't have energy to have jobs. It amazes me.

**J.G.** One of the prominent targets for your humorous satire is psychotherapy. In your fiction it is not considered very helpful.

**K.G.** I don't think it helps adults very much. I think it replaces anxieties with mantras. But I find it helps children. I read child psychology all the time, every day, because I grew up in such a screwed-up environment that I don't know how to raise children. I have to read to learn how to do it.

Ellen Foster had a sense of how to treat herself and how to doctor herself. She didn't need anybody to tell her how to do it.—I found that Emerson quote for the book, from his poem "Self-Reliance," very early into the writing of *Ellen Foster:* "Cast the bantling on the rocks / Suckle him with the she-wolf's teat." It became a real guiding thing for me.

**J.G.** Do you feel that you have returned to the Ellen Foster character, under new names, in your later fiction?

**K.G.** Yes, exactly! And I feel that I'm very lucky that no critic has caught me.

**J.G.** Except for comments to the effect that the narrative voice sounds much the same in your novels.

**K.G.** If you're talking about singing or acting, everybody has a style. I think that my style is finally emerging. My books are distinguishable from other people's books. You couldn't put Josephine Humphreys' cover on my book and pass it off as one of hers anymore. So that's happened. But I don't think I am going to return and do a correspondent sequel to *Ellen Foster.* The only one I have considered it with is *Charms for the Easy Life.* I am thinking of writing about what happens. People ask me all the time. The key is in the last line: "and waited to be found." She's called Tom and he is going to come and get her. The word "found" works in a literal and metaphorical sense. He is going to come and find her there. Find her as a human being, find her as a woman, and be a replacement for her.

**J.G.** There is a lot of matriarchal history in *A Cure for Dreams.* So much that it may get a bit tiresome for your male readers.

**K.G.** Yeah. Women love it because they feel left out of stories, except for romance stories and historical fiction. Women readers love to read literature about themselves. I do have many male readers, but you saw in Columbus, Mississippi [at the Eudora Welty Writers' Symposium, 1995], how many women that will come, as opposed to men. But men in the South are working at nine o'clock in the morning.

**J.G.** Women have always been the readers, haven't they?

**K.G.** They have been. Until Tom Clancy, I think, women were the readers.

**J.G.** Does the title of *A Cure for Dreams* refer to a cure for the dream of traditional family life?

**K.G.** I made that title up because the women in the book are very realistic. *A Cure for Dreams* is reality, a good dose of reality. The women in it have to deal with the real world and cannot stay involved in a dream world. There are plans for a movie, too.

**J.G.** I'm surprised to hear it. I don't think of the plot line in *A Cure for Dreams* as being all that strong,

**K.G.** I don't even *remember* a plot. It is an independent filmmaker. I think she will just follow the lives of the women.—The Civil War book will be six hundred pages long without a plot, except for the war. I am depending on the War to get me through.

**J.G.** I found Trudy to be the most appealing character in *A Cure for Dreams.*

**K.G.** I like Trudy. When I was growing up, I knew somebody just like Trudy, her name was Peggy. She would put her leg up on the dresser and shave it with a straight razor and Jergens lotion. It was amazing to watch.

**J.G.** Trudy refuses to conform. Her message is: go and do what you want to do! Don't be enslaved within a family. But Ellen Foster was desperately searching for a family.

**K.G.** Trudy is a renegade.—The woman who worked for me yesterday made the comment "And that was the first time I felt like I was in a family, and I was sixteen." It is important. And it is important in this house that we feel like we are in a family. It's important that everybody gets along. The most serious criticism a child can hear in this house is "You're not acting as a part of this family." We know who we are, we know what defines us. When somebody breaks out of that and runs over to the side, they have to redeem themselves before they can come back in the group.

**J.G.** You have just described your private family life, but that type of living is not reflected in *A Cure for Dreams* or in *Charms for the Easy Life.*

**K.G.** No.—They created a family in *Charms* out of barrel ends. And at the end of the novel Margaret is included in a new family of Tom's relatives. You know she is going to have family there also. I had to quickly create a new family for her at the end.

**J.G.** Margaret's initiation is over when her grandmother is dead. That's a nice story. I am left with a "and-then-what?" When I first mentioned this to you in Rennes, you said that you wrote *Charms* when you were very much in love. Is that why everything is so nice, so cute, and just a little sugary in the novel?

**K.G.** Well, it bought this house!—The mother is this unsatisfied creature, who is walking around trying to find the right man. And when she does get somebody, his ex-wife comes into town, and she has to be dealt with and run off. A lot of that book is transmuted reality that was going on in my life at the same time. I transmuted it and took it back fifty years. It is still, besides *Ellen Foster,* my favorite book.

The new one is just a serious leap, a major leap. The first line is "I did not mean to kill the nigger!" So it is starting out highly politically incorrect. I don't care about any rules while I'm writing.

**J.G.** I enjoyed the grandmother who keeps court in *Charms.* I would like to get to know her better. But isn't she unbelievably flawless?

**K.G.** She doesn't diagnose her own death, which she should have seen coming. She was having symptoms of a heart attack, and thought she had indigestion. Of all things she should have seen, she should have seen her own demise.—You'd be surprised at how many women that say, "My grandmother was just like that." They did rule.

**J.G.** That's what we tend to do. We go to reunions and find out about our relatives.

**K.G.** By anecdote.

**J.G.** Andrew Lytle also used the anecdote in his fiction. But Faulkner encouraged the writer to steal her grandmother's night shirt if necessary. I think he meant, so we could see the old woman, as she is, with wrinkles and all. But in *Charms,* seen through the young girl's eyes, the grandmother can only be a perfectly heroic person.

**K.G.** The grandmother in my new book, who is a lot like Charlie Kate of *Charms,* is raising a black child as a pet, as toy, all throughout this book. She thinks she's saving his life, but what she's really done is to take him over and to keep him from becoming a human being. She has no self-realization, and that's really hard to manage to write from the first-person point of view about someone with no self-realization.

**J.G.** The celebration of grandmothers is characteristic of Southern fiction today.

**K.G.** I think we tend to lionize those women, because we weren't looking for men to be role models. They were gone. They went out at sunup and came back at sundown. So we had to look somewhere, and we looked to grandmothers, who were usually living inside the house. We have not yet reached an age in Southern fiction that we cannot lionize those women. It's a trade habit.

My eleven-year-old daughter intimated to me a few weeks ago that she thought her grandmother had outstayed her welcome. She had moved in the same way, I guess the writer needs to move from that innocent all-adoring view of her grandmother to seeing her as a person who is around the house and needed to go on back to New York. I watched that transition. I was shocked by it, and said, "You can't say that, she is your grandmother! One day she's going to be dead, and you are going to think about that!" So, you see what I was doing, in life and art.

**J.G.** Are your grandmothers still alive?

**K.G.** They are both dead. My mother's mother is the main grandmother in *Ellen Foster*, pretty much. That's how she was. Whereas the mother in "Seasons of My Discontent" is not based on anybody I know but myself. We share a lot of the same attitudes. But I will listen, and she writes. That's the same way *Ellen Foster* was written. She's going to come out the same way.

**J.G.** So far, you have written on the immediate family past. It hasn't been Faulkner's or K. A. Porter's concern with the past of Southern history. But in your present project you are going back in history.

**K.G.** Right. It's not my own history. Half that room up there is full of diaries. I have bought every old diary I could find and have read those for history. I intentionally didn't use Mary Boykin Chesnut's diary, because she was too highly placed and too well connected. I needed somebody closer to the land. Those notebooks on that sofa over there are full of antebellum and period language.

**J.G.** In your last two novels you limit yourself very carefully to *this* relationship and to *that* situation. Did you ever consider having several plots at once?

**K.G.** I'm always going to write about *everything*, and then I will get scared to death, because I wouldn't know what I was going to write about next. I couldn't do several plots at the same time, and I wouldn't want to. Maybe one day when the children are out of the house, I can do that, not now. I have enough trouble remembering from day to day what I'm writing about. I always have to read yesterday's work to remember, because so much real life happens in between.

**J.G.** The Southern writer is expected to be concerned about the community. But I feel that you are becoming more and more focused on individuals.

**K.G.** I've found that characters do become more and more insular. But in what I am working on right now, the woman is a part of the whole South. She has to look at her own life in terms of what's happening in the community. The woman depends on the newspaper to tell her if she's going to have food. So there is a direct link.

**J.G.** Please tell me about *Sights Unseen* [September 1995], your most recent book.

**K.G.** This book was extremely difficult to write. Not difficult emotionally, but I had a hard time technically with that book.

**J.G.** Was it a much longer manuscript than the finished novel reveals?

**K.G.** Yes, it was two books in one. And I split it up, and it became *Sights Unseen.* I kept the other pages, maybe one day I will do something with them, but not now. I knew it was two books when I sent it off. My editor and agent called and said, "Do you know, you've got a problem here?" I said, "Yes, I know, I sent you two books." It was about four hundred pages. The way I type, it is almost the same in print. And I sat down at the dining room table and made stacks.

**J.G.** After I first read *Sights Unseen* I wondered, "Does this narrative have enough detachment to tell me something of lasting value, or is it all just for the narrator's benefit?"

**K.G.** Did you learn *anything*?

**J.G.** Later I realized that I had learned something about mental illness in ordinary life. I will be a little less naive if I have to face a similar situation.—I also think the mother–daughter relationship is very convincing.

**K.G.** The daughter has a very expectant and ideal view of what a mother should be. Her mother doesn't meet those standards. So the daughter meets with constant disappointment about that. That has to be dealt with and rectified in some way.

**J.G.** I suppose my initial disappointment has to do with the narrative voice. In *A Virtuous Woman* it is not your voice we hear but that of your character Jack. You demonstrated your negative capability by disappearing out of the narrating. But in *Sights Unseen* you never *become* Maggie Barnes. We always see her through the filter of the narrative voice.

**K.G.** I prefer it that way. That's probably why I don't write omniscient third-person fiction. I would have to become so many people in dialogue to make it believable. I am in so many ways a lot like Maggie Barnes. I have not been arrested for hitting anybody with a car, but I've become almost arrested for sort of the same thing. In my nonfiction I do make those confessions of how I was almost like her. How my own personal life fitted hers. When I wrote *Sights,* I had just had a year-long manic depression, out of control. I had a really fine memory of what it feels like to have that nonstop voice in the head. So when I sat down, I said, "Have Hattie write it." That's the way I put it. When I had her write it, I could replicate that voice, and then she could very quickly come back in her own voice. So she could provide this feeling of insanity without dropping the cover. I never, as a writer, want to drop my cover.

**J.G.** I feel that I have asked a question about something you did not write. I didn't intend to do that, although it is fashionable.

**K.G.** Yeah, that drives me crazy, when I read reviews and they say, "Well, that's fine but she didn't deal with architecture!" Or, "She didn't deal with the traffic!" Just anything. There is a lot you don't deal with. You write one book at a time, and you can only do so much.

**J.G.** Do you have time to keep up with the fiction of your contemporaries?

**K.G.** For two years I've read mostly Civil War things and mysteries. I read mysteries to relax, but mysteries with some literary merit, like James Lee Burke and P. D. James. I read E. Annie Proulx and Carol Shields. I read friends' books. I read Reynolds Price and Lee Smith's, Clyde Edgerton's books, and Barry Hannah's.

**J.G.** Have you read Edgerton's *Redeye*?

**K.G.** I haven't read *Redeye* yet. I heard him read from it several times. I read about books, I read all the reviews. There's a pile of reviews right there that I need to get to. Frank brings them home from work. And I read about books that are coming out. All the hoopla about bad books that are coming out.—I thought *Waiting to Exhale* was the worst book I ever read in my life, and now Terry McMillan has *How Stella Got Her Groove Back.* And they are paid phenomenal sums of money to write these things. I am getting more and more cynical about the books that are coming out. At least ten people up close have to tell me to read a book before I spend my time reading it.

**J.G.** Do you ever think about changing publisher?

**K.G.** Oh no! I'm highly overpaid at Putnam's. I'm really overpaid. The first time I saw a million dollars on a contract, I thought, "You are really overpaid. This is great, you should *stay* this overpaid." I would never change for money. If there were a bidding war, then . . . I'm comfortable where I am, and if I wanted more, they would give it to me, I'm happy.

When we talked about writing the second book after writing the first one, I left out one of the things that made it hard. It was that I fell into a lot of money very quickly. I mean, it is amazing. The books do so well over here and in France. It's real easy for me to do nothing all day. I could go for years without doing anything. I really have to find my self-discipline to get down and work and not write for the money. To have it keep being art and not turn it into Eugenia Price, bless her heart, she died, and not turn it into Anne River Siddons. I would rather go for the art and have the novels just happen to become popular.

When I'm writing I never think about accessibility. This morning I was writing, and I had the woman say, "I need to knit my ball-breakings." I do not intend to footnote it. They were what stockings were called during the Civil War. They can go look it up!

# *Interview with Barry Hannah*

◆◆◆◆◆◆

*Oxford, Mississippi, April 12, 1982*

Barry Hannah

◆◆◆◆◆◆

**Jan Nordby Gretlund** How do you select specific material for your fiction?

**Barry Hannah** The main part of my stories always comes out of life, I'm terribly affected by something, obsessed with it, or find it a situation I can't forget, and then the rest is imagination. But the emotional part is always something I've been through. That is why it always takes me at least a year to write a book. I have to do quite a bit of life or I just don't feel I have anything to say.

**J.G.** Could you give me an example of this out-of-life-and-into-fiction process?

**B.H.** Take my short story "Our Secret Home," in *Airships* [1978]. This is an episode that happened when I was teaching at Clemson University in South Carolina. There was a person in town who threw a party and nobody came. That's an old joke; but I was one of the three guests who showed up. It was terribly embarrassing. The hors d'oeuvres had been set out, the liquor was expensive and plentiful, and everything was primed for his friends to show, but they didn't. I was edgy for him, and embarrassed.

**J.G.** Why did you write "Our Secret Home" as a first-person narrative?

**B.H.** You always have to put yourself in another's shoes. That's why someone who writes hardly ever does the life story of someone else's interesting old aunt. I'm often asked to do so at parties: "I know the most interesting person; if you knew her you'd write a book!" I bet I wouldn't. There's nothing I can do about your interesting old aunt, because her life has not touched mine. But at Clemson this person's life touched mine, and he became my "interesting old aunt."

**J.G.** Who inspired you to become a novelist?

**B.H.** I met three really wonderful men at the University of Arkansas:

Bill Harrison, Ben Kimpel, and, though I took no classes from him, Jim Whitehead, the poet from Mississippi. I got a lot of "active" teaching in the poolroom playing with Jim. He impressed me as a man who took his art very seriously. In the South there's always a touch of the sissy about the arts. Jim was a big ex-football player. I was impressed that this brawny man gave a damn about his sonnets, and I got very serious.

Bill Harrison got me an agent; he told the agent I could write much better than he could himself. Bill is very unselfish; I would never tell an agent that about one of my students. All European literature that I know was introduced to me by Ben Kimpel. And I have an education in European fiction, especially, that I consider priceless. If you don't read Kafka, Dostoevski, and Kierkegaard, some Hesse, and Lagerkvist, you are missing a lot. But I don't read much while I'm writing, except for some nonfiction.

**J.G.** What do you think of taking *or* teaching a course in creative writing?

**B.H.** You can teach students by encouraging what is good. It comes down to the example—you show them it can be done. You *can* publish, you *can* say what you mean without hedging, you can even find your own soul in a creative writing class. I believe that's possible for the students. I found my "soul" in the writing classes I took, finally. You get somebody like Faulkner who doesn't need the school and it is a completely different thing. It would be ridiculous to say, "What would Faulkner have done with the Iowa

Workshop?" He would have ignored it, just like he ignored Ole Miss. He didn't need it. But the University of Arkansas was good for me; it turned my whole life around. Even if you just get self-educated around a university, it is good to have a few props and know some good books.

**J.G.** Does it mean anything to you to live here in William Faulkner's Oxford?

**B.H.** Here on Johnson Avenue I'm in the backyard of the house Faulkner wrote about in *The Sound and the Fury.* The idiot Benjy probably walked right through this living room. I don't go for the Faulkner Convention, but I love the real William Faulkner and the way he populated this land. If you're very cynical and arrogant, you might begin looking at the South as just existing for movies. That's how I think of Faulkner—I mean, he invented a beautiful cast; Yoknapatawpha is movie Oxford. It is imagination-land. I don't think it does any good for these Japanese people to come here and get on a bus and go out in the sticks to look for Eula Varner and the Snopes family. They're not there. They never really were.

**J.G.** Can you explain why Mississippi seems to produce more artists than any other state?

**B.H.** There may be more artists here per capita. I think Mississippians tend to feel knowledge more deeply than somebody who has it as his birthright. They are not as blasé about whatever they can latch on to. That might have something to do with it. You really have to fight for your "truth and beauty."

**J.G.** In your first novel, *Geronimo Rex* [1972], there is a Mississippian called Whitfield Peter. Did you know anybody with his strong prejudices when you were growing up in Clinton?

**B.H.** Anybody in Mississippi who's my age or older will tell you that such a character is hardly an invention. I grew up reading letters in the paper down in Jackson that weren't too far off the letters I wrote for *Geronimo Rex.* Mine were done from memory and imagination, but there were such virulent attacks from the right in the paper. There was a certainty that Jews, Commies, and Negroes exist synonymously for ill in these letters to the editor.

**J.G.** Are the Whitfield Peters dying out, or is it still like that?

**B.H.** It's not publicly like that. And there is a real difference. Nowadays when a black student leaves the room and the others say, "Yeah, that nigger!" they don't mean the evil, ugly thing their forebears meant. You can find a young black person who wouldn't believe me on that, but there *is* more compassion. The kids might make the old Southern joke about calling blacks "Indians" when they play on the team. But it is not with the nasty bias of my generation. You don't want to gloss that over, however. There is still some entrenched nasty feeling.

**J.G.** Why do most of your main characters have strong prejudices, not only against blacks but also against Vietnamese, Ohioans, and women?

**B.H.** I'm against prejudice in theory. But it seems to me that you can understand somebody much better by his announced prejudices than you can by his humanistic explanations. Of course, Ray would call the people he fought against "gooks."

**J.G.** Has the women's liberation movement reacted to your novels?

**B.H.** Yes, they are the shrillest of all, much more than blacks. An intelligent black person never complains when a guy in my fiction says "nigger." He knows who is saying it. But I've been boycotted. At Iowa, for instance, some girls wouldn't take my class, because they thought I was sexist. I heard that after I got up there. Well, it's all right; it's their point of view. It just amused me. I don't have anything to say about women in general. If I write about suicide, why should somebody ask me about my position on suicide? I don't know. Sometimes I love women; it goes with the day for anybody honest. And then there are times when we are categorical: "God damn women!" I'm not a misogynist, if it means anything, in spite of *Ray* [1980].

**J.G.** Does the success of *Airships* and *Ray* mean anything to you?

**B.H.** Of course it does. It means something to me every time somebody enjoys a short story of mine. Maybe I'm working more out of a feeling of unworthiness than some writers. Maybe I don't have to prove anything with my books, but as a Southern writer in Mississippi you're pretty sure the world thinks you're dumb—and you're going to prove you're not. The national acceptance has meant a lot, but it didn't mean anything for my mental health or habits. A success does not make you clean up your act.

**J.G.** Much Southern fiction is concerned with the role of the family in our lives. What has the idea of a family meant to you?

**B.H.** I thought the family was a curse for about ten years of my life, but I came back close to my folks in my early thirties. I always thought that a family with nephews and nieces was very important. In the South there's a sense of closeness and support in the family that's almost a religious feeling. I think that is very fine. I saw it denied a lot in California, where you don't even know where your granddaddy is.

**J.G.** Did you know your grandfathers well?

**B.H.** One of them died right in the room where I slept. His name was Rivers King; we called him Daddy King. The other one was dead by the time I achieved consciousness.

**J.G.** Were you already trying to define your own feelings toward the father figure in your first novel?

**B.H.** It is important to do that, and I give it its due. *Geronimo Rex* is about growing up, also about fathers and mothers. The *lack* of a father is significant to people. When you have to be your own father, you have to be your own captain. That's what Harry does, and that is why the father drops from the book.

**J.G.** Are there any major differences between Harry Monroe of *Geronimo Rex*, Raymond Forrest of *Ray*, and Barry Hannah of Oxford?

**B.H.** There's obviously a case to be made that my characters are much the same. I don't seem to be able to do another kind of book. I can occasionally write short stories where I venture into the third person. But for long-distance writing, I count on basic honesty and a hot moment. I don't seem to go for very long with a character that is completely out of myself. I can't sustain it. I have Keats's "negative capability" for a short story like "Knowing He Was Not My Kind Yet I Followed" but not for anything much longer than, say, twenty pages. It is not that I'm so arrogant that I don't think other people would be good as my protagonists, it's just that I have to have daily honesty or a base of emotion to write. I don't come in at eight o'clock and hit the typewriter till two every day like some writers. I have to feel something.

**J.G.** What do you think of your second novel, *Nightwatchmen* [1973], today, ten years later?

**B.H.** The book didn't have much response, but I still like it. That's probably my most deliberately Gothic book. It has murders, beheadings, and a killer stalking. *Nightwatchmen* does have some artificial characteristics that I have tried to erase from my art since then. I learned this from that novel: the more contrived a book I try to write, the more action I put in, the worse I become as a writer. I want to have a readable book, but without the conventions of plot. That is a tough thing to do, because even a good reader is going to want a plot, usually. Now I try to get a sense of discovery on every page, instead of over a long configuration of events.

**J.G.** It has been said that you have a Gothic sense of humor. Does that mean anything to you?

**B.H.** I am a little wary of that expression. It is accurate for the kind of people who read the *Literary Digest.* I will say this much, it is *not* misleading. But I have no interest in reviving the Gothic form. I don't think Gothicism describes my life. Sometimes my humor may run toward the black and the strange, but I am certainly not trying to jump into a strictly European Gothic tradition.

**J.G.** Some of your black humor could be called medical humor. Do you have personal knowledge of medicine?

**B.H.** I was pre-med in college, and I had a job as a research assistant in pharmacology at the Ole Miss Medical School in Jackson. That's how I supported my early first marriage. So I don't have a thorough education in medicine, but enough to write *Ray.*

**J.G.** When Mr. Hooch tries to kill himself in *Ray,* you could have been very sentimental about it. But instead it is a hilarious episode. Do you use humor to avoid sentimentality?

**B.H.** It could be. It seems more a question for a psychiatrist than for an author. But I really do believe that life is very sentimental *and* very funny. And just like Samuel Beckett said: "There is nothing funnier than unhappiness." Somebody else's unhappiness, that is. Mr. Hooch is the kind of guy whose attempted suicide would have been just as gimcracked as his life. It is consistent with what the guy is. It is not simply hilarious.

**J.G.** Are you writing any poetry?

**B.H.** No. I have written no poetry since early college. I like the ideal of poetry, but I like narrative even more. Poetry is finally too confining, and I like the looser environs. I don't think I was a very good poet anyway. It was a kind of beatnik/bourgeois thing for me, and I put no stock in my poetry. But in my fiction I practice it per sentence. I don't like a bad sentence; it irritates me if I think it is bad or not musical. It has got to go with the music of the paragraph. So I am a rough poet still.

**J.G.** With sixty-two chapters to only 113 pages, *Ray* looks like a poem. Could it be read as a poem?

**B.H.** Some of the critics talked about *Ray* as a long poem. A girl who was interested in buying rights for the movies told me:

"I think *Ray* is a little redneck poem!" I was insulted in a way, but you can see it that way.

**J.G.** It seems to me you could write more poetry, if you felt like it.

**B.H.** Poetry doesn't pay the rent.

**J.G.** From what I have heard of the novel you are working on now, *Maximum Ned,* it appears that you have no intention of toning down the sex and violence in your work. Do they pay the rent?

**B.H.** Sex and violence are both close to death in curious ways, and they are natural properties for me to write with. I find people more animated when they have a gun to their heads. And I like people in situations of stress, because then they tend to be frank and cheat less. It is a kind of psychodrama, because I'm not violent myself. And it is not that I have discovered effecting a revenge in my fiction that I can't get in the real world.

I just frankly enjoy violence. I find it cathartic, like, say Peckinpah's movie *The Wild Bunch.* I walk out of a movie like that feeling very clean. It is a problem that we have a lot of grown men sitting around with nothing to do with their bodies after about age 23. Denying violence altogether is a mistake. Critics ask me, "Why the violence? Why the sex?" They shouldn't be asking these dumb questions. Their life is not governed by the rational rules of conduct. These instincts are big powers, and you must deal with them in your work.

**J.G.** Why are your violent men constantly playing heroic roles in their imagination?

**B.H.** In my short stories I've also written about those who do not play the heroic role. "Constant Pain in Tuscaloosa" is about a guy very down and out. He is trying to get back his dignity and connect with the human race. But I don't know any young American who doesn't want to be heroic. Every punk in London wants to be heroic. I want to be a heroic writer, to win the minds and hearts of my generation. I don't know any honest writer who does not want fame and want to be able to sway people somewhat. There may be a few who hide their novels in trunks, but nobody I have met.

**J.G.** Narrator Harry Monroe in *Geronimo Rex* sees this character as a heroic figure: "What I especially liked about Geronimo then was that he had cheated, lied, stolen, mutinied, usurped, killed, burned, raped, pillaged, razed, trapped, ripped, mashed, bowshot, stomped, herded, exploded, cut, stoned, revenged, prevenged, avenged, and was his own man."

Aren't these peculiar qualities to admire?

**B.H.** It is strictly adolescent. Harry feels ugly, and Geronimo is not a gainly person. It is adolescent, all right. I think Europeans really think of American men as adolescents. They put down Hemingway, guys never getting over bullfighting or catching the big fish. And I accept that, because that is just the way I feel still. I don't feel very sedentary; I don't care about the library that much; I feel ready to go. It has always been an interesting question to me about growing up. I frankly haven't met that many old wise men in my life.

**J.G.** Is Hemingway one of the men you admire?

**B.H.** Yes, very much. I like his ideas as they occur in his style. It is like a guy in my new book says—the hero is writing a movie and there's this brown-eyed deaf man in it.—When you think about it, often it is not the profundity of an idea but its sheer velocity. That's what Hemingway means to me.

**J.G.** Walker Percy is supposed to have said that the South has so many writers because of the lost war. Will the defeat in Vietnam have a similar effect?

**B.H.** I admire Percy. He is a much deeper thinker than I am. I am more an artist of instinct than Percy, who is a good Catholic and an existentialist. The Vietnam War was a big subject in my youth. I didn't go. It was shocking for America to lose, and it took some terrific readjustments to get used to the fact. Maybe Percy was talking about the way losing the Civil War made you a spiritual outlander. Maybe what he meant was that defeat makes you eloquent, more eloquent than victory. And I write about defeated people often, people who are really down and out, distressed and poor, and *eloquent.* It is like that poor guy telling a story in my new book: he doesn't know whether to commit suicide or go bowling, but he is telling the story. You become eloquent in defeat.

**J.G.** Religion does not seem to offer your heroes much help. You don't exactly praise the religious attitude at Herdermansever College in *Geronimo Rex.*

**B.H.** No, not as it is practiced there. I found it to be rather fascistic. Besides, the teachers were dull, except for three or four. They had a kind of forced "Christian" education that says, "We are going to read this history, but we are going to believe only enough to substantiate our orthodoxy. We are not going to talk about these successful and happy souls who were atheists or Mongols."

**J.G.** To what extent are you a religious man yourself?

**B.H.** If I said that I believed in God, what would it mean? I proceed from the fact that there has been a great lie to me, from the word go. Somebody stands in the pulpit and says, "I have just talked to God." You get a little lonely when you realize at about sixteen that's not right. There's something too frantic about the present religious fervor, especially on TV. If somebody needs to be on the station twenty-four hours a day saying that there *is* a Jesus, they're protesting too much. Women are paying for these institutions. The preachers know that there are women at home who are vulnerable and capable of sending a hundred-dollar check to Jerry Falwell or Jim Bakker. They labor on the emotions of those gullible women, so they have the fancy living rooms from which they broadcast. The idea is, "Be a Christian and you can have a fancy living room, too." The money doesn't turn followers off; they *want* to see their preachers in the money.

**J.G.** There is one place in *Geronimo Rex* where you say that life shot through Harry "as if existence meant something." Do you often think of existence in terms of its meaning?

**B.H.** Yes, but I can't answer the question yet. It means enough to write about; it must mean something very deep to me, or I wouldn't be compelled to write about it. Because I don't see writing as show business, I see it as engaging life itself by finding and asking the big questions. Yes, I engage in these questions daily. I have always been more interested in the person who proceeded as if life meant something than I have in the philosopher on the hill.

**J.G.** Will you also try to express the meaning of your Hollywood experience in your fiction?

**B.H.** My new novel, *Maximum Ned* [*Captain Maximus,* 1985] is inspired by a Jimi Hendrix title. Jimi the guitarist was a gatherer of the atmosphere of his age, which I still live with. You do live with your youth, and you never get over it. When Hendrix died in 1970, my youth was probably peaking. And he is still an insistent reminder of a difficult and loud age. The novel is mainly about California.

**J.G.** What took you to Hollywood?

**B.H.** For one thing, I went there to get healthy, physically. And now I can continue to write without despising life every morning, like I used to. I had never been close to movie stars, but I got sort of close to movie people out there. And I started rethinking things in terms of movies. I didn't get heavily into film work, and I don't know much about it, but film offers some interesting ideas. I was working with Robert Altman on a movie, and once when I was trying for the smothered elegance of the way some women talk in a certain kind of situation, Altman said, "Sometimes being intelligible is overrated. It is not necessary to understand everything people say in a movie."

This is a point about art itself: it is not always necessary to understand quite what somebody says to know that it has made an impact on you. I learned a few things like that from movie work.

**J.G.** Though *Maximum Ned* is based on your California experience, it seems to be more about vindication through music than about California.

**B.H.** Jimi Hendrix's spirit is in it. But the main character is a writer just like me. It is the first book I have ever done with a writer as the main character. I thought it was time I did a fairly honest book about the trade. This guy is writing some films with Altman. The music of Hendrix was closely allied with LSD and extreme drug use, but it wasn't just that; he seemed to have captured an atmosphere.

**J.G.** Music has been important in your work ever since the appearance of Harley Butte in *Geronimo Rex.* Are you saying that if religion, sex, shrinks, war, violence, drugs, and liquor cannot help us, music and art may?

**B.H.** Right! I found that out after I got cleaned from heavy drinking. I couldn't listen to that music sober for a while. It just was not the same. And then when I got healthier, I found a Hendrix record and put it on. And I knew I was finally healthy because it meant the same thing to me even though I wasn't taking anything. It was a beautiful thing to listen to him and what he brought back bold as love.

# *Interview with Barry Hannah*

◆◆◆◆◆◆

*His home on Van Buren Street, south of Oxford, Mississippi, June 3, 1985*

*I'm ten minutes late, delayed by the place name "Denmark" on my way. Outside there is a big black Harley-Davidson parked conspicuously outside the Hannah house. He is sitting on it, smiling the Hannah smile, like the Cheshire cat, and holding a cup of what looks like Hawaiian Punch but does not smell like it.*

**J.G.** Do you consider yourself a satirist?

**B.H.** Yes I am. My main voice is against hypocrisy Baptist, Methodist, anybody who is a phony. You'd better believe. Yes, I am a satirist.

**J.G.** Are the characters more important than the plots in your books?

**B.H.** Yes, they are more important. But I write a good story, and I do not even write unless I know a good story. I use a little of the baroque, I guess it comes from my musical training. But I do not make phony stories. I tell the *exact* truth as I know it. The only time I play baroque is my trumpet, my drums, my piano.

**J.G.** Is there anybody you play in baroque music?

**B.H.** Mark Ferguson. He is a great trumpet player. See, I am not in shape with music now, but God blessed me with a relative pitch, not perfect pitch. I can play any instrument, I can learn it in a week. I can play all instruments.

That is why they wanted me to be a jet pilot, but I turned them down in Vietnam. I can speak French, I am a perfect marksman, but I just cannot shoot anybody. And so back to the baroque,—of course I like the baroque.

**J.G.** Are your characters really throwaway characters, created just to make a single point? Especially in the brief short stories. We see them do this. . . .

**B.H.** No! I do not write throwaway characters. You should know better than that! They are there to engage your emotions.

**J.G.** It seems to be very painful for your characters just to live. Is it *that* painful to live?

**B.H.** It is painful, because I have fleas on me right now. That's all. No, my life is not painful [sprays himself against red chiggers].

**J.G.** Do you consider yourself a humorous writer in the old Southern tradition?—Do you read the old Southern humorists?

**B.H.** I do not read *anybody.* I used to. I have a classical education. I read everybody in Europe, in America and et cetera.

**J.G.** Flannery O'Connor and Walker Percy are known as very amusing writers. It is a Southern tradition; do you see yourself in that tradition?

**B.H.** I do not see myself in *any* tradition. Both Flannery O'Connor and Walker Percy are wonderful writers, but—yeah, I am a comic writer, but I make up my own jokes, I do not copy from Walker or Flannery. Sure the best thing to do in life is laugh. I save myself through laughter.

For instance I got on a jet flight yesterday and then gave a reading at Tallahassee, drove my car thirteen hours, and the only way—Barry Jr. was with me, he took the whole trip. But I was so goddam bored and my back hurt. So I got back and just crashed. But you do not ever have to really crash, I get good sleep, of course.

The cops stopped me yesterday because I had some bourbon on my breath. I wasn't out of control or anything. Oh, this is just a young asshole with a Magnum, you know what cops are. And I took the breath test, and of course I had 2.4 on my breath. The only thing is, I raved at him, I said, "Don't you have something better to do than to handcuff me, you know I will make it home." "No sir, I am just doing my duty." So I got handcuffed and a five-hundred-dollar fine, which my lawyer will take care of. I am also going to blow him out of the water, the cop,—one thing about good connections is—Governor Bill Allain and I are friends, and the mayor of the town, John Leslie. So I am going to blow the officer's career away.

**J.G.** Isn't it better to put him into a story and kill him with some humor?

**B.H.** He doesn't *read.* I will write a letter to the *Oxford Eagle,* about how lousy they are about finding my guns and my Cutlass. So, fuck cops—in Oxford.

**J.G.** Your new stories are very condensed. They read like short prose poems.

**B.H.** I don't think I have time for a long book anymore. I make perfect sentences and poetry. You are *right.*

**J.G.** For me it seems that you found your own distinctive voice between *Nightwatchmen* [1973] and the stories of *Airships* [1978].

**B.H.** I am going to rewrite *Nightwatchmen.* It had too much dialogue. It was a lousy commercial failure; my next book will be called *Never Die* [appeared in 1991]. This one, I call *Captain Maximus* [1985], because that is the highest flying navy rank. I am just Lieutenant Commander, but it is the highest rank as a jet pilot, and Maximus is Ned Maximus. I chose it as a title for the whole book—I raised the whole book so it would be a silver bullet—see also *Power and Light* [1983]. It is the best book I have ever written.

**J.G.** Why would you publish *Power and Light* as a novella, when it is really a film script?

**B.H.** Well, I went out to California and got healthy, Robert Altman loves my work, I wrote it at a time he was going broke. I am kind of hoping he will see it again and shoot it, really make a movie out of it. But I don't ever write for anybody *but me,* never.

**J.G.** Was it *your* basic idea for a script?

**B.H.** No, it was Altman's idea:

four lady hard hatters. And they were all coming in there. One of them was Amy Shriver, another one was Jack Nicholson, and—*Rockford Files*—James Garner. I thought Garner should be the guy, the hero, who writes notes.

**J.G.** I admire the passage about Lou, the addict, who is shooting heroin to improve his writing.

**B.H.** I like Lou, too. There wasn't any particular actor in mind there.

**J.G.** The difficulty in reading a script is with the coherence, where is it going, et cetera.

**B.H.** It speaks for itself. I have no answer.

**J.G.** There is a lot of violence in your fiction, yet it is there for a purpose, you don't just indulge in it.

**B.H.** I don't. No. I have only killed one man in my life, at the new Allen Thompson Air Base. Grenade fragments—he almost blew my arm off, my arm was so bloody, I couldn't see, and I killed him with a .38 automatic. He threw a grenade at me. There were a hundred bullets in him. And I told the Navy, "I can't take it anymore." I just can't shoot anybody. I don't even know if I hit him. All I was doing was this:

[Covers his face with one arm and mock fires with the other.] Hell, all I want to do is to make music, sit down and ride my motorcycle, and write books, and meet friends like Jan Gretlund.

**J.G.** Listening to the music and riding the motorcycle offer escape. Do the sex and the violence do the same for you?

**B.H.** It is a ridiculous question. It really is. It is getting on my nerves.—Not *you,* but the question. [Hannah gets up goes to the kitchen.]

**J.G.** Is that a Bowie knife?

**B.H.** Terrible violence. Perfectly balanced. And I can do it. [He throws the knife at the door to the next room, fairly close to my head; it vibrates in the door for some time.] I don't use violence. I don't shoot anybody.

**J.G.** I am talking about the violence in your fiction. If you choose to put a lot of violence into your books, you probably have a pretty good reason for it.

**B.H.** Yes, I have reasons to put in violence, because even catching a big bass is violence. Even playing tennis is violence. Landing a jet is . . . *not* violence [indicating by hand a smooth landing, smiling the Hannah, or Cheshire cat, smile]. And—I will just go out and load my navy pistol for you and show you what violence is about.

*We go into the yard. Hannah fires six rounds of his .22 at some beer cans. "Got every one of them," he announces. As far as I could see, he got one of them. Then he loads his rifle with some difficulty. He is still drinking what looks like Hawaiian Punch out of a plastic cup. He is still in his briefs. He fires the rifle toward a tree with some targets on it. I take pictures. After he runs out of ammunition, he goes back to the living room to get one of his bows.*

*He shoots a couple of arrows and then lets me try it. I retrieve a few but decide to wait until he has shot the last one. Somebody calls, Hannah picks it up, but nobody answers. He gets angry and curses somebody he calls Bobby Lee, who is supposed to steal from his house when he is out of town. Hannah believes Bobby Lee checks Hannah's whereabouts over the phone.*

*Hannah goes to take a shower and comes back fully dressed and in a white sports coat, but he is dripping wet and does not seem to have toweled at all before he dressed. Still dripping, Hannah demonstrates he can play the drums to accompany Bob Dylan on an old scratched recording, after that he plays a few notes to another recording now on his trumpet; the pitch remains relative. Finally he tries to play his electric organ, but there is something wrong with the wires.*

**J.G.** People who read the violence in your fiction may not accept that it has the same cleansing effect as the music.

**B.H.** They are wrong. I am for music. I must exercise. In a minute we will go out and try to hit them with arrows. But, yeah, release, shit, our bodies were not made to sit around. Not sitting around working this typewriter, except if you love it. And my body is made, and yours is, for movement. I might make it to eighty years old, if I can give up cigarettes. But my dad is eighty-one, and he is still puffing away. I am just for having a good life, have some fun goddam it.

**J.G.** If you read Barry Hannah from one end to the other, it seems that the fiction is becoming shorter and shorter, and more and more fragmented, more and more condensed. Do you know what I mean?

**B.H.** Yeah. [He is picking up the arrows]. No comment.

**J.G.** Is the first story of this book, "Gettin Ready," based on a personal experience?

**B.H.** Yes. I was really broke at the time, and I caught the shark. It is a true story.

**J.G.** And you let it go?

**B.H.** Yeah.

**J.G.** The part of that story that I did not understand is about getting up on the stilts at the end, and telling everybody in their boats. . . .

**B.H.** Fuck you! Fuck you!—Well, he is out of his mind. And—. No comment. Goddam—just *read* it.

**J.G.** I will read it again and get it, eventually. It seems to me that as you have gotten older, you have also become more and more ironic in your fiction. [Hannah is almost asleep].

**J.G.** When you talk about the crab in this story, do you have T. S. Eliot's crab in mind?

**B.H.** No.

**J.G.** Do you want to go now? [We have planned to go to downtown Oxford to find something to eat.]

**B.H.** This guy is to call me back in fifteen minutes. Gotta wait for that.—If it is a short flight, I will take it. I am not gonna do any long flight.

**J.G.** I love the irony of the story called "Idaho," where the guy never gets to Idaho, and also the comment on the professors who work. . . .

*Hannah does not answer or show any interest at all. A call comes. It has nothing to do with flying. Earlier Hannah had told me of his experiences as a pilot in Vietnam. When I protest that he had told me earlier that he was never there but relied on his friend Quisenberry for his firsthand impressions, Hannah claims this is just a front so his son will not know that he flew in Vietnam.*

*I don't bother to argue the point. We go to town. We are all alone in the gumbo place; it is still early afternoon. Hannah orders some guacamole, but he can't keep it down, and he knows it is coming out the side of his mouth. We walk to the bookstore on the Square, he takes longer than me, he is being recognized. Hannah buys Tennessee Williams's autobiography; he has been waiting for it. We drive out of town.*

*On the way back to the house, we look out "for speeding niggers," as Hannah puts it, and make two stops; first at Walmart, as it turns out, to buy some ammo for his .22 pistol. We walk through the toy section and feel bad about it. The second stop is at the bowling alley. I thought he wanted to go bowling, but it is also a liquor store, and Hannah came for a fifth of bourbon.*

*Back at the house he is without his key but makes it in through a small window and opens the door. In the house Hannah strips to his shorts right away. He goes straight to bed, and he needs the rest. I promise to come back and see him.*

*It will not have escaped the reader's attention that the more ridiculous party in this comedy called "an interview" is the interviewer, who has traveled a long way and therefore, against all odds, remains dead set on getting his interview from his somewhat incapacitated victim.*

*The last time I enjoyed Barry Hannah's company, he was participating in my conference "The Best Reading Their Best" at USC Beaufort, in January 1999, and he did a wonderful job and behaved like the perfect gentleman he always was, in spite of all his antics.*

# *Fiction Is Like Fire and Flood*

INTERVIEW WITH MARY HOOD

◆◆◆◆◆◆

*Oxford, Mississippi, March 26, 1996; Woodstock, Georgia, October 30, 2000*

Mary Hood

◆◆◆◆◆◆

**Jan Nordby Gretlund** You demonstrate a powerful sense of place in your fiction, but the setting of your stories is not the setting of your novel.

**Mary Hood** I chose the place of the stories. Many of them could have been told in the place where *Familiar Heat* is set. Some of them could have been told in New Jersey. When I made my decision to bloom where planted, I was there in the North Georgia hills, and I looked around and I didn't know the name of trees, I didn't know the name of roadside weeds. There were trees that were unfamiliar to *my* eyes. I noticed them because they were different. The first things they ever saw were on the coast. When I go back to the coast now, I have a strong sense of being where I really belong, which is where the wide marshes are, very intense shade under live oaks, and the enormous dazzle of the beach, the marshes, and the sky. So you have mostly horizon, then a little bit of land, and, way off, the headland. This is the Georgia coast.

I went out West for a few weeks and everywhere that I saw sky, it looked like the coast, there where the marshes are. I liked the South Dakota high plains, anything with sky and grass, and I thought this is the marsh. I'm looking for the marsh. It is my native place of Brunswick, Georgia, Glynn County. The intense shade under the live oaks and then the sudden opening of tunnels into just glory! I still think that is the way everything should look, because that is how it started out. I had gone out thinking I might find somewhere else to live. But on the way back, well, the first place you pick up atmosphere and a little humidity in the air was Oklahoma and things were a little greener, but it was still so dry, and when you got to Arkansas suddenly those little tiny hard leaves on the trees became these flapping large poplar leaves and there was humidity to spare. The trees have to transpire through these big leaves like elephant ears, and it looked like—home. It scared me. We crossed the river at Memphis, and we were back, and I thought, if I went into any of those little white houses, I would know what was on the mantle, I would know what's hanging on the nails, nailed into the mantle, I would know what's in the kitchen and I could name something in one of the drawers. And I thought, well, I am doomed to be Southern. I will just travel and look, but I don't have to move away.

I thought the stories all had to be about the same place, and I wrote about my neighborhood in *How Far She Went* [1984]. I took the stories that I know from other places and made them fit where I was, which is Cherokee County in North Georgia, where I live. There is no reason why that's not the way one should do. Persons who might paint would paint out of whatever was driving them to paint and paint what they see out of the window. What the painter is about and what the picture is of might or might not be the same. But the painter could still succeed in the painting without anyone ever realizing that the artist was from somewhere else. I think that is also true about fiction.

I was born on the coast, but my mother's people were from the area I am living in now. My father was born in Manhattan. He was second generation but was raised by an immigrant grandmother from Ireland and the immigrant grandfather from Sweden, Mary Margaret O'Dowd and William Wenlöf. He was a Lutheran and she was Irish Catholic, so it must have been a very interesting household, and they brought my father up.—There is nowhere to go back to for me in the North to say, "This is home." But half of who I am is Northern. I was born in the South and brought up here, but the home that I lived in was half his and half my mother's, and we never had that Southern thing of a house filled with cousins and all that, a thing that I write about that seems so Southern, we didn't do that. We lived in many places, but I never lived in any town where we had relatives—that's not Southern.

**J.G.** Maybe in that sense you are a modern Southerner? Josephine Humphreys writes "there are no normal families."

**M.H.** A home was made.—My mother's father was a Methodist minister, so he was itinerant. Every two years or so, at that time, the church moved the man on. My grandmother said, once she was counting up, she was in her seventies then, that she had had more addresses where mail came to her than she had had years of life. I wanted to be Southern, because I saw my mother was. And the wonderful stories she could tell, she is a wonderful storyteller. Her name is Mary Adella Katherine Rogers Hood, she was named after all her grandmothers. Everything in the family was done to propitiate ancestors and the Katherine just because they liked it. And I am Mary Elisabeth.

**J.G.** Besides the sense of place and family, many Southern writers also demonstrate a keen religious sense, but you do not focus much on religion in your fiction, do you?

**M.H.** My mother is Methodist, and my father was brought up Episcopalian, or Anglican, and baptized in Trinity Church in New York City. In fact, his home where he was born is where one of the Twin Trade Towers was built. But we did not attend Episcopalian churches. On days when he felt obligation, or holidays, he would come to our Methodist church.

**J.G.** Flannery O'Connor is, of course, *the* famous writer from Georgia. But she was out to save our souls, and you are not.

**M.H.** Don't you think so?—I was out of college before I actually began reading. My family didn't know I was interested in writers. I was in college during the time Flannery was in Atlanta during her last illness. I didn't know that and I didn't study in school, so I had not heard of her in that way. And when I began to read in books, I read stories by a person named Flannery O'Connor. I had read Flan O'Brien, I had read European writers. One of my favorites is Frank O'Connor, the Irish short-story writer, I absolutely love him, and V. S. Pritchett for just the suave way he can tell a story, and I love Elizabeth Bowen. I know she and Eudora Welty were good friends. But when I first read her, I didn't know Flannery O'Connor was a woman, and I didn't know it was a Georgian. I read a story and I thought, "This person can write!' We must watch this person. At that time I was studying poetry, and I was caring more about poetry than prose, but I was struck by the story. I think it was the one about Julian and his mother, "Everything That Rises Must Converge," I'm sure it was. It was a torment to me, the story embarrassed me because it was so good, and I read "Revelation," it was exhilarating. But I came to a place where I thought "she doesn't like me." I felt like I was that person, Mrs. Turpin, "the warthog from hell." But everybody tells me that is okay, I am a *redeemed* warthog.

I went and I got more. I found all by the same writer and found it was a woman, it was a Georgian, and what is terribly sad, it was already over, the life was over, and I was reading everything. One night on television I saw Bob Giroux talking about her:

"I never saw anyone get as much better as quick as she did between this story and this story." And I envied that. She didn't misstep the way you do when you think you have life to burn. I wanted that said about me, but it wasn't. I was a very slow learner. So in my thirties I was still saying: am I, can I, should I? Ought I to quit now? Just hang it up? This was before I had published.

The first that was published of mine was a story in *Yankee Magazine* [New Hampshire, September 1978], which has not been published elsewhere. It wasn't soft, I am not a soft writer,—I don't repudiate it, but it was a treatment of family stories in which I allowed hope. Later I wrote about Aunt Goldie, who had begun to cry and cried for five years. At the family reunion she was a broken sweet person. It was in "A Country Girl," but I've told that story without saying why she cried or anything. I left it more that here was more of the truth. Whereas in the story for *Yankee Magazine,* I stopped the story before there was any reason to cry. I changed the names of the mountains in Georgia to the names of mountains in Maine, and instead of cotton it was potato fields. I just changed that and they went for it, because the story was a story from anywhere.

**J.G.** So your first story was a family story?

**M.H.** Yes, I was sitting at the dining table, and I had been writing poems and poems. And I had been working on histories. I love the chronicle of the conquest of Mexico by Hernándo Cortéz. I had found somewhere the actual chronicle. I was reading it and was doing the Spanish and the translation, and I was making like a cycle of poems, this was all what my mind was involved with. I think the way my mind works was that when the fence broke under the weight of the roses in the chronicle, I saw it and thought it into "prose" in a kind of epic way, and instead of its being about Mexico,

I dreamwalked to my table and wrote a simple family story, very much *not* like the conquest of Mexico.

**J.G.** Did you ever publish any of the poems?

**M.H.** Yes, I published poems, but I went ahead and put them in the stories, so they appear as paragraphs.—I don't think it hurts anyone to study poetry. My students now do not read poetry. They will say, "Oh, I don't have time." "What do you have time for?" I ask. I would want them to read Shakespeare, and a Russian poet, Marina Tsvetaeva, that I find wonderful, but it may be because she jumps around in my mind just like that. She is absolutely fabulous, but she is advanced. I've been teaching myself Russian, but I'm not anywhere from where I would know what it is that is so brilliant in the way she has done it.

**J.G.** *Familiar Heat* shows that you know Spanish well.

**M.H.** And Latin, from those two I read everything else in the Romance languages. I just work it out. I wanted to know what the big deal was with Dante. I would sit and read Virgil until that was not anything I had to go and look up. Then I had the feeling of that, the pattern, and then I went and read Dante. I had the English translation, I don't know whose, but then I just read out loud the Italian as though it were Spanish. I just read it and I listened and listened, and I said "Oh!" I didn't even need to know the meaning, although I usually knew. And after a while I saw what had happened to the lines. These enormous chains had broken and he had song. I saw suddenly that instead of this rhythmic-like horseback, he had song. To realize how anything like that is done is bound to help. It is like school figures in skating. You wouldn't go out and skate a figure 8 for a program, but if you can do that there is something in the discipline of being able to. You need to have form. Even if it is pointless, it can be good for you.

**J.G.** How long did it take you to write *Familiar Heat?*

**M.H.** I began writing it shortly after I finished college. I had an idea from when I was a child. It was the first time death had stolen anybody from me, and I felt that I had been cheated. I was about eight years old when I saw a beautiful man. I had seen men and women and children and dogs and cats and birds and trees and houses and Christmas and everything in the world that was beautiful and wasn't. I didn't have any idea what ugly was especially, but I had never seen the male person as beautiful, as glorious, and he was! It was the last time I saw him. It is hard to explain this, the book is not about this, but the feeling that I worked from was.

After World War II we did not have a new car for a while, as you couldn't buy one. In 1954 we got our first new car, it had been ordered, and it was wonderful! Someone in town had a son who was going away to the service, and they wanted it for him. They asked Daddy if he would sell it, because they didn't have time to wait for theirs to come up. He didn't really want to do that, but, it was superstition I guess, he didn't want something that someone else wanted, and the man gave it to his son. That's who I saw that day. He came to our house to thank my father, and I looked up and he was standing with the sun behind him, which I did not mention about Cristo in the novel. It isn't at all like the same story, but at Christmas he was killed on leave—in the car.

The money we had got for the car we saved over the weekend until the bank opened. I think it was put in a canister of coffee. And we were told not to think about it and not to tell anyone it was there, and we didn't. I would go and stand enchanted before the cabinet that a car could become a roll of cash and the cash could be buried in coffee, and you weren't to think about it. I can't explain it. It was like a tree going back to a seed.—But at that time we didn't know what would happen to the boy. It was months before . . . , and the money had become furniture.

We had two wooden barrels, at that time they were as tall as I was, with a piece of plywood over them and one of my grandmother's crocheted cloths and a blue vase with goldenrod and lilies from the ditch. And I was so afraid that I said, "Mama, are we rich?" I was afraid, but it was beauty! I didn't understand then that beauty is not cash. Cash bothered me. I had heard some preaching I guess. I was in Sunday school from the beginning. And my grandfather Claude Rogers baptized me. That was at Echota in North Georgia, an Indian town; it means "new town," and it was the capital of the Cherokee nation. I don't know what it was, but the rich man's son sorrowing because he was to go and give away everything he has, and everyone knowing that he wouldn't. He wouldn't get in, and that bothered me. And I remember asking, "Are we rich?"

**J.G.** You have actually taken the trouble to "dream up" a plot in your novel, it has a plot, it is telling a story, which is not really the fashionable thing to do nowadays.

**M.H.** I had hoped it didn't have a plot, isn't that funny? I didn't want minor characters, that was going to be ruled out, no *fichelles,* Henry James's little paper dolls, there was not going to be any of that, I thought that was false. And everybody said Henry James is the big cheese, he is the one to beat. And I can't read him—. But we would be impoverished without Henry James. I remember and know the world by sense impressions. If you said to me, "What day, or what was the history lesson?" I might say, "I don't know but I remember that it was raining and they were burning the seashells at the oyster factory and the air smelled like," et cetera, and then say, "I think we were studying the Thirty-Year War." The book would have meant nothing, but the ambiance! That is just how I take in the world, so Henry James was verbal and not sensory. I finally realized that I had to read him, I wanted to know what "the figure in the carpet" was. I had been reading interesting things about writers and that we had one, even if we don't know what it is, and I thought, "I will have to read that, won't I," and I bought the book, and I suffered so! It is not at all Joseph Conrad, *his* is a physical world.

Elizabeth Bowen helped me a great deal:

"Plot is the knowing of destination," that helped me to hold back before I began writing the words down, to just go ahead and think through the pictures. I read her *Eva Trout,* her last novel [1968], I didn't understand it, but she is fabulous. I think it is at the end, this ungainly, strange Eva Trout is about to get on the train in Victoria Station and this son that she's had, for whatever reason and no good reason, says something and she says, "What is concatenation?" The next line changed the way I wrote. It reads: "Her last words." She was assassinated by her son at that point. *What* was that all about? That was such a shock. It was like turning that page in Virginia Woolf's *To the Lighthouse* and finding out that Mrs. Ramsay was dead these many years. I thought: you can do that?

**J.G.** Does your sense of place include an awareness of biracial living?

**M.H.** Some of my characters are black, but I don't say so. I don't say when they are white either. And in *Familiar Heat* you discover that Ben is black. He is in *And Venus Is Blue* [1986] the family in "Finding the Chain" and I couldn't let Ben die in the novel until I had him say somewhere else that he had a happy time. I knew that he would die in the boat, and it was years before I could figure out how I could allow that to happen. There's a part of me that still believes that fiction is like fire, you can hold the animals at bay. Light up a story, it will either change the outcome or it will keep the things away, keep death away.

And so I made the story with Ben and his family, and I *knew* when I had written that that it was the last story I wrote for this collection, I did it the last two weeks. I wrote the stories one after the other, and that was the one I saved for last. I had thought the collection would be called "Finding the Chain." But when they read the novella *And Venus Is Blue* they thought that it was stronger and changed the title for it. I put everything I had into that—that was what home was. People always ask me, "How many times does he die, in that story?" And I say, "He dies once, but on every day of her life." He dies on the day he dies, he dies because Delia remembers it into the future, and he dies on every day of her past because every memory is tarnished by how the story came out. The idea is that tragedy attacks the past as well. Imagine a bullet aimed at a photograph album, and it burns a hole through every page. Now that scar is on every page in the memory.

**J.G.** You don't seem to be agonizing over civil rights or brooding over Southern history in the Faulknerian manner.

**M.H.** I think it is very possible that it is unrealistic, what I have abstracted. I thought I was abstracting truth. If I believed it wasn't important, then I believed it wasn't necessary, and therefore I wrote stories that were not about racial disharmony but about people. Perhaps I am wise enough still to do so in the book I'm writing about what went on in the South in the 1960s. I do not have the courage to tell what I know as the truth, except by lying about it as truth. I think it is very difficult, it is a compromising thing to have moved around, as I have, and made friends in new places and then discover that, either during the time or after, I did not see things the way others saw things. And yet I was friends with the people with whom I did not agree, and how could that be? It made me feel treacherous, two-faced, and disloyal.

**J.G.** Few of your stories are humorous, and your novel is not much so. You are not really writing in the tradition of Southern humor, are you?

**M.H.** The years of the stories were dark for me. Because of the things I worked out in *Familiar Heat,* I will certainly never be the person that I was. In the first two books I still believed fiction could make up for things, but I came to a conclusion early on that it was impossible. "Inexorable Progress" taught me that in some way I had saved something in fiction, or I had given it another chance. I was writing to save what was already lost. I'm always writing against death and the complete shock of things changing that you do not intend to change. But that is what life is. I hate death. I hate the surprise of bad news. I hate corruption and the inevitable decay of the high moment.

My grandmother saved the letters my mama wrote when I was just learning. She said that my first uncoaxed word came when I was in another room, and mama heard me say "gone." I was probably either looking at a bird, and it was there and it wasn't, or it was sunlight and it wasn't. Already then something was and then it wasn't.

**J.G.** In *Familiar Heat* you don't work in a Mark Twain–type humor, do you?

**M.H.** Well, I can't say. What is Twain's humor? Frankly I think I am a hoot. There is much that makes people laugh in my first novel, some of it intentional! The novel I'm doing now is, I think, so dark—and yet it is so funny. As regards my short stories, the collection I am writing is almost legendary now just by its title:

*Survival, Evasion, and Escape.* A story from the recent *Georgia Review,* about a Navajo girl, will be in it. The collection will have stories from all across America, and there will be three stories, I think, about a Jew from Poland; one story will be set in Europe and two in America. The stories are not Southern in the sense that they are set here. One of the things I realized was that I did not wish "to sound like myself," meaning "imitate." I want to *be* myself. There are always new stories that I want to write, but years went by, and, coming back to the short story and reading the army manual that gave me the title, I realized that the new stories were really about modern American life. I want to show how you survive, evade, and escape in American life and how we are isolated behind enemy lines in so many ways. And in the new South this is certainly going to be an issue.

**J.G.** Have you also been thinking of writing a new novel?

**M.H.** The new novel will be linear, the plot will not be curlicued around. It will be based on something I thought I saw one afternoon on a roadside, as a girl, and probably misinterpreted. And it is inspired by Hurricane Alberto that dumped twenty-four inches of rain on Albany, Georgia, in 1994, and a flash flood developed and cemetery vaults let the water in. The caskets were sealed, but about five hundred or so flew up out of the cemetery like rockets almost. And the hydraulic pressure would pop the lids off. I thought to myself: the dead rise, it is Judgment Day! I covered this for the *New Republic* [August 1994]. They required forensic experts to put the bones back together, so they got another shot to find if somebody died from natural causes or not. And in my mind I made fiction going back to what I "saw" on the roadside. An old flood occurs in my next novel, I call it "The Other Side of the River." It is both a biblical and a Southern topic.

◆ ◆ ◆

**J.G.** Did you have a happy childhood?

**M.H.** I enjoyed my life. There were moments that were hard and dark, family moments, there always are. And my family had volatile, strong personalities, with strong differences.

**J.G.** You frequently attack male chauvinism, and there are several egocentric men in your fiction. It was a surprise that Faye Rios in *Familiar Heat* would choose the chauvinistic Captain over his much more positive brother.

**M.H.** But wouldn't it be nicer if the terrible brother learned something?

**J.G.** You do not give us much insight into the Captain's mind.

**M.H.** No, I never did. There were several things that I did—I had time to be intentional. One of my absolute masters in instruction in fiction is Joseph Conrad. He impresses me greatly with his effects. How they are achieved I have never been able to know. His effects of light and dark and the action being seen in a lightening flash. Is it in *Lord Jim—A Tale* where the woman holds the torch through a window, she can't see what's going on in the shed, but they are killing each other. And in one little flash of light you see that and it is gone. How he did that, I don't know! His people are so real that you can follow them in the dark. The physical presence of his characters delights me, and the maleness of the males. I have no objection to masculinity, I really approve and encourage it, unless it is churlishness, or bad manners, or rudeness.

**J.G.** Or wife beatings?

**M.H.** Well, I think I am pretty rough on that! Wouldn't you be? That is not a very pleasant thing to go through. The story I wrote about that, "The Goodwife Hawkins," is a pathetic story about the mortal combat between those two. And all she does to extricate herself is nothing.

**J.G.** Her doctor prescribes valium for *her!*

**M.H.** But she lets him die! That is what it amounts to. She is very sorry, because what she thinks is that she is going to get another chance, and she doesn't. And that's something she has to live with, which is personal responsibility.

**J.G.** The feminism that celebrates the family of women and the matriarchal heritage that dominates Southern women's writing is not reflected in your Faye Rios character, and it is not a focus point in *Familiar Heat.* Why not?

**M.H.** I always try in everything I do in my books to tell what people do. How they work. My pulpwood cutter is a very true glimpse of what it is to be a valiant human man. But this man is out in the woods cutting, not because he *wants to,* but that's everything to him. That's all my politics. Anything you would ever want to find about me, you can read in that story called "Moths." That would be my democracy—that would be my religion:

"Love one another!" That's the text I live by, and that's right out of the mouth of Jesus. Whether it has to be beaten over your head, the way Flannery O'Connor did, or that one is condemned by one's Protestantism or salvaged by one's Catholicism seems to me to be a question that rather floors art.

If Flannery has succeeded, I think it is *in spite of* her religion. She would be very hurt to know that, but I feel rather strongly about it—people compare us. I think she would disapprove of me deeply in a personal sense. But I wrote about Catholics in *Familiar Heat,* and I wasn't trying to prove that they weren't what they should be or that they were. The black people were black and the Catholics were Catholics; it wasn't such questions I was writing about. In that sense I understand how you say that I am not racially entangled, or religiously or gender-politically *entangled.*

**J.G.** Your novel shows that you know a lot about Cuban immigrants. How did you learn about them?

**M.H.** Well, I've read and read, but I was in school in Atlanta in 1964, and there was a sizable Cuban exile community in Atlanta. In my classes in Spanish, which I just kept taking, literature classes, I wanted to become fluent. What's the use of knowing a language if you can't even read the literature? So I just kept taking "the literature of Spain and South America," at Georgia State. I majored in Spanish, it is my degree, in Spanish literature. I like the poets very much, I like Pablo Neruda tremendously, and I have always loved Garcia Lorca. I think that Gabriel Marquez's *Love in the Time of Cholera,* the first section of that book, and what happens on Pentecost Day, is just so amazing and it is wonderful the way that's written, and it is an inspiration in English or in Spanish. Among my classmates there were three or four English-speaking people, the rest of them were Cuban exiles, who were taking the courses because they wanted to talk about *their* literature, so I saw this. I also saw attitudes within the school and I saw brothers—that got me started. But then where I live, I see how brothers compete. Human beings are fascinating. The Cuban brothers, the American brothers, the North Georgia brothers, you name it, I loved watching, and after a while I just would have had a file in my mind on how brothers behave and how brothers compete.

*Familiar Heat* is not the first novel I have written, it is the third. The first one did not involve me at all. I was able to write a story, begin it and end it. I shaped the fiction. I haven't read it again, but I looked back later and I thought that the two main characters should have been one. The conflict would have been within a person instead of across boundaries, and it would have been tighter. Now I can see that, but at the time it was: you have this, you have this, and I had fiction. It was not a challenge, except that I finished.

Then I wrote a book called *Racing's Precinct.* That involved a man among men, and also Delia's father from "And Venus Is Blue," that was the same man. When I sent it off, I received comments that I had good characters but trouble with point of view. I didn't understand what point of view was! It was a term I didn't know. Being self-taught, you can overdo this, I thought New York was saying I was provincial and that I was Southern. I didn't know you could be cherished for these very qualities, if you come from the right part of the country. I thought, "I guess I am provincial," and I started reading "the Great Books" of the Western world.

I was reading on my own and started at the first one in the set. It took me a long time, I'm dyslexic, I toiled. I had other things to attach to because one of my heroes of prose, and I think of philosophy, too, is Sir Thomas Browne, I absolutely adore him. So there were things along the line that I would think, "Oh, soon I will get to it." And I loved Aquinas, but by the time I got to Aquinas, I had already been reading Flannery's mentors. I had read Jacques Maritain, and I was deeply moved by "The Responsibility of the Artist." I had a sense of triviality. Was fiction trivial? Was art trivial? What "good" did it do? I felt that reading Maritain was very important for me, because he said: you are allowed to do this if you care, and it is *not* trivial. You are not helping lepers, but you are not crocheting something to cover them with either.

**J.G.** Were you disappointed with the reception of *Familiar Heat?*

**M.H.** I was not disappointed in my readers, and I feel my work with it was successful. Like Miss Jean Brodie I was a little surprised that my season was so short. But it had three printings and then a paperback in several printings. I don't think it was a failure, and I don't think it was artistically a failure. But commercially it was a challenge because I never received money after I turned the manuscript in.

I had the advance, which I was paid over about eight years. It took me that long to finish it, and then since the day I handed in the last piece of my manuscript there was no more money from the book. The paperback sales went against the advance. That was a huge shock to me! It wasn't that there was anything wrong—it is just that I hadn't prepared myself. How would I survive until the next one was finished? And that is one reason I am working at Kroger.

**J.G.** You wouldn't want to live off another advance?

**M.H.** I would like New York's ideas about that to change. I would like publishing to change. I think the idea of blockbuster and bestseller and midlist and university and all of that ought not to be how you decide what's a success or a failure. And one way we can stop the madness is to stop asking for payment in advance. I don't think it is right for literature, I think a lot of times books get written that do not need to get written, just to keep it going. I left Knopf, I had a two-book contract, and I was supposed to publish short stories with them, but I asked to be released from that contract. Fortunately, it turned out that I had an editor-out clause, and my wonderful editor Barbara Bristol had left.

It has been several years, about twelve, since I wrote a short story. I laid them down to finish my novel, but I just wrote a new one that is coming out in the *Georgia Review* this quarter [fall 2000].

# *Interview with Mary Hood*

◆◆◆◆◆◆

*Commerce, Georgia, October 29, 2014*

**J.G.** Let me ask about your mother, who was so kind to me when I visited with you in Woodstock.

**M.H.** She passed away in 2004.

**J.G.** I am sorry to hear that.—I had the impression that you discussed your fiction with your mother.

**M.H.** We didn't talk much about my writing. She read it, but we did not discuss it. It was not like I rushed in to show it to her.—No! She liked Barry Hannah, and we drove many miles to go to his readings. Facing his elderly fan, he was absolutely astounded. He thought she had come to throw holy water on him, as on an incarnation of evil. But my mother thought he was wonderful; which, of course, he was in many ways.

**J.G.** Are you able to think of *Familiar Heat* today? I mean, can you think of it as a novel, without thinking of all the time you spent on it?

**M.H.** I haven't read it lately.—I am proud of it!—At the time, I wondered why it was held against me. I now think it was because Florida isn't the South. I could have placed the action on the Georgia coast, which I know well, but I needed the Cuban fishermen.—Besides all that might be wrong with the novel, I am still pleased with it. But I will not make a complicated book like that again. It was really three novels in one.

**J.G.** It was a Herculean labor. —Yes, it could easily have been broken up in parts.

**M.H.** When I saw those new stories by Ron Rash, I thought, "So that's coming on." And it still helps when people write stories that are about the truth, we can see the generations. I agreed very much, and I have recommended his book. He didn't need my help, but I just think he is a . . . waugh!

Before I wrote the foreword to Pam Durban's new collection, titled *Soon,* I reread everything. And reading it all at once, I would see connections. One of the wonderful things I trust her with is the way she narrates. It is very steady, very deliberate.

I live in a house where I have battery-operated clocks. We put batteries in, and we don't hear "tick-tock" sounds. At the farm where I had a "writing house" in this county, I rented in a farm house, and they had all sorts of wooden-gear clocks, which had the timing slightly off and the chiming would move from room to room. I was a guest there, and at night there was that presence and stir of time, which I find very attractive.

**J.G.** Some people might have found it distressing to listen to the clocks all the time.

**M.H.** I think I would have too if it were brassy, but it was mellow. If it had been in a small store with hard walls and all the clocks went off at the same time, it would have been terrible, like somebody dropping pans. My father built a grandfather clock, and it is in my brother's house. Durban has that steadiness—it is like a pulse. There is an orchestration in the way she uses time, and that is important in reading her.

I prefer to hold a book when I read, but on a Kindle I can do a word search on phrases that kept coming up. I thought, "Is this in another book?" It was one particular set of things, and I used that in a sentence or so in my "Foreword." I am sure she didn't know it. I hope this is not going to make her all tangled up now.

**J.G.** I know the story "Soon," but others may not know that this is only one story. I would probably have added "and other stories." I think that some of the other stories in that collection are just as good, if not even better.

**M.H.** "Soon" is an acclaimed story, and people know that, she has won prizes for that. I noticed Durban long ago when "All Set About with Fever Trees" was in the *Georgia Review.*

**J.G.** And it became the title story of an earlier collection.

**M.H.** If you enter the world of Pam Durban's books, you will come to realize that it has no beginning or end to it, in a way it is like a map. She is a Faulknerian in that every story has five or six ways you can look at it. The reader can't see that at first, because each story is so distinct, but over time you begin to see that not only do some characters tend to pop up again, but so does the theme. To me it just runs through it all—like a cord.

**J.G.** I am pleased that the USC Press asked you to write a foreword to *Soon,* and I am happy that *you* did it. Introductions are too often written by people who know too little about the craft.

**M.H.** In *Georgia Review*'s issue commemorating Stan Lindberg, there were an interview with me, an essay, a new story by me, and a selection from twenty years of letters to the former editor. After that issue USC Press contacted me. They wanted to see my stories but couldn't believe that I don't have an agent.

**J.G.** In general it is getting more and more difficult to find a commercial publisher of fiction—in particular for collections of short stories. It is fortunate that there are the university presses.

**M.H.** I make more out of the sale of individual stories, but it is great that they are collected and appreciated by some presses. The stories we are talking about are what I began in the '90s. It was a collection that I referred to as *Survival, Evasion, and Escape.* I had a contract with Knopf. I left Knopf, partly for financial reasons, I was much surprised I did not qualify for an advance payment, but mostly because Ann Close had left the company. Fortunately, I didn't have to break the contract, as I had an editor-out clause. She was not somebody insignificant to have as your editor; she was also Alice Munro's editor. To make sure that I know what I wrote *after* my Knopf years, I am now dating all I write. I actually live and have lived frugally. I didn't squander the money I was paid for *Familiar Heat,* but to work on one novel for ten years is a long time, and my father was ill. After I lost my publisher, I wrote and I wrote, but I wasn't publishing *forever,* it seemed.

When I sent my new stories to USC Press, they immediately wrote back and accepted the manuscript for publication. They sent me the peer reviews, and I am pretty sure one of them is by Ron Rash.

**J.G.** There is an impressive group of writers in the South today, and they all seem to know the others' work.

**M.H.** Yes, maybe it is a bit too much. But I accepted to write the foreword for Pam Durban's collection in order to pay tribute to her.—They mentioned that they are working on a new imprint, which will be called the Story River Press. One of their first books is called *The Story of a River,* which of course sounds fortuitous. Pat Conroy will head the new imprint, and he has read my manuscript and accepted it.

**J.G.** One of your plans for fiction was, as I remember it, to write about lives in a high-rise building, with focus on all the lives in that building. They all have very different individual lives and fates, and I have been looking forward to seeing that in print.

**M.H.** That is coming along. It will be micro-fiction, a suite of tiny finished stories, all on the people in that one building. And it is called *About Time,* as each story has a quality that is about time. In a Jewish family they are waiting for the first light and ready to light the candles and for the Sabbath to begin. At the same time other types of life go on in all the other apartments. In one of them there is a child's room, but the child never came, so now they keep a collection of watches in that room. What matters to all these people, now that the big house, the land, the silver, the furniture, et cetera, don't matter anymore? Something has to matter in the lives of the people in the building.

**J.G.** Let's talk about what was called *Seam Busters.*

**M.H.** Buster is a name for a good ol' boy.

**J.G.** It reads as a novella in the Katherine Anne Porter tradition, too long for a story and too short to be a novel.

**M.H.** Porter is wonderful.—She is one of my teachers!

**J.G.** She was a tough woman, really tough.

**M.H.** Yes she was.—When I worked at Kroger as the coffee person, I joined the union. I asked whether it was like the teamsters, but my boss reassured me. I used some of that in *Seam Busters.*

**J.G.** You didn't want to end up with your feet in a concrete block.

**M.H.** Exactly!—Once again I was writing an ad for sunglasses. They are in the kit for soldiers. You can't buy these in their actual frames with the wrap-around. They are made for soldiers at tremendous expense; they help save lives as shrapnel bounces off. You can buy some that look like the originals, and it is considered pretty cool to be wearing those. I wrote text blurbs, tiny articles of 340 to 600 words usually, and at the level I worked, it was at 1.5 cents a word. I had moments when I had to write an article very quickly and sell it. I did the research in the morning and wrote it at night or got up early to meet my deadline, usually twenty-four hours. And in a month I would have made an appreciable amount of money, up to four hundred to five hundred dollars. It is hard work, and I began to find that it interrupted my creativity, but it also fed my creativity.

Somehow I found out about the new "camou," that is, camouflage material. I had a friend whose daughter who had just come back from a tour of duty overseas. She had had tours in both Iraq and Afghanistan, and she was the only one I could ask about the new camou. It is crispy, doesn't wrinkle, and you can't wash it in ordinary detergent. The troops were having trouble with the enemy's night vision; they could see our troops in the dark. Even the patch with the flag on it is now black, and you wear that in the field. The field dress was just one item; in camp you had a different set of everything. You had to remove your insignia in the field, but back in camp you had to put them back on. To do it quickly you had to use Velcro, because zippers were destroyed in sand storms. And pants laces did not help in the desert. To keep changing around was cumbersome, and you had to keep up with two kit sets. I borrowed a uniform from my friend and had her fighting gear hanging for a while. I studied it; I had read that the sand was also bad on the Velcro. The soldiers used their gun-cleaning brass brush to clean the Velcro. All these tiny details were changed in the field dresses, and they were the origin of the camouflage factory in *Seam Busters.*

Then I was influenced by the milieu when I worked in the Baker and Taylor books warehouse. Most of the women I worked with there had had other jobs. Some admitted they had stolen and would tell you where they had sold. The mother of a friend told me the story about the inspector for her sewing and how another seamstress had taken her good sewing and passed it on as her own by putting her stamp on it. So the good seamstress got the other one's bad work back. But she knew she hadn't messed it up. So *she* changed the thread on her machine to red, and the thief never noticed and was caught.

**J.G.** Did you have factories like that here in the Commerce area?

**M.H.** Yes. But they are all closed now. There were the Wrangler jeans sewing plant and there was Blue Bells, and the thread mill was just down the street. They would spin the cotton into thread and weave it into cloth.—I found that there are plants in South Carolina that are still sewing. Most everywhere else has gone now to China. They took machines and everything and walked away, it is called outsourcing! America is taking a real hit! So when this happened, I was thinking, I know they are sewing in Atlanta, there is a plant doing the pants of the field dress battle gear. And where else, I thought, it got to be in Georgia because I am writing about it.

**J.G.** I think the fact that people really cannot make both ends meet on a farm anymore, so they have to go and look for factory work, is an important part of the book.

**M.H.** That and benefits, such as insurance, are what drove the women out of the house into the plants.

**J.G.** And there is the irony you put into the story: the woman's son may be coming back in a coffin dressed in a camouflage uniform that may have been sewn by his mother!

**M.H.** The women knew that.—At Baker and Taylor we were not sewing, but we were repairing books, right here in Commerce at the end of these tracks, and we knew the books were sent to the troops. I worked there for exactly three years. But then I went back to teaching at Oxford, Georgia, Emory and Mercer, and that got me going again and gave me time for my own work. I didn't go back to factory work where you had a belt moving and everything was about how you use time.

**J.G.** So now you have ten stories ready to be published as *A Clear View of the Southern Sky.* And the title story is about a woman who is an assassin and in prison for having killed a man. And then there is *Seam Busters,* which is also ready for publication. So they are out of the house.

**M.H.** They have already been edited.

**J.G.** So what are you doing now?

**M.H.** I just finished the Pam Durban "Foreword."—So, what am I doing? I am writing another story about time, one that was in my mind for some time. But the other day when I was typing, baking, and taking notes, the story was there. It is about a woman in her eighties, who has to get on the road if she is going to do what she said she would do. She goes on a mission trip, and it is about what happens to her on that trip. I know that woman well.

I am not immune to criticism, but now I think I'm getting the benefit of it. I have the sense of it, if not now, when? Nobody can distract me, except myself. I have to stay on track. We are still young. The package is just the wrapping.

## *The Excitement and the Mystery of the Immediate*

INTERVIEWS WITH JOSEPHINE HUMPHREYS

◆◆◆◆◆◆

*The Confederate Widows' Home, Charleston, May 26, 1993; January 27, 1996; May 9, 2000; May 2, 2001*

Josephine Humphries

◆◆◆◆◆◆

**Jan Nordby Gretlund** *Dreams of Sleep* seems to me more poetic than your other novels.

**Josephine Humphreys** I haven't looked at that in a long, long time. I don't like to. I suppose *Rich in Love* is most fresh in my mind because of my involvement with the making of the movie.

**J.G.** I hear there were some negative reviews of it. How much did you have to do with the making of the movie?

**J.H.** Well, I had little to do, officially. But I was there all the time. I didn't write anything or make any decisions, but I watched. And I loved it—I thought it was very good.

**J.G.** You are not just saying that out of loyalty?

**J.H.** No! I mean there are some differences between the movie and the book. And then there is some oddness about the movie. It never made me uncomfortable, but I could see from the beginning that it was going to be unusual, in that it is very much an *even* movie, in terms of action and emotion. It is very balanced and controlled.

**J.G.** Is it more controlled than even the novel?

**J.H.** Yes. And now I like that aspect of it because I do think it is unusual. It makes the film stand out, to me.

**J.G.** In your first novel the main character is obsessed with her husband's secretary and mistress. She seems to accept the infidelity and just watches the affair as an interested observer. What makes Alice so different?

**J.H.** I thought of her as almost pathologically detached. Actually, I think her fascination with Claire is her strongest emotion. She has a kind of focused fascination with children, but it is still not a personal involvement.

**J.G.** Is she really in greater psychological trouble than it appears?

**J.H.** Oh yes. What also interested me about her—I don't like to talk about these characters as if they were real, because I feel it is not really honest to do that. I mean for my own interior self it is difficult for me to bring myself to say: "Alice is this," "Alice is that," but I have gotten used to it because those are the terms in which people discuss books. But that was a big hurdle for me at first to do that.—As she took shape she interested me as a narrator. She doesn't really narrate, she is not a first-person narrator, but mainly it is her book, I think. And she worked well for me as a teller, as a watcher, because that's all she does.

**J.G.** Are you an observer of Charleston in the same way?

**J.H.** After my sons have left home I feel the need to acclimatize myself better. It leads me into an accord with my own city that I never really had before. After more than fifty years I understand it better. It is a very proud place. People here feel they are better than anybody else, especially the rest of South Carolina.

I can see the diversity within the city, in fact, within one little part of it. I long to feel at one with it, but I feel like a watcher and an observer within my own home.

**J.G.** I see a parallel to Walker Percy's character called Lancelot. Interest seems to be the only "emotion" left for him and for your Alice.

**J.H.** That's right.

**J.G.** As critics we have the urge to place writers in categories, and for me you are a Southern existentialist writer and a city writer. You describe people who are trying to find "a realer life," and this is, I suppose, something that Percy (or maybe Faulkner) started in Southern literature.

**J.H.** Yes. He did to me.—I always loved "the other" Southern writers, as well. But I didn't lose my heart to them. I admired them, Eudora Welty, Flannery O'Connor, and big Faulkner books, *Light in August* and also Reynolds Price—all wonderful and great. And yet I never really recognized their South. I recognized it more as matching one of the other writers' books than as matching anything I really had ever experienced. Or matching something I had seen from a car window driving through rural South Carolina but not corresponding to my life or what I was seeing every day. And then suddenly there was Walker Percy. But you're right, there were some existentialist concerns in Faulkner.

**J.G.** Do you associate your writing with or disassociate yourself from Walker Percy as novelist?

**J.H.** I really don't do either. I neither associate nor disassociate, but I simply love his books. That is the association for me. I have read all his books, except the essays in *Message in a Bottle*. I think I have read all the others. I do surely like them all.

**J.G.** The fact that there is a veterinarian in *The Fireman's Fair* called Dr. Percy is probably not an accident?

**J.H.** No, it is not an accident.

**J.G.** Are you paying a tribute to Percy's existentialism?

**J.H.** Yes, in the most informal and humble way. You know, I couldn't even tell you what existentialism means.—I used to, but I no longer deal in that kind of business.

**J.G.** It is just a word.

**J.H.** Right, but to me the important thing about a Percy novel is the importance of the moment and the excitement of the immediate—and the mystery of the immediate.

[We are immediately interrupted by the sound of a garbage truck, possibly from Porlock, working the street.]

**J.G.** But you do write about the malaise, the decay, the rottenness at the core, the long pain, and the emptiness at the heart of things. All standard existentialist expressions for people who have a hard time finding any reason to exist.

**J.H.** Those are also terms that you could discover coming from the mind of anyone who had ever suffered from depression. In addition to being philosophical terms, they are also psychological terms and are real to me, more than they are ideas. Those are real feelings that I have had and suffer from, contend with, and enjoy. I think that is why, when I read *The Last Gentleman* and the other Percy books, that they spoke to me so strongly.

**J.G.** As a Southerner you would mention *The Last Gentleman*—whereas the outsider would mention *Lancelot,* as a more successful novel. But it is unpopular in the South.

**J.H.** I like *Lancelot!*—I like the journey in *The Last Gentleman,* that is really what grabbed me and what fascinated me. I also like the attachment of this young man to a separate family. I have done that in some of my works. I like the idea of a stranger coming into a family.

**J.G.** The philosophical father in *Dreams of Sleep* seems to be the kind of stoic person that Faulkner and Percy wrote about.

**J.H.** Yes.

**J.G.** Was the father right? Is there nothing after the assassination of John Kennedy?

**J.H.** As a matter of fact, I always say that my work is completely fictional, not autobiographical. But if I go through one of them, I can find something on almost every page that is actually absolutely true. And those are the words that my father said to me when I did call him that day in 1963. "Was he right?" Certainly it was true in terms of my vision versus his. At that time I was eighteen, and I was enslaved to the dramatic. I mean, everything had meaning, and everything was very important to me, and he was almost the opposite. I thought that an event like that would have such repercussions that the whole world would change. He knew that it would not.—And now, I think I am somewhere between those two.

**J.G.** The father in the novel did not believe in "progress" either!

**J.H.** My own father actually does—and I don't. But the notion of progress is a look at how things change over time.

**J.G.** For some Southerners such as the Agrarians, "progress" was almost a dirty word and certainly a Yankee notion.

**J.H.** Yes.—But weren't those men for the most part rather wealthy? I think that there was actually another school in the South which clung to the idea of progress, economic improvement, people desperate to get out of the poverty that made living so hard.

**J.G.** The question is what has to be given up for the material progress?—Alice's father sits around while the world tumbles down, and his stoic reaction is "I told you so!" In that sense he is a William Alexander Percy character.

**J.H.** Yes, he is!

**J.G.** Walker Percy tried to come to terms with the stoic tradition all of his life. I wonder how strong this tradition was in John C. Calhoun country and especially among Charleston's upper classes.

**J.H.** As a point of view stoicism has its advantages, but I think I am an enemy of it—as a way of living. It is a protective stance, and I think those are always bad.

**J.G.** Isn't it a Southern stoic attitude that you do the right thing in order to be able to stand yourself?

**J.H.** Yes. It is a survival technique.

**J.G.** Is North Carolina then better than South Carolina?

**J.H.** Yes.—From the point of view of things like education—in particular education—North Carolina has in my memory always had better schools, from elementary school up through college. First of all, they are willing to spend money on education, which we have not been. And, secondly, I think that for some reason there is not so much anti-intellectualism in North Carolina as in South Carolina. It is more acceptable to be educated and intelligent in North Carolina.

**J.G.** Some of its industrialized areas, like the Triangle Area, have the pace of the frightening North nowadays. It is not very Southern.

**J.H.** No, it's not. But that is true actually even in Charleston and has happened in the last twenty years. Just because of migration and people coming here from other places. It is hard now to find people who were born here if you go to the grocery store and just take a sampling.

**J.G.** They don't sound right?

**J.H.** They don't sound right, that is right. But I am glad that that happened, you know. Whenever you lose something, an accent, or closeness to history or traditions, it is sad, but I like the new city better than the old one.

**J.G.** What do you mean when you say "the old one"?

**J.H.** The old one was a city where the highest value was placed on ancestry and genealogy. There were not many other values; it was *the* most important thing! It was a very rigid, stratified society.

**J.G.** It was better to have a creek named for your ancestors, like Allen Tate, than to be rich.

**J.H.** That's right.

**J.G.** On the other hand, you point out that people keep to themselves in their houses Bayside now, here on the peninsula. The poor whites have disappeared from the city, and the blacks are being forced out. Is there still a project?

**J.H.** Yes. Now of the ones that were in the city, one was vacated because it was dangerous—it was very low-lying. The one that was the model for the one in *Dreams of Sleep* is just blocks from here, and it is blacks only. I don't know that for sure now—obviously it is open to black or white—but it is primarily black populated. And it is still there, and it is very pretty. I walk in places that I'm not supposed to. I go to black churches I enjoy. I feel I shouldn't go, but I do go to about five black churches.

J.G. Isn't it a sad result of the new city that the rich people of Bayside isolate themselves in their houses.

J.H. Very sad, yes! You know, *Dreams of Sleep* was published in 1984 and took five years to write, and the city has actually changed a lot since then and is now more open. I think people are coming out of their houses.

J.G. It seems that you have an intimate knowledge of both poor whites and blacks, for someone who has grown up in a privileged home.

J.H. When I grew up, the entire city was poor. There were only a few wealthy people. I was in grammar school, I went to a public school which was segregated, it was all white, but with people from different kinds of white backgrounds. So I was always in school with very poor children. And they were my friends, so I did know them.

J.G. Were there Iris Moon types, practical girls?

J.H. Yes, exactly. And I didn't know any black people. I didn't begin to know black people until —really, until I was an adult. There were black students at Duke when I went there, but not many. There were three girls in my class that were black, they were the first ones. But then when I came home, in my twenties, I taught English at the Baptist College here for seven years, and that is where I got to know black people well. Most of my students were black.

J.G. Do you think that the interracial relationship, which wasn't possible for Iris and Emory, is possible in Charleston today?

J.H. Definitely.

J.G. Getting to know black students as a teacher doesn't really explain your knowledge of black family life and black history.

J.H. I have read a lot of black history, and, in fact when you are teaching English to teenagers, you do get to know families, because that's what they are worried about. Also I had a lot of students who were adults and who wrote about their families.

J.G. Do you feel that black people are still being exploited by white people and do not have the opportunities we have?

J.H. No, they don't! Obviously there are a lot of good changes, but all of America is still quite racist in terms of how white people think about black people in general and in terms of what doors are open to black kids. There have been wonderful legal changes, but white people hardly ever talk with a black person. The changes have not happened in the city's social life. Charleston resists change of any kind, but the bigger the change, the more violent it is.

**J.G.** Is it hard to find a school that is evenly integrated?

**J.H.** It is very hard in the city. There aren't any. There are two schools now that have opened the last five, ten years that are magnet schools, where they have special programs. And they are getting in good teachers in order to attract white kids. So there are two, an elementary school and a high school program. But the regular schools up in the city are completely black.

**J.G.** Do you at times use black characters as yardstick characters, almost the way Faulkner did? Rhody in *Rich in Love* seems to be such a character, she seems to know more.

**J.H.** That is how I personally feel. I am not happy with the way that happens in all my books. I mean, it is okay, but I see that the black characters are more like a chorus to the protagonists, and that's what I wanted to do, because that is how my life has been. It has always been a central little white drama, and black people around it, who to me always seemed to know more and to understand things, family life better, to understand troubles better. I would like to be able to have black characters that are the protagonists. And in a way Rhody became that towards the end of the book.

**J.G.** I see progress in fiction that can see black people as not just stereotypes but as individualized human beings with separate identities, as you do with Albert Swan in *The Fireman's Fair.*

**J.H.** That's what I want to be able to do.

**J.G.** Is the New South of your everyday like "Ohio warmed over," that is, the plastic-columned South?

**J.H.** There was always a threat that was very clearly perceived here in this city. We depended on tourism for income. And yet you could see slowly that if you welcome tourists to your town, the town will change in order to please the tourists. And then you lose the authentic city, I don't mean the genuineness of it, but you lose that excitement of a real place. So I think that for a long time Charlestonians have been aware that there was this danger in pandering to the tourists. And yet we have always welcomed people.

**J.G.** Ohio-bashing is, of course, prominent in fiction by Walker Percy and Barry Hannah.

**J.H.** Actually, I did it, because I looked around one day, and, my best friend here is from Ohio and has moved here, my sister married a man from Ohio and they came down, and my husband's family, which was originally from Illinois, all moved to Ohio. Suddenly there was a lot of Ohio in my life. I really just picked it to make private jokes. Also I was at Sea Island, Georgia, which I used in *Dreams of Sleep,* which is one of the old Southern resorts, and half the people there were from Ohio. And they told me there is a reason for it.

If you are in Cincinnati, and you want to get to the beach, to the Atlantic Ocean, one of the shortest drives is to the Georgia coast, to get to a real seashore beach. So it is not that they are going out of their way.

**J.G.** Aren't the men in your fiction all ineffective, overly sensitive, emotionally stunted, and potentially violent? And all are unable to face reality?

**J.H.** Let's see. That sounds right. That's accurate [laughing].

**J.G.** Driving to Charleston, I heard on the radio a woman stating with some passion that she was "looking for a construction worker whose hairs on his belly should match the length of the hairs on his legs!" This is not the male type we meet in your fiction.

**J.H.** No!—I have not known many men in my life. I have no brothers, so we were a real girl-household, growing up. And then I was terribly shy as a teenager. I never had any male pals. I only knew boys that asked me out, and there were not very many of those. And I went to an all-girl high school. My husband and I started dating when I was a freshman in college. A lot of my knowledge of men comes from my father and my husband, those two people that I have known, plus reading. I like the men in Walker Percy, I like the men in John Updike, and I find both of those sets of men to be very attractive. If their chest hairs are not long enough, it doesn't bother me in the least. I like the reflective men. Also, I have two sons, and watching them grow up, I made a lot of discoveries about men—or, at least about these two men that I have, the ones I own.

**J.G.** Did you discover that there are gender differences right from the start?

**J.H.** Yes. And I discovered it at a time when the conventional wisdom out there, or the political wisdom, was that there was no difference. But there definitely is. And I believe there were differences I never heard anybody else talk about before. I think that my own sons were far more honest than my sisters and I were, more concerned with justice, the idea of justice, and moving more towards that ideal than we ever were, and more romantic than we were. We were very cynical, and they are not.—They have a good cynical streak and sense of humor, but when it comes to friendships or love involvements, they are very romantic. That was a shocker to me.

**J.G.** When I learned that you had written on William Cowper and are interested in sixteenth-century poets, especially Thomas Wyatt, it occurred to me that your ideas of modern men may have their origin in your knowledge of those early English poets.

**J.H.** Probably.

**J.G.** I'm impressed with your male characters Will Reese and Robert Wyatt. They are very convincing; whereas Walker Percy never created a very good woman character, unless they were mentally disturbed.

**J.H.** They were all nuts . . . goofy!

**J.G.** But most male readers can identify with the men in your novels.—Are you still reading sixteenth-century English poets?

**J.H.** Not really. I have not gone back to them for quite a while. But Will's fragmentary memory, in terms of being haunted by lines of poems, is what happens to me. I have forgotten a lot, but now and then a line or stanza of Wyatt or Donne pops up in my mind.

**J.G.** Miss Welty told me she was taught by "a Swift and Donne man" (and I had to think about that wording for a minute).

**J.H.** You thought it was a Southern colloquialism.—Exactly the same thing happened to me. My beloved teacher at Duke, William Blackburn, who taught creative writing, also taught seventeenth-century poetry. I adored him, I just really loved him. And he loved the poetry, so I loved the poetry, too.

**J.G.** One thing you have in common with these early poets is a quest for real romantic love, a true love.

**J.H.** Yes.

**J.G.** If you grant your characters romantic love, you are faced with criticism of sentimental endings.

**J.H.** Yes, I know . . . I mean there's just nothing I can do about that [laughing]. I don't think they are sentimental. I think I do have problems with the endings of all three books in that they are fast. They are too quick, and they are rather contrived, they are manipulated to end there. And, you know, every time I do it, I think, "Well next time I am not going to do this." But I might, anyway.

**J.G.** Do you simply get fed up with them and want them to end? Or do you have a set length you are working toward?

**J.H.** It is more the last, although it is not physically a set length I'm working toward, but it is like a horse heading back to the barn. Once he knows that he is going there, and it is time to go, and he knows where it is, he is on the way and just fast and straight. I can't make myself slow down. Because I generally write without a plan, no outline has been prepared. So it is very slow going at first, I don't know what is going to happen, and then toward the end of the book, when it is clear what has to happen, and I know it, I just rush toward it. I think that I am not working toward a happy ending, I think I'm just working toward an ending that is temporary equilibrium, and that things will go on.

**J.G.** When you began to write, you spent a long time writing your first novel. It is my impression that you may have finished the next two books faster than you intended. Was there pressure on you from the publisher to follow up on the success of *Dreams of Sleep*?

**J.H.** There is no pressure from the publisher. I feel that "pressure," which is not the right word, but I feel an *obligation* to my agent. I have a really close relationship with her. And I am always afraid that she is going to start to worry. And I want to deliver something to her. It is a personal kind of obligation I feel. She is also Reynolds Price's agent, and Saul Bellow's agent, and do you know Richard Bausch, she is his agent. She is great!—The agent is really important. She has been such a help to me and has really encouraged me more than any other single person.—Right now I'm just moving slowly, and the only thing that makes me nervous is thinking about Harriet and thinking she is probably up there in New York thinking to herself. . . . So that's the pressure, but my publisher has never said, "We want this soon." Possibly because, though I have the same publisher, I have had different editors. There is such a turnover [at Viking]. I have had five different editors. They have all been wonderful, really good editors, but I haven't had with any of them the same kind of relationship that I have with Harriet.

**J.G.** Do you think you will use more time on the novel you are writing now, in spite of your agent?

**J.H.** I already have.

**J.G.** Now that we are here talking in the old Confederate Widows' Home in old Charleston, it is perhaps appropriate to ask you, why so many of your characters are afraid of growing old and the loneliness that at times comes with it. Are you worried about old age?

**J.H.** Of course! Well, I'm not so much worried about old age as I am about the decay. It would suit me fine to be ninety if I can think and walk. I would rather think than walk. But I would like to be able to do both of those things. But actually more than my fear of old age, I have an enormous consuming fear of death, and have always had, my whole life. In fact it is so big that I'm very comfortable with it now, and it doesn't debilitate. I think it is in Will's thoughts in *Dreams of Sleep*. What is terrifying about the idea of dying is the idea of no longer being around to watch.

**J.G.** You are talking about your basic curiosity! You want to see what will happen to your sons.

**J.H.** You're right—totally right (laughing).

**J.G.** Even if you're afraid "to spot and clod," as you put it, and waste away, doesn't old age have a charm of its own?

**J.H.** I look forward to any kind of lively, engaging, interesting old age. In fact, I am probably happier now than I have been. I like the age I'm in now, and I probably always will. But I like life and I don't want it to end, that's the problem. I have found interesting things about it, and advantages in it. If you really are frightened of dying, then you are simply aware of your mortality and that energizes the rest of your life, what you have, and you hold on to it.

**J.G.** Do your sisters think about death in the same way?

**J.H.** One of them does. I think the third one never thinks about it.

**J.G.** Neta, your grandmother, as you describe her in your essay "My Real Invisible Self," seems to have lived a full life, also as a grandmother.

**J.H.** Yes, she did.

**J.G.** A law of increasing reality, as worded in *Rich in Love,* reads:

"The older you get, the clearer you see, the clearer you see the more you need to forget what you saw. So people smoke, drink, stuff things up their noses, eat, and screw." Do you, yourself, believe this?

**J.H.** Yes.

**J.G.** This can perhaps be related to the carpe diem idea expressed by Wayne in the same novel. Wayne looks rather ridiculous, with his sexual urge, but is he necessarily ridiculous? He seems to be honest about his emotions.

**J.H.** Honesty, truth and honesty, is something I think about a lot. I told you I found my sons to be more honest.—I couldn't say whether I am honest with myself or I'm dishonest with myself. I'm either very honest with myself, or I'm not at all! I'm not sure which one it is. It is very hard for me to recognize truth. That makes the writing of fiction interesting, because I don't know. Even in a made-up story there are true things, there are both true facts and truisms. And being honest about your emotions seems to be so critical—a really important thing—if you are going to live with yourself and make meaning out of your own life. The dishonesty would be more to you yourself than to anybody else.

**J.G.** I believe I finally tricked you into expressing a typical Southern stoic idea.

**J.H.** Oh, it is? [laughing]—Well, if you are actually deceiving yourself, then you can't proceed. If you are fooling yourself, if you're not constantly struggling to remain emotionally honest with yourself, you are losing that thread of meaning that will unite your life and the very meaning that will allow your whole experience to make some sense.

**J.G.** As Marcella [in *Dreams of Sleep*] is honest to herself?

**J.H.** Yes, and Louise [in *The Fireman's Fair*] is certainly not. And it does require a kind of a struggle to be honest with yourself, because how do you know? You are the only judge. You are both the storyteller and the listener, and you don't know where the truth lies. And that's part of this law of increasing reality. I thought, what could be easier than to be honest with yourself, to know your own notions, but with experience it is very hard to do that, hard to know what your feelings really are.

**J.G.** Does history fade? Are things falling apart? Is that the only lesson we can learn from history?

**J.H.** No, not at all. That is what Will thinks.—I actually have gone through a cycle of interest in history. I was not interested in it as a child. I was not interested in the study of history at all, I didn't like the unrelenting interest in it what surrounded me here, and the valuing of history *over and above* the present. A lot of so-called facts turned out to be fiction, and I grew suspicious of it. So in college I avoided studying history. I had never been interested in the Civil War, in reading about the battles, and was not interested in the family history. Because it was used in the wrong way! It was used to defend segregation, it was used to make the South into something that I thought it wasn't and to glorify something that no longer existed. I just didn't want to have anything to do with it. But now luckily I'm much more interested in Southern history.

The teaching of history has changed, there has been a revolution in the ways history is presented and in the kind of history that is told! I like reading about real people, I mean historical, real people, and also common people, ordinary people: women, blacks, poor people. That kind of history was never being taught when I was in high school and college. If you took a history class, all you studied were battles, treaties, and politics. And now in universities, my son is a history and literature major, and they don't do the wars. They concentrate on the real, what we used to call "social history," but now they consider it "history." From that point of view it becomes a living thing, a real thing, and an important thing.

**J.G.** Are there any books of this type of history that you could recommend?

**J.H.** This kind of book is being written all over the country; it's not an unusual book. That is what all this is up here on the shelf. This is all history. There's no literature. There's no fiction. This is a book about families in rural Georgia. Black and white families that intermarried with photographs and accounts of what happened to their children, whether the children then entered the white culture or the black culture, and how it all worked—letters and photographs.

**J.G.** Will this changed view of history influence you in the writing of your next novel?

**J.H.** Well, I hope so. And there's a little bit about it in *Rich in Love.* Lucille talks about the past, she says the same things I just said.

When *Dreams of Sleep* was published, the first foreign rights that were sold went to Denmark, and then to Sweden, Norway, and Finland. And that's all that was ever sold, up until recently. And I said to my agent,

"What is this?" And she said, "Oh, Scandinavians love depressing Southern novels!"

**J.G.** Many Scandinavians find it sad to see the disappearance of the Old South, as reflected in the golf-course cemetery, the frozen food, et cetera.

**J.H.** That really is terrible. It is not just a joke to talk of that development as being awful. But it is hard to talk about now, because we have been thinking about it for twenty years and we haven't done anything about it. And it is still happening. It really is bad. I don't think it can be stopped. I think when there is a lot of money involved, you are just not going to get people to put a halt to it. It has happened all over America, and what can you do? The only hope for stopping it is some kind of catastrophe, like an economic depression, that will stop it. But there is nothing else that's going to stop it.

The environmental movement has had an effect in the South. We will probably be able to preserve some little pieces of our rural countryside and our wilderness, but only little, tiny little pockets. The place is just all but gone. It is the loss of the wilderness that really bothers me more than the loss of the cultural, self-made culture. Because I think human beings will always have some kind of interesting culture. It may be for a while uncomfortable, maybe crime-ridden, and maybe not what we want, but that is an ongoing and ever-changing thing. We couldn't have ever kept Southern 1940s town culture alive.

**J.G.** One of the culture killers among us seems in Southern fiction of today to be TV—also in your novels. Are people who watch television emotionally dead?

**J.H.** They are. TV is just insidiously destructive. It is destructive to me.—I had the courage to get rid of it for twelve years and to raise my children without a TV in the house until they got to be around twelve. Then they began getting schoolwork assignments to watch something and write a report on it. And we couldn't do it. But it is a thief, as it robs you of your mental energy. It is just a very alluring kind of immediate entertainment. We know from watching rats in experiments that they will go for immediate gratification, and so will we.

**J.G.** Your main characters are always, even if troubled, people we can recognize as being good. I wish you would give more space to fascinating disagreeable characters, like Owen of *Dreams of Sleep*.

**J.H.** Marcella started as a *not* very good character. If I do spend time on them they turn good [laughing], which I actually think is true, in a way. If someone is not crazy, then I think you can expect to be able to find goodness at the heart of a person. I believe there is always something there. When I go through my daily life, I think I am fairly suspicious. But given a little time, I think that people can have faith in the hidden. What people hide from you is sometimes bad, but it is often good. That's because goodness is vulnerable and they don't want to reveal that they are vulnerable.

J.G. Other people, who are perhaps not so good, also live in your place. Belonging to a place makes you responsible also for others living there. Isn't that frightening?

J.H. I don't think it is frightening. I think it is complicated, and that's what I like about places. I am really in love with places. Not just this place. I love to travel, and when I go somewhere, I usually decide that this is where I should be living. I went to Australia, and it was very hard to come home. I really just wanted to stay. And what a complicated history, there is not much good in the early history of Australia.

J.G. The general optimism that you exude is, of course, also what makes the books so amusing. Have you read the old Southern humorists?

J.H. I have a good sense of humor, and it is a very broad, vibrating sense of humor. In college I read a lot of Southern humorists, early 1820s, Longstreet, Baldwin, and Twain.—Twain is the greatest writer ever. I love *Huckleberry Finn,* I have always loved it. And I like the letters and *Pudd'nhead Wilson.* I like to think of him as a Southern writer. I also love Walt Whitman, and he is not exactly a funny boy. Those two I think of their brains as being five times bigger than mine. As they were able to do this, I mean they were geniuses.

J.G. Eudora Welty's concerns of love and separateness seem also to be your concerns.

J.H. I like both of those concerns.

J.G. Can you have both?

J.H. Yes, you can have both.

J.G. Thank you.

J.H. [laughing] It takes a little bit of thought and energy to arrange it so that you can have both though.

J.G. Will Rob Wyatt find both love and separateness with Billie Poe [in *The Fireman's Fair*]?

J.H. I think that will be a problem for those two. I think the separateness should be a problem. They essentially came together because they have not connected with the rest of the world. Those people are coming together to ally themselves against the rest of the world, and that is not a good basis for love. I, on the other hand [laughing], got married because I didn't like the weather in New Haven where I was living, and Tom was in Texas. So I called him in Texas and asked him if we could get married. That sounds like a terrible beginning to a marriage, but it worked.—I think the sense of humor is really important for a long life together. I would like to write about the long marriage, I think it is a really strange thing and is becoming rare, but it is still interesting. With Jack and Maud, I was writing about the phenomenon [*The Fireman's Fair*].

**J.G.** And Maud gets such terrible treatment, because she is a woman with imagination.

**J.H.** Yes, but even this terrible treatment, and long years of terrible treatment, does not spell the end of the marriage. I think there are always possible paths out of trouble in a marriage. What is needed is just a going forward down the path. Obviously there are marriages that ought to end, but sometimes when I see people that are in trouble, I feel towards them the same way that I felt when I was a little girl and heard about men who in 1929 jumped out of their office window when the stock market crashed. I wanted to just say to them, "Why don't you wait a while and see what's going to happen?" I mean you envision disaster, but next week things just might look different. And that is how I feel about the endings of novels, too.

**J.G.** In most Southern fiction, including yours, religion is not very important. It seems to be a subject you can't mention.

**J.H.** That is what my religion was. It was Episcopalian, which means you don't mention it. The South, I think, has always been very religious, but there were different faiths and different styles of worship. I actually think of my work, not my novels, but my work writing as being a spiritual activity with somewhat the same goals as religious ceremonial rituals. It is the searching element, the looking for meaning that they share. I like the notion of mystery in religious thinking.

**J.G.** I see the absence of the religious dimension as one essential difference between you and Walker Percy.

**J.H.** Right, but I am not saying this about the novels, but, writing, you can see it that way, the doing of it. What gets into the novels is still extraordinarily limited, restricted, and restrained. And it has not come from Southern Protestantism, but it comes from John Donne and John Milton and their poetry, through William Blackburn at Duke University. It is more a *Paradise Lost* sort of construct than it is fundamentalist faith.

**J.G.** But you don't offer the existence of mystery as a hope in your fiction.

**J.H.** No.

**J.G.** Nobody in your novels finds an answer to their search in religion—there is no Kierkegaardian leap into faith—and yet, religion is an element in your own life?

**J.H.** It would be misleading for me to say that it is an element in my own life. I mean, I don't go to church anymore, I have lost that connection. But what

I have is stronger, the sort of faith that I have is stronger, a thousand times stronger than what I had when I was actually going to church and professing to be religious. It is now much more simple.

**J.G.** Is it that your faith just doesn't fit into any denomination?

**J.H.** Right. I have not been able to find one, so far.

**J.G.** In your fiction you move forward in Kierkegaard's pattern from aesthetic enjoyment to irony and ethics and on to humor, and then you stop, poised for the leap of faith—but your characters do not make the leap.

**J.H.** Well, there is Maud, Rob's mother [in *The Fireman's Fair*]—I am not even sure that is still in the book, I may have taken it out—but toward the end of the book she confronts her husband and son and says, "I am not a heathen. Just because I don't go to church, you think I'm not religious. I am. Yes!" Her husband, Jack, is a churchgoer and very active in the church, and not for social reasons. I always thought of him as being a real normal, regular, faithful congregation member of a standard church. Whereas hers is much more a renegade faith that can't find expression in those churches, and therefore it gets sort of stuck inside her, and nobody else knows about it. Because it never pops up, never comes to the surface, it is all enclosed in her. I think that is more like me. I identify with Maud.

**J.G.** In that novel a passage about the church that has been changed to a blues place calls attention to itself. Is that your comment on what is happening to religion, black religion?

**J.H.** I think black religion is still extraordinarily strong. I know that it is. Though it is assailed by, I mean at least overburdened by, the crowding of problems of the young people in black religion. But the church is still one of the few institutions of hope in the troubled communities. But it seems to me that there are some other church things in my novels. Such as a former church transformed to some other use, or in *Rich in Love* there is the church picnic ground, you never get inside that church, but you are outside, that is where Lucille and Wayne meet. There is in that novel a description of a statue of Indian warrior Osceola. A hollow statue filled with bees. In the original version that was the statue of Mary on top of the church; I changed it from what it was.

**J.G.** Do you know why you changed it?

**J.H.** Yes. I was envisioning an actual church near where I live, which is Stella Maris, a Catholic church. There are other places in the book where the church comes in, for example the picnic ground; so there is the statue, there is the picnic ground . . . and at the last minute, I go through prepublication, I go through this little period of insanity, paranoia, and anxiety. I worry that something I have said in the book is going to offend. And my husband is Catholic, and his family is Catholic, and I felt that they can think that I am really talking about their church, their connection to the church. So I took out everything Catholic, or changed it. The choice really had nothing to do with religious denominations; it was just a choice that had to be made.

**J.G.** You took the life out of Mary and put it into Osceola.

**J.H.** [laughing].

**J.G.** You do not seem to take a great interest in your character Louise [*The Fireman's Fair*]. I find her a very interesting character.

**J.H.** I do, too.— Sometimes when I start a new book, I start with something left over from the old book, I think, I could start with Louise, start with somebody in her situation on the last pages of the novel, and take up her story.

**J.G.** But that is not what you are writing now?

**J.H.** No, I am working now on a book that I started after *Dreams of Sleep.* And it is just hard, and I quit at that time.

**J.G.** It has been suggested that you probably wrote *Rich in Love* before *Dreams of Sleep.*

**J.H.** I read that. It was so funny to read, because I hadn't. But in a way there is a truth in that claim, because when I began writing *Dreams of Sleep,* I knew that the expected thing of first novels would be: a first-person coming-of-age story about a young woman. So I decided not to do that, though it is tempting. There is a reason we expect that from first novels, because it is perhaps a novel that has to be written that any writer wants to write. So I made a conscious, willful decision not to do that, and then when I had finished *Dreams of Sleep* and went on to the other thing that didn't work then, I thought, well, why don't I go back and do a first-person story? So, it is a first novel in form, in spirit, but I just did not do it in that order.

**J.G.** How important is Billie Poe, in *The Fireman's Fair,* and why is she named Poe? Did Edgar Allan enter into this, at all?

**J.H.** No, when I name people, I do sort of check over what any name is going to call up of connections in a reader's mind. And I mentally run through anything that I can think of that is going to occur to someone. After I chose the name of Poe, I thought, well, is it Okla.? It will make people think of Edgar Allan Poe.—Actually, I chose it because it is in the South a sort of lower-middle-class white name. Obviously, that is not always true, but it has that ring to it.

**J.G.** One critic suggested that the name really means "pore" as in poor?

**J.H.** Oh, [laughing] that is great!

**J.G.** Maybe the true Poe connection is in the infatuation with really young women.—Like Iris and Lucille, your other young protagonists, Billie Poe seems to have been born with an innate knowledge of life that most of us need years to acquire.

**J.H.** I think that more people have that knowledge, more than we realize. More young people are wiser than we believe, or than they want us to know! They do not want us to know that.—There was a review of *Rich in Love* in the *Washington Post* by Joyce Johnson, and she said that the character of Lucille was completely uncredible, because it was a seventeen-year-old girl thinking thoughts of a forty-year-old woman. And that upset me—I went to bed for about a week, when I read that. Because I thought it was possible that it was true, because I wrote it at age 40-something. But I thought about it and finally decided she was wrong. Because I do know girls like that. And then I began to get these letters from young women all over the country. The book is just hugely popular with seventeen-year-old girls. So it can't be a not-credible character. It is a not-credible character to an older person who has forgotten or never knew that secret side, that noble side of adolescence. People think that people that age are just silly and troublemakers and rebels or troubled in some way. But the young women who write to me made me forget Joyce Johnson's review in the *Post.* They really just latch on to this character!

**J.G.** Why do you take reviews so seriously?

**J.H.** I'm just that way. I am very aware, and I'm very shy and very aware of the criticism. I am incredibly sensitive to the opinion of others.

**J.G.** You are not like Cormac McCarthy locked in his motel room.

**J.H.** No!—It just slays me, I mean, at that moment. But then over a long term, I do pretty well.

**J.G.** It also means that, unlike some other writers, you go into a dialog with your critics.

**J.H.** Yes, I do.—What if they are wrong! I think I take the time and try to decide which ones are wrong, which ones are right. And I do sort it out. But I'll always have some difficulty with criticism. In fact that is why I no longer show unfinished work to a reader. A lot of writers have a friend, husband, or wife who reads as the novel progresses. I have never been able to do that. I did try it.

**J.G.** Did you try it on your sons?

**J.H.** No! I don't think I could stand it, because it was bad enough with my husband. What would happen was always the same. I would give him a chapter to read. He would read it, and he would say, "This is really good." And that was nowhere near enough! I wanted so much more praise, I wanted more elaboration. Oh, it is killing! And then what happened after that was that I would throw the chapter away. Because I thought that it was bad work. And then I would regret it.

**J.G.** In view of what you have done so far, shouldn't you just insist on what you have written?

**J.H.** Well, I don't think those books are good. I hate to look at them. There is some of the writing in *Dreams of Sleep* that I like a lot. And there are sentences in every book that I like. But that is as far as I can go.

**J.G.** In *Nowhere Else on Earth* you are preoccupied with the nature of history and of fiction. What is the relationship between them?

**J.H.** I'm still worrying about that. When I undertook to write the book, one of the questions was how to handle the story that is not only true in its basic outlines but also important to the people to whom it belongs. And I didn't know where the limits of fiction would be in that case, how far I could go to elaborate and flesh out and detail scenes that in the documented history were only skeletal.

**J.G.** Did you feel that the lack of historical information came to be a straitjacket in the creation of the characters?

**J.H.** No, that was not the problem. If I felt constrained, it was not because I didn't know enough about them but because I did not want to misrepresent them to their living descendants. All the characters in this book are real, they all lived.

**J.G.** Is it true that the basic story of the Lumbee Indians can be found in a *Harper's* from 1870?

**J.H.** Yes, not only *Harper's* but also the *New York Tribune* wrote a series of articles about the Lowrie outlaws and the seven-year Lowrie war, and the *New York Herald,* another national magazine, also covered it. And the Wilmington and the Robeson County newspapers wrote about it. In the novel all characters, except two, still bear their real names. I changed two names because I felt that those became probably not true to the original. One became more evil, and the other one became more ridiculous, a comic character.

**J.G.** Did you change the names of Postmaster Barnes and his brother?

**J.H.** No, those are still the same names.

**J.G.** The reason I suggest this is that the brothers Barnes appear in my favorite chapter in the book, where they have to kill an ox with nothing to kill with. It is great tragi-comedy. People can picture the physical effort of doing "the honorable thing" of killing the wounded ox.

**J.H.** What I was trying to do was to understand Barnes. There are two real villains in the story, James Barnes and Brant Harris, and Barnes is the more interesting of the two, because he began as a friend to the Indians. Writing for me is always an attempt to figure something out, and in chapter 2 I was trying to understand why he may have changed and why he turned from friendship to betrayal. The whole scene of the killing of the ox was not really planned very much, it was all written in a day, and I knew when I came in that morning that I was going to follow Rhoda down to the postmaster's house and that she was going to be able to see him in some kind of weakness. So that she would gain some understanding of villainy and how it has causes. He has trouble and he is in trouble and it is serious. I don't think that what Barnes did was justified, but it is understandable. But Harris was roundly vilified by everybody who has ever looked into the original "story"; no one thought he had a good bone in his body.

**J.G.** Do you believe in absolute, inexplicable evil, as Flannery O'Connor did?

**J.H.** I think of it not as evil but as failure, mental or physical disorder of some kind. I don't believe there is a force of evil at work in the world. Whereas I do, maybe, believe in a force of good.

**J.G.** Were you concerned that the characters in your novel should be true to the historical characters?

**J.H.** Yes absolutely. But I *had to* elaborate, probably 98 percent of the book comes from my imagination, because you can gather all the written history that exists about this and it wouldn't be more than five pages. And everything that's known about Rhoda Strong would be even less than that. So there is no question about whether it's fiction or not; it is certainly fiction. But it is historical fiction, it is grounded in truth, and that just raised a lot of really interesting questions, ethical questions about what you can do and what you are allowed to do in fiction.

**J.G.** Do you feel in retrospect that you worked too close to the historical reality for a novelist? I'm thinking of the creative license traditionally adopted by historical novelists, such as Charles Dickens or Madison Jones, in writing fiction set during the French Revolution or the Civil War.

**J.H.** This is a completely different situation. This story has been made into a novel before, but there are a lot of French Revolution novels, a lot of Civil War novels, and there are only two other novels about the Lumbee in the 1870s, so the responsibility was a lot bigger. I mean nobody is going to go to *A Tale of Two Cities* to understand the entire French Revolution, and in fact most of his characters are totally fictional. You have one or two big names that represent historical characters, but Madame Defarge is not a real person and didn't exist, so Charles Dickens had no duty to her really. I felt a connection in my novel in a wonderful personal way to the characters and to *their living descendants,* who represent to me a continuation of the novel.

J.G. It was a peculiar situation the North Carolina Lumbee found themselves in, during and after the Civil War.

J.H. People hadn't succeeded in classifying them in a comfortable way for the rest of the community. They still didn't know quite who these Lumbee were.

J.G. I always admired your ability to create convincing male figures, but whereas Rhoda Strong does come alive in this novel as a believable individual, you somehow leave Henry Lowrie alone.

J.H. It is more about her than about him. My mental note to myself as I was writing was: what would it be like to be married to and in love with someone whose primary passion was not you, that is, someone whose mission in life was a higher calling? I'm still interested in that. I think it goes back to Milton. I remember reading Milton's description of Adam and Eve; they lived differently, he says, he for God only and she for God in him, and I thought, what does that mean? And I rejected it then when I was young, but now I do think that women tend to find the first interest in their lives in their families and in their intimate connections. Men tend to find their first interest in the outside world: causes, deeds, abstractions, and hunting. Rhoda wants to protect her little family, but Henry's cause is not abstract, he wants to protect everybody in the tribe. But this doesn't exclude the possibilities of people learning new ways and learning from each other. And I wanted to show how Rhoda became interested in the causes that he felt so passionately about and that he also becomes a man who really does understand the importance of romantic love and family. I wanted to see those lines cross. But Henry is a figure who remains mysterious to me.

J.G. Does the heroic creation called Rhoda make the novel *your* contribution to the gender debate?

J.H. Rhoda's character is certainly an important part of the book, but I can't predict how people will interpret her. I see her as I see him: strong people, who under normal circumstances would live an interesting but normal life. They find themselves being in a position where they are needed. It has never happened to me, and I don't know what I would do. If you were needed by the people you live with and called upon to take a community role, I think that changes the shape of your life in a major way. But we don't know until we are in that position whether we will be able to do it or not.

J.G. If you started writing *Nowhere Else on Earth* immediately after you finished *Dreams of Sleep,* you have researched your material for a long time. Didn't you ever feel that it was too cumbersome, even exacting, to get the right word, expression, and phrase for the time?

**J.H.** It was fun to try to figure out or imagine what the language would have been, or something close to it. I really loved doing that. I found some letters in Robeson County, North Carolina, that were written in the early 1900s that I figure were pretty close to the language of the time. And I also found hours and hours of oral history that were taped fifteen years ago. Interviews with very old people in the community, some of them actually knew Rhoda Lowrie. It was exciting to hear people speaking who were talking about her. And I spent a lot of time listening to and talking with people who live there now. Forty to eighty thousands of them are still alive.

**J.G.** How did they react to the novel?

**J.H.** I was really worried about that, because they had said many times in the newspaper and other places that they don't want white writers telling their history. But two weeks after the book came out, the Robeson County Indian newspaper, *The Carolina Indian Voice,* had an editorial about this very same thing. The first two paragraphs said, let's have no more white writers coming in telling us who we are and what our story is, but then it said, there are exceptions to this rule, and here is a book that we should all go and buy right away. And they have bought it by the thousands, and they organized a reading for me in the gymnasium of the high school where they had ordered the books. Viking was very reluctant to ship them 250 copies, which is how many they wanted. Viking said, you'll never sell that many, but they were sold in under an hour. People buy this book for their children, they buy it for their three-year-old granddaughter, they buy it for their grandmother, and *they* like the authenticity of it.

**J.G.** The detailed passages about how the Lumbee produce the turpentine made me think of Melville's long chapters on the art of whaling. Are the passages on the production of the turpentine a way of counterbalancing the passages on the microcosm of historical individuals?

**J.H.** I put it in because I loved it, and that is usually my reason. It was so interesting to me that there is this elaborate process that they were giving their lives to. It clearly wasn't going to last, and it was a false hope for them. It was a complicated process leading to an ultimately useless product that whole lives and acres and acres of land were being sacrificed for. Turpentine is a product, it is not like a medical product, it is not like a great human invention, and it is one of these things we could certainly live without. It became for a while extremely valuable, but after the war it was a steadily dying trade. The industry moved then down into Georgia, Florida, and

Texas, because it eats up trees. But I have always found it interesting what a culture or society does to earn money.

**J.G.** All of which may indicate that you *are* crusading in the novel. You try to preserve the true memory of the tribe, and you indirectly attack people who nowadays exploit nature in a similar way. You do champion a cause, you are not just telling a story about Rhoda, you are telling the story of the Lumbee and their industry. When I look for art for art's sake, you give me politically correct fiction.

**J.H.** I don't want politically correct fiction, but I don't want art for art's sake either. I want art for human beings' sake. And I think that art for art's sake is a luxury that is not mine. It doesn't make any sense to me. I wouldn't be writing if I didn't have things that I wanted to say, and this novel has no more of a message than the earlier ones. It may be harder to see in some of them, I don't like it to be too visible, for the story is always the most important part of a novel. But a story has other significance beyond entertainment. If it is simply entertainment, for instance when it is just to make you laugh, then it has no use as literature. If it illuminates and elucidates human problems, then it has a use. And most stories do that, it is hard to find a story that is pure entertainment or purely art. In fact, I can't think of one.

**J.G.** Mr. Poe is always blamed with writing exclusively for art's sake.

**J.H.** I think you may be right, and that may be what is wrong with his work [laughing].

**J.G.** Your first three novels were always funny. But in this novel you don't allow yourself too many amusing scenes. I say "allow" because often I expect you to make fun out of a situation but then you don't. But you do have the scene with the Yankee soldier who is easy to love as long as he is unconscious. But there are not many scenes like that. How has the public and critical reception been of *Nowhere Else on Earth*?

**J.H.** Both the critical and the public reception have been better than for my first three books. So that has just made it more fun. Even though you don't think so, most readers have found this book to be funnier than the first three. It is that soldier chapter more than any other, and some of Rhoda's father's scenes are the ones that reviewers have singled out. I'm uncomfortable with that soldier chapter, I almost took it out. But I'm glad that I left it in there.—For me the book is a lot about race. That is always the most interesting thing about the South to me, and I think that is what fuels Southern literature and makes it continually interesting, enriching it all the time in a number of different ways.

It is not only the "racial problem," but the whole question of racial identity and who Southerners are, and who are the characters in the big story we are dealing with here, and where did we come from? I think that is what Faulkner was writing about in the whole big Yoknapatawpha picture. The way that people connect doesn't always match up with the way they are truly related and connect on other levels. That's always been one of the things that drove me to writing, and I've been writing about in all the books. The variety of people in the city of Charleston was the subject for the first three novels.

**J.G.** You intimated once that this is not the only historical novel you were planning.

**J.H.** I have another one that I have started. I've two going, one that is historical and one that is not. I really have enjoyed writing this book more than any other, and I've enjoyed the publication of it more than any other. And certainly I have liked doing the research and learning the stuff, so I'm probably going to go ahead with another historical novel, but I won't be as nervous about doing it this time. I feel like I know more the kind of book that it will be and the kind of writing that I will have to do for it.

# *Interview with Josephine Humphreys*

◆◆◆◆◆◆

*Charleston, South Carolina, October 21, 2014*

**J.G.** When you create a fictional character, is it because you try to see yourself in context and measure yourself against the fiction?

**J.H.** Yes, sure.—Although I try not to do *any* measuring.

**J.G.** Can you avoid it?

**J.H.** Yes, you can avoid the excesses of it. And the truth is that I never googled my own name and probably never will. I *feel* the publishing and the public nature of being a writer.

**J.G.** When you go somewhere to give a reading, do you feel like you are somebody else?

**J.H.** I do.

**J.G.** You *become* somebody else.

**J.H.** Yes.

**J.G.** Do you like that somebody else?

**J.H.** Yeah! [laughing]. That somebody else is a performer and a joke-teller—and I am really much more shy.

**J.G.** But you don't have an audience at home anymore.

**J.H.** I have a husband and a dog—I *am* really shy. And when I am talking with you or with other people, I feel it is not really me. The only real *me* is the one that writes.

**J.G.** Can you have *two* "real me"?

**J.H.** You can, but I know which one is the real me, and the only real me is the one that writes.

**J.G.** Is that because you feel that you can be more honest when you are writing?

**J.H.** I'm not performing when I am writing. When I perform—read—it is a minor aspect of my real self.

**J.G.** At the European Southern Studies Forum meeting at USC in Columbia in 1993, you gave a reading and quoted Robert Frost's statement on his art—"The principle I believe in is this:

'No surprise for the writer, no surprise for the reader.'"

J.H. It is from the introduction to his *Collected Works*. Frost's idea is that you can't plan ahead of where you are, *not* a paragraph, *not* even a line. To me it is a great adventure to find out what the next line is going to be, and that is the main reason I write. It is an exploration more than anything else, and something *je ne sais quoi*. The most famous part of Frost's introduction is where he compares a poem to an ice cube melting on a stove.

J.G. Do you write here in your office, or do you write at home? Or, do you just write wherever and whenever you are inspired?

J.H. I didn't write when Daddy was very sick, at all, but now I am back at it.

J.G. Did you feel like going back to the writing?

J.H. Oh yes! I am miserable when I'm not writing.

J.G. Is it your goal to *disrupt* the present apparent order, as Danièle Pitavy-Souques suggests in *The Southern State of Mind*, in order to revert to an older, more subversive, richer, and more creative disorder?—I suppose that this would fit in well with *the duty to surprise* the reader and even yourself.

J.H. I have a definite rebellious streak in me. I think it is important to disrupt everything. When I was young, I had a conflict with that idea, because I was also extremely well behaved.

J.G. So you were brought up traditionally.

J.H. Absolutely!

J.G. You were, in other words, a severe challenge for any young man who could sense your wish to disrupt and surprise, and perhaps that you were interested *but* brought up above all to be well behaved.

J.H. *That* is really true, truer than you could possibly know. I was a straight-A student, and I was never in any trouble of any kind growing up.

J.G. So, you don't have *that* to write about.

J.H. No, I really don't.—But I like to look at things so closely that they kind of turn upside down. I feel I am doing exactly that when I am writing.

J.G. Does your writing disrupt your everyday life?

J.H. Writing *is* my everyday life! It is what I do to disrupt. I'm still well behaved, but *in my head* I'm not so well behaved. I like troublemakers, and I like people who upset the order. I think it is important for every individual and for every culture to do that and to look closely at what we are doing. It is important that we don't do something just because we have done it before—we must reevaluate.

J.G. When you advise people to be aware of what they are doing—as in *not* to copy past ideas blindly—your advice still has an element of the didactic.

J.H. That is interesting because it reminds me of an objection that Reynolds Price once made:

"Reflect on her adultery!" I thought at the time, "What is he talking about?" That was probably a pretty good comment, but I just did not feel *that* was what I wanted to do at all. I am not here to reflect on people's sins!—It made me realize that in Reynolds Price's own novel *Kate Vaiden* [1986] there is a lot of adultery but not much reflection on it.

**J.G.** We are sitting in the middle of history, actually in one of the rooms in the Confederate Widows' Home in Charleston. Does this overpowering presence of history in your office rub off on the fiction?

**J.H.** What I like about history—and I do love history (whereas I rarely read today's history books)—is to dig into what I consider "more personal narratives," such as letters and memoirs. I want to know what people's lives were like. In some ways I feel I can get a better idea of humanity and the roots of human life by reading *their* historical records.

**J.G.** People of today are distracted by electronic gadgets. But maybe people in the nineteenth century could sit down and, without too many distractions, record the facts of everyday life.

**J.H.** In *Nowhere Else on Earth* [2000] I was really looking for the past, because I had heard something about this story, and about this love affair, and about this "criminal"—I heard something about it, but it *wasn't* in history books, so I had to go find it. And I became obsessed—but that is the only reason I write anything, that is, if it takes over my brain when I focus on it.

**J.G.** Do you still visit with the Lumbee People in Robeson Country, North Carolina?

**J.H.** I keep in touch with Louise Maynard. She is the Lumbee woman who came to me in the middle of my writing the novel. She is a wonderful person, and she kept me going and really helped. The novel is dedicated to her.

**J.G.** Will Reese of your novel *Dreams of Sleep* sees marriage as being worthless.

**J.H.** To me marriage is *a mystery.* That is a word I use a lot. I picked it up from Reynolds Price, who was my writing teacher when I was at Duke University. He said, "In our lives we encounter some mystery every day." That was the reason he gave for wanting to write. He used it in a religious sense—I use the word about everything. I think marriage is one of the really interesting mysteries, and I like to write about it.

**J.G.** You have been married to the same man for the duration.

**J.H.** Yes, for *hundreds* of years. And marriage remains a mystery.

**J.G.** It *is* a mystery why we tend to find one person to attach ourselves to, in theory, for life.

◆◆◆

**J.G.** What are you writing now?

**J.H.** My next novel will not have any history in it!

J.G. Can you avoid it?

J.H. Yes, because there are two projects on my desk. One is going to be a novel and the other a Haitian "thing"—I don't think it will ever be a book, just a something I got to do.

J.G. It is difficult to work on two unrelated projects at the same time.

J.H. Yes, that's *hard,* but I don't want to let either one of them go.—But I would like *to finish* them, because I have other things I want to do. And I can't until I got these projects cleared up.

J.G. Are you worried about the reaction to either one when it *is* published?

J.H. No! I learned quickly that the publicness is bad for me. Whether there are good or bad reviews, it is bad for me. Publishing is like being in a beauty contest, and I feel I am participating in a contest when a book of mine is published. It is a terribly warping thing, a bad phenomenon, to be in a contest knowing that the girl dancing or giving a prepared monologue is not really you! But I like the life I have; it is very entertaining, and it is a lot of fun to be me.

J.G. But your public persona life is not much fun?

J.H. That part is fun, too, but it is *not me.* I see a lot of "mirrors" wondering which one reflects *me.*

J.G. As in "will the real Josephine Humphreys stand up!"

J.H. Right! I think of this a lot, but I haven't come up with an answer yet. I don't think I have the same need for recognition that I had in my thirties.

J.G. You have proved that you can write a good novel, even repeatedly. But you just do not like to be lionized.

J.H. I certainly do not!

J.G. You are not alone. Think of J. D. Salinger and Thomas Pynchon. But didn't you want your first novel to sell?

J.H. I didn't *want* it to sell. I never wanted any of them to sell.—One problem was that I didn't have to earn a living. Ironically, I think that has been a handicap for me. If I had had to earn a living, I would have wanted the books to sell. I'm embarrassed about that in some ways, because I know that artists work hard and should be paid well. But I told my publisher, "I never want to know how my books are doing."—As I didn't care whether the novels were a success or not, I left all of that to my agent. I still don't care if people do not like a book, and it has always been like that. I realize I am one odd writer.

J.G. All good writers are liable to become odd, maybe because they spend so much time in their own company.—Several of the great writers, such as Sir Philip Sidney, and arguably H. D. Thoreau and Wallace Stevens, wrote to please themselves and considered themselves the best judges of their works. A good many did not depend on their writing for an income but wrote anyway.

# *Out of the Garden Forever*

INTERVIEWS WITH MADISON JONES

◆◆◆◆◆◆

*Auburn, Alabama, June 3, 1978; January 12, 1981*

Madison Jones

◆◆◆◆◆◆

**Jan Nordby Gretlund** Are you "a regional writer"?

**Madison Jones** Certainly! It is pretty obvious to me that I *am* a regional writer. And there's nothing negative or even limiting about regionalism. I don't know of anyone who would consider Faulkner's regionalism a limitation in his creation of Yoknapatawpha County. My own regionalism is most obvious in *The Innocent.* A definite sense of place is very helpful as a guide for my vision. It helps me to know what is true. I don't always understand the full meaning of my images of place, but I always know when I am lying about them. They warn me when I am dishonest in my writing.

**J.G.** How has your early life as a Southern country boy influenced your fiction?

**M.J.** I feel a strong attachment for the country of my childhood. Most people do in the South, probably more than people from other parts of the nation. Our sense of history has a lot to do with that, and for me as a writer this attachment to place has been indispensable. The familiar place offers inspiration and images to embody my ideas. Some images I remember from my childhood, and they retain a certain mystery for me. I could, of course, have seen fields of briars and buckbushes stretching to the horizon in other places. But I saw them in Tennessee, and for me they will always be associated with the country of my childhood. I hope that the mystery I feel in connection with the remembered images has been retained in my fiction.

**J.G.** Was there anything or anybody in your childhood that inspired you to become a novelist?

**M.J.** There were no writers or intellectuals in my family anywhere. They were mostly oldfashioned Presbyterians, and I'm afraid they considered writing a frivolous waste of time for a man. It wasn't considered serious work. I think they thought that it bordered on the effeminate. My family read the Bible and not too much else. Of course, it never occurred to them to read it as fiction or even as poetry. My grandfather, who was a very old man, born before the Civil War, lived with us when I was a boy. He read stories to me by the hour from the Old Testament. That's the literature I knew best. So if there's a great author who had a decisive influence on me, I guess it is Moses.

**J.G.** Have you ever attended a tent revival or a faith healing meeting in Tennessee?

**M.J.** Yes, I've been to some of those meetings. I went to some when I was young. I haven't been to a faithhealing meeting in quite some time. But it hasn't been too long since I have been to one of those tent revivals, and they are still quite common. In middle Tennessee, in the country, it is still an Old Testament world, as I've tried to show in *Passage through Gehenna.* It is "Jesus, Jesus" all the time, but in a way the Old Testament has an almost equal status—in some cases even more influence. To Fundamentalists every word in the Bible is literally true and the real emphasis falls on the need for personal rectitude. Grace is, of course, insisted upon, but the main emphasis was always on rectitude. And, of course, I was trained that way.

**J.G.** What do you think of faith healers and their miracles?

**M.J.** They do produce these things, these faith healers. I don't know any explanation for them. Many of the illnesses are obviously psychosomatic, and you can count on that being the case. But then in other cases it seems to go beyond that. When somebody mends a broken bone, as they sometimes do, you wonder what is coming off. Salter in *Passage* is in a well-authenticated tradition, I guess you could say. You can still find plenty of these preachers not only in Tennessee but also in Alabama, Arkansas, and throughout the South, in fact and in the rural Midwest, too, for that matter.

**J.G.** Does it seem grotesque to you that the backwoods of the South in our day and age are still peopled by Fundamentalists?

**M.J.** We probably have a good deal more than our share of unusual people in the South, even today. But I think there is a great deal of "grotesquery" in other places in this country. New York City seems to me to have more grotesque characters than the whole South does. We still have a lot of backcountry people, though a lot fewer than we did. There are still some enclaves around the South where the people would, by regular standards, be considered peculiar. But I never thought of them as "grotesque." It is a word I learned when I started reading about Southern fiction in books by Northern critics.

**J.G.** How do you select specific material for your fiction?

**M.J.** In a way I am always walking around with my material. Usually, I *am* my material, for unconsciously the selection of material is determined by the problems and discords of my own life. Serious fiction is in a way autobiographical, but, of course, you can't really see that in the finished novel if it is any good. *The Innocent* is close to my own experience. I began with my own background, but I ended with something entirely different. The setting, the horse, the moonshiner, and traits of the protagonist are borrowings from my early life in Tennessee. But in the novel these elements end up as fictional facts. Step by step they change physically and in psychological effect. It is the idea behind the writing that transforms the autobiographical material so it becomes part of the artistic reality of the novel.

**J.G.** Why did you call your first novel *The Innocent*?

**M.J.** I can't remember when I first thought of that title. But at first I saw Duncan Welsh as a social victim. Then I brought in McCool, the moonshiner, and the title took on a different meaning for me. I realized that my protagonist is really a victim of a flaw in himself. He rejects life as it is with Evil as a prime fact, and he tries to return to the innocence of Eden. But he finds that Satan is there now, and Duncan is destroyed. The flaw in him is that he wouldn't accept the existence of Evil *and* that man has been forced out of the Garden forever. But this change in the meaning of the title only dawned on me as I was writing. The story came to life and talked back to me.

**J.G.** Your second novel, *Forest of the Night,* is my favorite. Why did you choose to take us back to the frontier life of the early 1800s?

**M.J.** Well, I was a good deal younger then than I am now, and a bit more ready to believe people would listen to wisdom, or what I thought was wisdom. Here was an exemplum of the idea of American innocence encountering the wilderness; he, the hero, was going to bring light into its dark. You might say there were ideological commitments behind the novel; it is a sort of philosophical fiction. The story is largely imagined. There is a little about the Harpe brothers on record, but very little. We know what kind of men they were and a few things they did, but we don't even know with certainty what their end was. But I hope this much is clear: the virgin forest has become a forest of the night for the enlightened hero and the confrontation issues in the near extinction of his real humanity. His is the fatality of badly misreading the nature of things.

**J.G.** Is there a connection between *The Innocent* and *Forest of the Night*?

**M.J.** Although I wasn't fully conscious of it, I created Jonathan Cannon of *Forest* in the image of my first hero. But, as I said, the novel is also about the Harpe brothers, the bloodthirsty outlaws who lived near the Natchez Trace at the time. After *The Innocent* I could see what there was in the subject of this murderous pair, for me, fictionally. My imagination was excited by the traditional accounts of them. It was an advantage for me that so little is known about them with any certainty. I saw the Harpes as innocents who return to the Garden to serve the new master there. But I had a hard time with the brothers; they weren't human, they were just monstrous freaks. I couldn't credit them with any intellectual stature. I finally decided to keep the Harpes in the background, as a reminder of the evil potential of man. What really interested me was how the brothers had come to be what they were. So I brought in my innocent hero. He is a disciple of Rousseau, Jefferson, and Paine. And his background has prepared him to see Evil only as a product of factors external to human nature. In the rest of the novel I illustrate the making of "a Harpe." Jonathan comes to see his fellow men only in their brutal aspect. He is finally identified with Wiley Harpe. I hope the novel illuminates the moral steps by which he loses his humanity. In this way you can read *Forest* as continuing a theme from *The Innocent.*

**J.G.** What do you think of *A Buried Land* today, after almost twenty years?

**M.J.** In a way it is the dimmest in my mind of all my novels. I am unhappy with Percy Youngblood, the main character. He is just too cold and too callous. But at that time, in the early 1960s, I was angry at the Tennessee Valley Authority, angry at what they were doing when they flooded large areas of Tennessee and northern Alabama. They destroyed a lot of good farms, entire communities, and much rare wildlife. I wanted to write a novel about that destruction, but also about disintegrating lives, minds, and relationships as a result of the physical destruction, which, of course, was meant to stand for much more than the immediate destruction. Percy works for the TVA and he destroys his relations with his family and the community. He also lets a girl be killed by an abortionist to ensure his own happiness.

**J.G.** Do you think in retrospect that *A Buried Land* was too much of an attempt at being topical?

**M.J.** No, not really. The novel is primarily about a spiritual bankruptcy, and not so much about the TVA. As I indicated earlier, writing is a form of self-discovery, and my subject is therefore always basically myself. This is my true topic, and I must be directed by it to keep my integrity as a writer. I have to ignore questions about reader interest in my fiction. I may sweat a bit if nobody will buy my books, but when I write, sales are irrelevant—I don't worry about them. It would be something else if I wrote "entertainments." Then I would have to consider what the public will swallow.

**J.G.** Your novel *An Exile* has been a popular success. I saw the film version "I Walk the Line" with Gregory Peck, and I think it is well done. Has the Hollywood success influenced your writing?

**M.J.** I am not consciously writing for the movies. When I wrote *An Exile,* it didn't even cross my mind. But since that book was made into a movie, the possibility has naturally occurred to me while writing other books. But it has never been any influence. I tend to write in visual scenes; that's just the nature of my imagination. It is not because of any design like "when I do this, it will be suitable for the movies." Of course, I would like for them to make a movie out of *A Passage through Gehenna.* But a wish like this has never had any part in my thinking about how I was going to handle a scene. I am sensitive to scenes and to visual things—that's why there are lots of "'film shots" in my fiction.

**J.G.** Your novels tend to be grim and pessimistic. They deal with "man's failure to submit himself to the limits of the human condition," as you have phrased it. Have you ever expressed your view of mankind in more comic tones?

**M.J.** I wrote a picaresque novel about fifteen years ago. It was never published except for two sections. Humor doesn't seem to be my strong point, but that novel was intended to be entirely comic. One of the sections that was published is farce, a whorehouse farce. There is a woman who has a jealous husband, so she puts the psychiatrist on him to remove the jealousy, whereupon she proceeds with her whoring. It ends up that she seduces the psychiatrist. I think it is quite a funny novel, but my humor didn't go over in New York. Like lots of other things about me don't go over in New York.

At this point at least one of the large episodes is out of date. It was more topical, you know, based on particular events. There is a part on civil rights. You can imagine why that part wouldn't be published. I called the whole novel *Tales of Dixie.* I had a picaresque hero. He meets a young man, a novelist, who has been hired by a Northern newspaper to come down and report on the civil rights trouble in Mississippi. It is partly making fun of the Northern idea of what was going on. But that episode, at least, is dead now. At the time I'm sure it made a lot of publishers angry. Now the trouble with it is that it is out of date.

**J.G.** In your fifth novel, *A Cry of Absence,* you write about the bitterest period of the civil rights struggle in the South. Why did you publish a novel about civil rights as late as 1971, and during the Vietnam War?

**M.J.** As I see it, the history taught to young people all over the country and in the South presents everything from a Yankee point of view. Young people down here are taught to feel guilty about our past. This is sad and probably dangerous. You can hardly ever hear "Dixie" played in public places anymore, or couldn't for a good while. If we were to believe Yankee historians, all Southern resistance to the civil rights changes of the 1950s and 1960s was based on racist or economic motives. Nothing could be more wrong, and that is one of the reasons—though only one why I wrote *A Cry of Absence.* I consider it my best novel.

A main factor behind our resistance was our impulse to hold on to our identity, to preserve our Southernness. Racial segregation was seen, at least in part, as one of our last links with our past, as maybe the one really fleshly link surviving. This is not to defend an inhumane system but to put a strong reaction into its proper perspective. In *Absence* I try to give an objective statement of this problem in the setting of a small Southern town in the 1950s. It is a story about the old conflict between family affection and duty to the law. But of course this whole statement indicates only one aspect of what I was trying to do in the book.

**J.G.** I read *Passage through Gehenna* as a return to the dark vision of *Forest of the Night.* What gave you the idea to write *Passage*?

**M.J.** I read a French novel by Pierre Choderlos de Laclos called *Les Liaisons dangereuses;* it is late eighteenth century. It is about two ambitious seducers—not only out to seduce but to sow malignity with those seductions. Mostly those of the woman, who is about as evil a person as you can find anywhere outside of Shakespeare. That is where *Passage* ultimately came from. That's what started me down the slide.

The novel has a history I couldn't even describe to you. It was so different when it started out: it was about a boy who had a religious conflict with his father—and the book just wouldn't go. And then I wrote this piece about Salter, the country preacher, and thought about it a while, and then I rejected it. And I still had the woman, Lily, but she was doing something else then. I sent the book to Monroe Spears when I had first written it. It was originally in first person. He didn't suggest that I change it, but he speculated about the idea.

I ultimately decided to change it to the third person. I brought some of the characters over from my unpublished picaresque novel. And in this manner it went through four or five different versions.

**J.G.** What is the true character of this Lily Nunn?

**M.J.** People in Hallsboro think this and that about Lily—they can't agree whether she is ugly or handsome. But the sexual magnetism is clearly there. Her name is, of course, meant to suggest the flower. But her name also recalls Lilith, the wife Adam is supposed to have had before Eve. In legend Lilith is said to have been of the devil's brood, and she preys on children, murders them. In my novel her origin is obscure; her father is named North, which in the context may, I hope, hint at satanic connections. You know the devil comes from the North. That is not Southern ideology—traditionally the devil comes from the North. I think of Lily as a witch, deliberately doing the devil's work.

**J.G.** The discovery of the existence of Evil by an innocent young man has been the theme of your novels since *The Innocent,* and it is also the theme of *Passage through Gehenna.* Why do you return to the theme?

**M.J.** I don't know if I am becoming more optimistic or not. But at least I like to think that *Passage,* if you can call that progress, doesn't leave you with nowhere to go, as I think my earliest novels did. I think of it as a turning to a more complete version of the theme; one that puts the emphasis on grace and sacrifice, as compared with the boneheaded determination to be perfect that Jud Rivers started out with. With his original attitude he couldn't do anything but try to stare the devil down, which can't be done. The devil is simply stronger in a headtohead encounter. But learning to love is part of the theme of *Passage,* and something Jud didn't really know about to start with. At the end presumably he has the means to make himself a whole person. I hope it emerges that Jud is at least capable of love when he asks why somebody else should have had to go through Gehenna, or hell, for him, so that he might learn to love. I guess that happens all the time.

**J.G.** Why is there so much violence in *Passage*?

**M.J.** The violence is off stage. *Passage* is half as violent as the work of Aeschylus or somebody like that. The novel is not as violent as a typical Shakespeare play. I have more violence in *Forest of the Night.* Violence happens. It happened in the rural world that I used to know, and it seems to me characteristic of life.

**J.G.** Who are some of the writers you have learned from over the years?

**M.J.** I learned a lot from the Agrarians, and Fugitives at Vanderbilt, especially from Donald Davidson. He confirmed my belief in the lasting value of Southern culture. Another major influence on me was Andrew Lytle. He guided me when I specialized in creative writing at the University of Florida at Gainesville. And, of course, I admire William Faulkner; he was the big man, the man of genius. He could animate so many kinds of things and bring them in, really integrally, to the whole being of a book.

Faulkner wasn't afraid of relaxing at times in his books. It is maybe a fault that I can't stand when I perceive a loose moment in my own books. I work very hard to reduce all unnecessary elements—words, events—between the climactic parts. In *Passage* it worried me that Hannah's death comes so quickly after the abortion. But there just wasn't any way around it. I always try to build things as much as possible. But I'm satisfied that I couldn't; if I had waited a long time to decide what to do, have made any more preparation. I knew it was right what happened. I simply wished at the time that I had a way to hold it back, to get more of a sense of time passing, so that the event could ripen. But there just wasn't any way to do it and still keep the novel moving. The tension is always a primary consideration for me.

**J.G.** Flannery O'Connor speaks very highly of your novels in several of her letters collected in *The Habit of Being.* How well did you know her?

**M.J.** I knew her over a period of about seven years. It began when she wrote me a kind letter about *The Innocent*—an act entirely typical of her. She was such a good writer. And she was awfully courteous and hospitable to me and Shailah. We went to see her once in a while at Andalusia, near Milledgeville. She gave us a lot of ducks and geese and so on. From the time of that first letter I went to see her, off and on, until she died. She was a gracious, witty, and pleasant person. I appreciated the way she was trying to help me get more notice as a writer.

I remember how certain critics used to consider her fiction cold and without feeling. Most of them have changed their opinion now, but if anybody needs further testimony of Flannery O'Connor's warm feeling for her fellow man, he will find it displayed generously in her private letters. She is surely the best writer the South has turned out for twentyfive years. Her writing is clear, straight, unpretentious, and full of humor. She had an integrity and courage that impress me and inspire me. Flannery had a dark view of the human condition, but she also had selfknowledge, humility, and real human compassion. Unfortunately, I lost some of the best letters she wrote me.

**J.G.** What do you think of Truman Capote, Norman Mailer, and Tom Wolfe's nonfiction novels?

**M.J.** For me a novelist is a man who is at liberty to shape the material he chooses from real life—exactly as he wants to. The way I see it, he must make the facts speak in his voice, so that they reflect his personal vision. In nonfiction novels the facts are supposed to speak for themselves. Capote and Mailer are not responsible, it seems, and the vision is left to the reader's predisposition. If a writer has no vision to communicate, he can't choose his facts according to it, and the account, the story, will fail to come really alive. This doesn't mean that a traditional novelist is free to distort facts, on the contrary. But he must bring a vision to his facts so they will be able to speak to him.

My book *Season of the Strangler* has a sort of journalistic origin, in the way of Theodore Dreiser's *An American Tragedy.* There are twelve stories all related to the central matter of a local strangler—as a symbolic figure—so the whole has somewhat the effect of a novel. The stories are portraits of people who, in a nonliteral sense, and for personal reasons, strangle their own lives.

*The Reed House, Chattanooga, Tennessee, April 18, 1999*

**J.G.** When we talked about your novels back in the 1980s, *Season of the Strangler* was just being published. It is one of your best books, but it never got the attention it deserves.

**M.J.** I think the stories were difficult, for one thing. I sent the book to Robert Penn Warren, and he wrote me back, "No doubt these are powerful stories, but I'm not sure I know what they mean, or what the whole thing means. But it takes a lot of reading." I think that most people do not like to do a lot of reading. I mean heavy reading. I think maybe it is pretty thick soup. When you speak of reading Henry James, you speak of heavy reading. It is closely knit, rendering more than most people want to bother with. Maybe my book has more description, more details than people generally want to deal with; that may be the case. I had not thought about it until Warren said that.

**J.G.** Is *Season of the Strangler* more densely textured than *A Cry of Absence?*

**M.J.** I wrote *Strangler* in the rather flat voice of a detached narrator, whereas in *A Cry of Absence* the voice, voices, in this case, reflect the qualities of my participating characters and are more precisely fitted to individuals. In *Strangler* the narrator's voice, a single voice, is constant all the way through.

A lot of people seemed not even to notice that there was a fictional narrator telling the stories. I should probably have developed him more.

**J.G.** After *Season of the Strangler* it took you seven years to complete *Last Things* [1989]. Was there a particular reason why you took your time after *Season of the Strangler?*

**M.J.** In fact it was almost that long between *A Cry of Absence* [1971] and *Passage through Gehenna* [1978]. *Passage* is the book of all my books that caused me the most trouble. I would start it, throw part of it away, work and work on the first part again. I thought I was never going to get it right. And then after I got it finished to my satisfaction, I had a time getting it published. The New York publishers didn't go for it, though it seemed for a while that Farrar, Straus, Giroux was going to take it. I finally sent it to LSU Press. It was the first LSU "original novel." But years were consumed in the process.

**J.G.** How important was the father–son relationship for you in the writing of *Last Things*?

**M.J.** Are you thinking about my own father and me?—My father was nothing like that! He was nothing like anybody in any particular book I have written. He was a very honorable, upright man—and stern, although he had some humor and lightness, too. But he was stern about principles.

**J.G.** Was he a religious man?

**M.J.** Yes, very much so. He was intelligent, but he did not have the breadth of mind or the kind of education that gave him much tolerance of different ways of thinking. I have his name, which was that of my great-grandfather, and I have a son also named Madison Percy Jones. Wendell Corbin of *Last Things* never did have communion with anybody, including his father, who was hardly worth communing with. But after all Wendell went through, he found, at last, a communion with what he was and with what his father was. It is a kind of a moral or spiritual regeneration to be able finally to communicate, if not with a whole community, at least with somebody who is difficult to love.

**J.G.** I had the impression that we had read an account of Wendell's slow moral disintegration and that he comes to a bad end.

**M.J.** At the end I intended that he would be on the way to a regeneration. I think he is subject to legal action at the end of the book, but at the same time he's got his foot on the right path again, morally and spiritually.—I don't know if anybody spotted it, but I did something in *Last Things* that I had not done in any other book, in suggesting ghostly experiences. For instance, there is a preacher in the book, a fundamentalist hellfire type, and he comes to visit Wendell at one point in this old dark house, upstairs. I tried to write the scene so that you cannot tell whether it is really the person in the flesh or not. I tried to write it with that sort of ambiguity. This was meant to bring a supernatural element into the book, which I hoped would give it a spiritual dimension. Also, in the part where he goes upstairs and is thrown out the high window, it is really like a possession. I tried to create that effect. When he is lying under the window on the ground, semiconscious, the young black man named Cat Bird is talking to the car dealer, who is described in various reptilian terms. They are talking on another-world plane. The effect, I hope, is a bit like some passages in Hawthorne where we overhear spectral voices talking abstractly from somewhere. The car dealer's name is Jason Farrow, which suggests pigs. He is the satanic force that has been in control of Wendell. But Wendell breaks with Farrow near the end of the book.

**J.G.** What is the meaning of the title of *Last Things?*

**M.J.** I intended a theological connection. Last things are death, heaven and hell, the last things to be considered in a life.

**J.G.** Were you satisfied with the reception of *Last Things?*

**M.J.** No! [laughing] It did not get enough press notice. Only a few, very few, seemed as though they saw what I was trying to do. But I never have had really satisfactory responses on a large scale. I have had lots of good reviews that I was delighted with, reviewers that I thought really understood the book and liked it, and so forth, but just never enough of them. If your book is going to prosper, you have to have the reviews hit the streets pretty close together, and a lot of them. I have never had that happen for my books. You need something in *Time,* something in *Newsweek,* something in the *New York Times* and *Chicago Tribune;* the reviews have got to be all around.

**J.G.** It seems obvious that *To the Winds* means more to you than any other novel.

**M.J.** It was based on the farm near Ashland City [Tennessee]. After my father sold the farm, a family that had worked for us moved to a cabin over across the Cumberland River in the hills there, high above the river.

**J.G.** Why did your father sell the farm?

**M.J.** For one thing, he needed the money, I think, *and* I was no longer up there. My brother was concerned with the farm he lived on, the one where my father's home was, and raising cattle. It had got to be more than my father wanted to fool with, and I think he was beginning to have business troubles about that time. I was thirty-three when he sold it.—The family that inspired the novel had eight children. In my book they are pretty changed from what they were really like. The father was not the kind of irresponsible fellow that the character is in the book. He was very responsible and very religious, a man I admired. In the course of the book the family is destroyed, both as a family and as a representative community. Those kinds of hill folks ceased to exist. They all went away, scattered all over the world, and lived in trailers instead of on farms.

**J.G.** The clashes between the hill folks and the town people are memorable in *To the Winds.*

**M.J.** You are thinking about the chapter where the daughter gets seduced by this fancy boy. It follows a scene where the young hill folks play jokes on the university boys and give them some peppering with a shotgun,—birdshot! And then finally the older boy gets tarred and feathered by the university boys.—The conflict is with the "modern" element, now dominant.

**J.G.** Does the seduction of the girl become symbolic of how everybody in the hill community is "seduced" and exploited by the new people who move in?

**M.J.** I hope so. I don't know about "everybody," but certainly the poor who are relatively defenseless are subject to a flashy exterior, as this young man illustrates. Not the older generation, not the parents, but the girls are excited by this, and that sort of thing has gone on back through history [laughing].

**J.G.** The clash between the farmers and the adult town-people, including the law, seems to be more alarming.

**M.J.** The urge for big money is corrupting, and the sheriff has fallen to it. His individual corruption is not necessarily everywhere, but it is common enough to where it is something to be looked out for, I think, in all such small communities. The family on the farm was subject to it because of their relative helplessness and ignorance. It was no longer the kind of world that could accommodate them.

**J.G.** Isn't this what makes it a tragic story? It is clear that they will lose everything, including the family unity.

**M.J.** It is the conflict within the family that begins tearing it up. The older brother wants to turn in Uncle Clarence, who has come back home, escaped from prison. They need money so badly that the older brother feels that he is in a way justified in betraying the uncle.

Otherwise they will lose the farm. So he is not entirely a rascal for so doing, even though his younger brother "Coop," who almost turns out to be the protagonist of the book, finally comes to hate his older brother as a traitor to the family. The two conflicts seem to mesh there.

**J.G.** Is it the throwing to the winds of the old culture that makes the book special to you?

**M.J.** If you remember chapter 4, it is almost like a folk narrative, it is the mother's history. She came from the last intact hill culture. The narrator describes her youth and her background, what it was like among the hill people. And the woman tries to maintain those values in her family. But her husband turns out to be pretty worthless, although he is well intentioned. He doesn't have much of a chance. So the mother is of the last generation that tries to maintain the original values of the hill people. She fades away, too, of course.

**J.G.** It is obvious that you have seen this life and lived it in Tennessee.

**M.J.** Yes, in a lot of ways. Like that cabin that they lived in, which they expanded considerably, built onto. I knew that cabin when a man lived there alone. We wanted shakes, wood shingles, to put on a roof. When we took the smokehouse and made a little outdoor bedroom out of it, we wanted wood shakes. People used to cut those with axes, and this old man still made them. He lived up in that cabin in the woods, and we got those shakes when I was maybe fifteen or sixteen. He was, I suppose, as far back as it went, history that still survived.

Somebody was still making shakes that way.—I well remember that cabin. And then later one of the boys from the family bought it and the little property around it. He lived up there alone for a while, but then when my daddy sold the farm, the young man's family, or what was left of it, came to live there. Through them I got to know the place well. I used it, the imagery of it all, in *To the Winds.* It was almost as if I had lived there, especially because I knew them so well.

**J.G.** In spite of all the experiences and private emotions you invested in the book, its sales are not impressive.

**M.J.** I was not surprised really, because I have had that experience too many times. But I thought that it had a chance. I was hoping that the kind of humor that is a part of the novel might have general appeal; its first eighty pages or so are episodes that are only connected by happening to the members of the family. These present an aspect of what that life was like. I thought that a lot of people who appreciate the old Southwestern humor would like it very much. Some did, but one reviewer liked the book only *after* that part was over! I had hoped that I would get readers who would like both that and the sort of detective story that follows—which I thought was an exciting story.

**J.G.** Your change of the mood in midcourse from humor to suspense may have irritated some readers.

**M.J.** As soon as the uncle comes in, when they discover Uncle Clarence, it changes everything, because they are harboring a much wanted criminal. The change doesn't seem to me to jerk you around, it just falls into their life, the way accidents do all the time and all of a sudden poison everything. I did not feel it give a wrench to the book. Suddenly they were outlaws for harboring an outlaw, and in a sense that is symbolic of what they almost had become anyway, "outlaws"—not so much as criminals but as people no longer living *within* the law. They couldn't imagine, for instance, not being able to bury on the place. Suddenly, here is the law saying you can't bury this dead boy here! You have got to do it in accordance with the legal code. They didn't know anything about that; they just thought it was natural that when somebody died in your family you buried him close by.

**J.G.** With "Familiar Spirit," the final story of *Season of the Strangler,* which is a Civil War story, you seem to open up a new topic in your fiction.

**M.J.** Yes, that's right. Although I had written another version of it long before. I published it, I think, in *Delta Review* about thirty years ago.[1] It was a magazine that only ran briefly, a few issues, I think, then conked out. So I had written that story essentially, though I rewrote it for *Season of the Strangler.*

**J.G.** After a lifetime of complex fiction on complex issues, you write a plain and simple Civil War novel, and it becomes your perhaps greatest critical and popular success. Were you surprised by the praise for *Nashville 1864: The Dying of the Light?*

**M.J.** Yes, but do not overstate the success, because it got almost no notice in the North. In great part surely because it was published by a small Southern publisher, that was one thing. In fact, a member of the committee in Chicago that awarded me the T. S. Eliot prize, partly for *Nashville 1864,* said that he saw the book and thought it must be just something I had wanted to get rid of and had published with a small publisher. And I am sure lots of people said, "Oh, why review this book, there are ten more from Random House, Harper, and wherever." So it was almost completely ignored in the North, except for those journals that review them all, like *Kirkus, Publishers' Weekly,* et cetera. But nothing in New York or Chicago or any place like that.

**J.G.** A change for the better was Jonathan Yardley's review in *Book World* of the *Washington Post.* I remember that he did not like *Season of the Strangler.*

**M.J.** Washington is not really the North, and the novel got reviewed by a Virginian. I have heard him described a number of times as one of the best two or three book reviewers in the country. I think that's probably true. But he reviews a lot of books, and occasionally he just doesn't like something, and he didn't like *Season of the Strangler.*—But *Nashville 1864* could have used a lot more reviews than it got in the South! For instance in the Atlanta paper, which off and on has given me good reviews. They never did review it. This was just after the appearance of the issue on me of the *Chattahoochee Review,* an Atlanta journal, that was wholly devoted to my work. The fact made no difference to Atlanta newspaper reviewers. But now that *Nashville 1864* is in Penguin, it has a chance to meet up with readers in, presumably, other parts of the country.

**J.G.** How did *Nashville 1864* come to be picked up by Penguin?

**M.J.** I guess it just had the good fortune for somebody to read it who knew about good books [laughing].

**J.G.** What is successful in the novel is the combination of the topic and the style. You always write in a superb style, but here the simple everyday realism of your style walks hand in hand with the classic account of days in the lives of two boys.

**M.J.** I have gotten a lot of praise from people, not just my good close friends, who referred among other things to the style, as Yardley certainly did. As a matter of fact Fred Chappell told me that the book "really knocked them dead."—Anyway, they all mentioned my style here, which was a surprise to me because I was just writing a simple story and hadn't thought about the matter. Incidentally, in the process of writing I never give a thought to style but only to the best way to say a thing. Many people think of style as being the way such as John Updike writes, or William Styron, with hopped-up language, rich and often esoteric images, and so forth. In my case here, the essential simplicity of my subject dictated the way I wrote about it. I couldn't have written it differently. In fact, it was easy writing for me; I wrote faster than I had ever written before. It used to be, if I got a good solid permanent page, or 350 words or so, in a day's work, I was satisfied. I hardly ever got much more, but in this case I could often get two or three finished pages. I don't often revise later. Except for *Passage through Gehenna,* I have rarely done more than minor revisions on any of my books.

**J.G.** We are talking about style and pretending to be innocent of the book's provocative contents. But the novel is a deliberate provocation on your part, isn't it?

**M.J.** If so, only to some small degree. Are you talking about the memoirist's, the fictional author's, opinions? Yes, I knew that some things I had him say were going to provoke, at least in the present climate of thought. You and my wife held the view that I should delete some of the things I have my memoirist say about life in the Old South. I put the question to another friend, David Bovenizer, who is an editor and a great collector of memoirs, some from his own Virginia family. He thought my handling of the matter perfectly characteristic and convincing, typical of the memoir form. This pleased and continues to please me, even though it certainly has cost me by giving offense to the politically correct. I admit to pleasure in taking licks at the established view of the Old South. Whether I did too much in the book might be reasonably debated. Nevertheless, it should somewhat balance the opposite view, which holds it impermissible to speak of anything except the horrors of slavery and the wickedness of those who owned slaves. As an absolute statement this is just not true, and I was anxious to say so. If, literarily speaking, that is an intrusion on my part, it is too bad. I think it enriched the book.

**J.G.** *Nashville 1864* is about two boys and the War, but it is also about the idea of slavery becoming clear to one of them. Isn't this what makes it more than a boys' book?

**M.J.** Yes, Steven comes to understand the racial situation, but that is part of his growing up, and surely that was so for most people who grew up in a slaveholding family. William Faulkner makes the same point. I didn't borrow it from him, but it is in *The Unvanquished.* He talks about how Bayard Sartoris sleeps beside his black friend Ringo, and so forth, when they are boys, but at a certain age suddenly the difference between them becomes manifest and relationships change. That is what happened to Steven, it is just a part of this historical material. It wasn't meant to show the horrors of slavery but simply the consciousness of the situation that comes at a certain point in life.

**J.G.** The novel isn't really about the Battle of Nashville, is it?

**M.J.** It is about the destruction of a way of life. I try to depict that life as best I can in the early stages of the book and in the comments of the memoirist. So it is about the wiping out of a world, and Steven's coming to consciousness about his difference from Dink, his black friend, is just a part of the consciousness of that world. I think of it overall, as a rendition of a society that has vanished from the face of the earth. The War is mainly a vehicle.—I appreciated Fred Chappell's review of the book in which he ends by saying that I show the reason why Southerners' memories are so full of regret at the loss of this world, with its faults and its virtues and everything else, but still a world that seizes the imagination and certainly produced many lovely things.

*Auburn, Alabama, November 14, 2000; January 4, 2003*

*The final section of the interview is on Jones's novel* Herod's Wife, *which was published in 2003. The telephone interview was added on January 4, 2003.*

**J.G.** Why are the people in *Herod's Wife* so burdened by anxiety? Has the Lakepoint community become estranged from itself?

**M.J.** The loss by displacement of community in the real sense of the word is most openly symbolized by the change in the name of the town, from Loretta to Lakepoint. Before, presumably, there was a workable moral coherence. But this was drowned out and replaced by a population with no common past or *values* fully deserving of the name. This, as I see it, is generally typical of our time. Without a past, including a religious inheritance, choices will be ill defined, producing anxiety, confusion, and, ultimately, distrust.

**J.G.** Is there a deliberate parallel to the estrangement of the Heltons, a parallel between community conflict and domestic strain?

**M.J.** A parallel exists, I hope, between the community at large and the marriage of Hugh and Nora Helton. A ghost of the past haunts Hugh and so, with bitterness, his wife. It should be remembered that the word "religion" has the root meaning of rebinding.

**J.G.** The "new abortion clinic" and violent disagreement about it in Lakepoint are brought up, and you show racial tension in town. Cap Waters and young Qualls come to life but quickly disappear out of the novel. Were you tempted to dwell on abortion and racial issues?

**M.J.** The several instances of radical disagreement in the town (racial, religious, and otherwise) are there for the purpose of illustrating the general moral incoherence. Further development of any one of them individually would have defeated my overall purpose in *Herod's Wife.*

**J.G.** Shouldn't we feel some compassion and pity for Nora Helton? Don't you share her doubts about Christian faith? Is she a victim of basic human curiosity about the sinful and forbidden, or is she simply evil?

**M.J.** Abstractly speaking, given the prevailing moral and spiritual climate, there is room for some compassion and pity for Nora. Bishop Wells puts it succinctly:

"'Nothing' is the word. Our Word." But Nora's total acceptance of the bishop's despairing assertion, whether or not it inspires the reader's sympathy for her, is an open invitation to the spirit of evil. For evil's personification, Satan, is, after all, a nihilist. Take him for real, as a person, or not, his destructive aura whatever its provenance is a presence in our world. And Nora is obsessed, or possessed, by this presence.

## NOTE

◆ ◆ ◆

1. "A Modern Case," *Delta Review* 6 (July–August 1969): 42–52, 72–75.

# *A Good Man with a Good Voice—*
# *"You can lead a mule to water"*

## INTERVIEW WITH MARTIN LUTHER KING SR.

◆◆◆◆◆◆

*The Ebenezer Baptist Church, Atlanta, Georgia, June 1, 1978*

Rev. Martin Luther King Sr.

◆◆◆◆◆◆

*On Auburn Street in Atlanta, "Sweet Auburn," as the local people call it, there is one of the biggest tourist attractions in the American South: the Ebenezer Baptist Church. The church became known worldwide as Dr. Martin Luther King Jr.'s point of departure. Today a memorial for the civil rights martyr is located next to the church, complete with a pool, shaped like the Reflecting Pool in Washington, D.C., where Martin Luther King, Jr. gave his most influential speech, "I Have a Dream," on August 28, 1963.*

*Now an eternal flame burns on Auburn Street to remind us of the murder, on April 4, 1968, of the most beloved black leader of our time. But Dr. Martin Luther King Jr. is not remembered only through symbols. Down the street are the headquarters for the powerful civil rights organization the Southern Christian Leadership Conference, which in the 1960s became synonymous with the King family name. Across the street from the church there is the Martin Luther King Center, which has meant much for Atlanta's black youth. The center was for a time led by Coretta Scott King, the widow of Dr. Martin Luther King Jr.*

*The King family have been ministers in Georgia at least since Dr. King Jr.'s great-grandfather. And one of his grandfathers became the first leader of the Georgia branch of the NAACP. It was, however, Dr. Martin Luther King Sr., father of the city's famous son, who more than anybody decided developments on Auburn Street in Atlanta. He pastored the Ebenezer Baptist Church when the SCLC was founded there in 1957 to support nonviolent social change. "Daddy King," as his friends called him, became a legend in his own time. He was not tall but was powerfully and solidly built, and he had a voice that could awaken even the hard of hearing. He was always actively involved with the struggle for civil rights. It is partly his achievement that black teachers receive equal pay in Georgia.*

*Dr. King Sr. was a determined and an effective leader, and he was also an open and friendly man. It was not apparent that his later years were full of personal tragedies. Besides his famous son and co-minister at Ebenezer, who was shot in Memphis, the old preacher lost another son in tragic circumstances. And it must have seemed totally absurd to him when his wife was shot in Ebenezer by a madman, who may have been aiming at Dr. King Sr. himself.*

*The June 11, 1977, escape from the Brushy Mountain State Penitentiary in Tennessee, of James Earl Ray, the man convicted of the murder of Martin Luther King Jr.; Ray's recapture and repeated professions of innocence; the racially divided reception accorded the NBC film on the life and death of Martin King Jr. in the fall of 1977; and the mixed reactions to the issue of a stamp honoring King Jr. on January 15, 1978, were just some of the events that were on King Sr.'s mind at the time of the interview presented here.*

*Rev. King Sr. was the only one left in a position of power on Auburn Street. He was influential among America's black voters. Thousands took his advice when it was election time. For years he has been the friend of Jimmy Carter. By actively campaigning for him, Daddy King helped the former governor of Georgia win many black votes during his campaign to become president. In August 1976, when Jimmy Carter was nominated, King led the Democratic Convention, meeting in New York City's Madison Square Garden, in the final singing of "We Shall Overcome." And he conducted a special service to mark Carter's inauguration on*

*January 20, 1977. The old parson in the Ebenezer Church was one of the few men in the United States who could always reach the president.*

*After I had tried for a long time, by phone and letter, to get to talk with Dr. King Sr. and all my efforts had been ignored, I mentioned my problem to Jack Etheridge, a white judge and professor of law in Atlanta. "Oh," he said, "would you like to have his private number?—Or, maybe I'd better call Daddy King to introduce you." His phone call worked like magic, and I was invited "to come to the Ebenezer Baptist Church to see Dr. King."*

*The time of my visit with Dr. Martin Luther King Sr. was right after President Kaunda of Zambia had received the Martin Luther King Peace Prize on May 23, 1978. The campaign to make Dr. King Jr.'s birthday a national holiday had begun, and so had the efforts to reopen the investigation of the assassination. But Dr. King Sr. wanted to talk with me about other things, subjects uppermost in his mind.*

**Jan Nordby Gretlund** In the South, the rivalry among the Protestant denominations is keen. Doesn't the competition among Methodists, Presbyterians, and Baptists do more damage than good for the Christian faith?

**Martin Luther King Sr.** I have now found the man who is going to take over, after me, as minister of my congregation. I have been looking for a good human being with a good voice, a man who will be respected by the congregation. And the new minister for the Ebenezer Baptists has been raised and educated as a *Presbyterian.*

As you see, we know very well that various affixed names are inessential. It is the human being and his Christian temper that count.

**J.G.** Your son became famous as a Southern minister and as a civil rights activist. Are you now satisfied with the progress after the segregation days? Or was your son's sacrifice in vain?

**M.L.K. Sr.** During the '60s many white people joined our church. But today we only have two white families who attend regularly. The others were also good people, but they were forced to leave the congregation by pressure from their friends, neighbors, and employers. But still, the racial situation here in Georgia has improved much since the '50s. I don't think my son and his friends have worked in vain. The good results of their work are everywhere about us. Black wages have gone up, the housing situation has improved, and our children get a better education.—But there is still a lot to be done.

**J.G.** Are there still members of your congregation who "go North" in search of the land awash in milk and honey?

**M.L.K. Sr.** No.—The great exodus to the North began in 1917 and continued all the way *into* the '60s. But today our sisters and brothers are coming home.

Why should they prefer the North? Wages were the original reason why they headed north. But now the pay in Atlanta is about the same as the pay up North. So now they are coming home by the thousands. There are many in the North who now see the South as the land of golden opportunities. And it is true, of course, that the South has everything. The oil wells are here, in Texas and in Oklahoma. And Atlanta, New Orleans, and Houston are the future, and the American Negro wants his share of that future. That is why they are returning from the big cities in the North. All Chicago, Detroit, and Boston can offer today are economic problems and racism.

**J.G.** Do you feel that white people still divide black Americans into "good" *or* "bad" blacks?

**M.L.K. Sr.** It seems to me that the image of the black American in literature and also in magazines and newspapers is positive on the whole. I don't read everything, of course. It is difficult to keep up at my age. Both white and black publishers send me a great many novels, which I don't have time to read at all. But I read my son's books on nonviolence again and again. And I also keep up with the many new actors and writers who work for TV, such as Alex Haley. But I do not have time to keep up with all the new literature.

What the white part of the population really thinks of their black neighbors? It is not for me to say. TV transmissions from our civil rights demonstrations created the popular opinion that finally gave us the civil rights legislation. I am convinced that today most white people have a positive opinion of integration but not all—far from all.

**J.G.** It seems to me that most black people exclude all whites from their everyday lives.

**M.L.K. Sr.** It is the task of the Church to teach everybody about neighborly love. I have just told you how difficult it is for a white person to remain in our congregation. The Church has failed, also the black Church. The racially most segregated hours in Atlanta are still Sunday mornings. You can invite people to come to church, but even if they do come, you can't force them to seat themselves next to each other.—You can lead a mule to water, but you can't make it drink. We cannot force people to like each other through legislation. But it is the job of the Church to show the congregation that it lacks in basic neighborly love.

**J.G.** In many big cities, black citizens live in separate sections of the city. Are you living in an integrated part of Atlanta?

**M.L.K. Sr.** Yes.—At this time there is housing enough in Atlanta, and only little discrimination even in the best housing sections. If we hear about an area that is not integrated, we will help the NAACP integrate it.—But right now we do not receive many complaints.

I still remember my first protest actions in this town. One of the first was to integrate one of the lifts in the courthouse. It was Fulton Court House, which had three lifts for "Folks" and one for trash and black people. The sign said "Garbage & Colored." But we have changed all that.

As a black American you can today travel from Atlanta to New York, Chicago, or Los Angeles and be treated like everybody else. But on the way you pass a lot of small societies, where absolutely nothing has changed in the relations between the races since the War [the Civil War]. Racial prejudice is today first and foremost a problem in local areas in the country. So the next goal of the civil rights movement is to integrate all those rural societies. In spite of court orders and legislation, almost nothing has changed in the country.

**J.G.** Is there a tendency toward militancy among the young black people in Atlanta?

**M.L.K. Sr.** The young black people of today know and understand more than my generation did. When our young demonstrate, they do so together with young white people. I am convinced that the young will solve the old problem. But once in a while I fear that the young lack a clear sense of direction. Violence is certainly not the answer to anything. But violence is the result of the greatest problem of the young: *the high rate of unemployment.* Our young people are in the worst situation. It seems that nobody needs them. There are three times as many unemployed blacks as there are whites. It makes the young bitter—and violent.

**J.G.** Is it possible for educated black people to find a job in Atlanta?

**M.L.K. Sr.** People come from Chicago and Detroit in big buses to visit the Ebenezer Baptist Center. And often they don't want to go home again, even though they just came here as tourists. This is also true of some of the well educated. In such cases we help them find temporary places to live. And at the moment we can also help find some jobs.

**J.G.** Are you satisfied with the pace of integration in Atlanta's school system?

**M.L.K. Sr.** Most people in Atlanta know very well that we have only a token integration of our school system. I think that busing is still a necessary evil in the effort to integrate the schools. But the great problem is, in the school as in the church, that even if we do manage to get the children into the same school and into the same classroom, we still cannot force them to like each other and become friends.

We also force people into the same neighborhoods, but as to make them see each other socially! As I said earlier, the Church must do more to make the races love each other.

**J.G.** Are black school children in Georgia today offered an education that can equal that of white children taught here?

M.L.K. Sr. The reason I talk of token integration is that white people resist integration of schools in every possible way. The situation is that white parents are desperately trying to escape to the suburbs, out to the expensive houses and private schools! The scandal is that now that we, thanks to legislation and busing, have succeeded in integrating the public school system, almost only black children are in the public schools. It is the pattern for most of the large cities in the South. It goes without saying that the best teachers are hired where they make more money.—The whole thing demands a real change of mind.

*Through a window in the office I see a group of tourists move about in the church, all dressed in colorful, apparently African costumes.*

J.G. Are the Baptists in Atlanta in touch with nationalist movements in African countries?

M.L.K. Sr. It seems that many from Africa identify with my son's nonviolent philosophy. In any case, when they come to the United States, Atlanta is the first city African students head for. More African students are in Atlanta than in any other American city.—The African politicians also come here. The president of Zambia has just visited the church and the memorial.

J.G. Do you see a future cooperation between Africans and black Americans?

M.L.K. Sr. Our problems are in America, and they must be solved by Americans. But we are certainly not blind to the value of international connections. As Americans, we have to think of where raw materials are going to come from in the future. We can't just hand Africa over to the communists.

J.G. Other minorities in the United States feel they are treated unfairly. Does the NAACP ever work together with American Jews, locally?

M.L.K. Sr. We try and have often tried to. But our problems are not quite the same. We the American blacks have the power of eloquence but no financial power. Jews have "green power." If they are treated badly in a hotel, they simply buy the hotel!

Martin Luther King's facial expression shows that he considers his last statement a joke. Our conversation has lasted for about an hour, interrupted by several phone calls, and Dr. King chooses to end our session. "Would you like to see the church?" he asks politely. After a quick tour of the church with the mementos from the great civil rights battles of the '50s and '60s, Dr. King escorts me to the church door and takes his leave:

"I hope you were satisfied with my answers." Dr. King's ringing "Goodbye" must have been audible at the other end of "sweet" Auburn. He is indeed a good man with a good voice.

Walking down the street from the Ebenezer Baptist Church, I realize how lucky I was to have been granted an interview with the extremely busy, highly influential, and obviously overworked black leader. I wondered why my Atlanta friend had been able to set up my visit with Daddy King after just one phone call (without looking up the number), when all my other efforts to see him had met with nothing but silence.

After some questioning, my friend the judge admitted evasively that he had relied on a long-established connection between the King and the Etheridge families. His uncle, Paul Etheridge, had many years ago employed a young yardman named Martin Luther King, who stayed around and married the maid, and that had been the start of a lasting friendship between the families. That is also the biracial South.

# *Laying the Ghost of Marcus Aurelius*

AN INTERVIEW WITH WALKER PERCY

◆◆◆◆◆◆

*Covington, Louisiana, January 2, 1981*

Walker Percy with Jan Nordby Gretlund

◆◆◆◆◆◆

## I. Kierkegaardian Stages

**Jan Nordby Gretlund** To what extent do you consider your first three novels "a gloss on Søren Kierkegaard"?

**Walker Percy** That's my own expression. It is an exaggeration, but I wanted to pay due homage to Kierkegaard. Insofar as one thinks in a philosophical frame of reference, when I was writing *The Moviegoer*, also *The Last*

*Gentleman,* and maybe also *Love in the Ruins,* I was thinking in terms of the three spheres of existence. It is a very convenient frame of reference, particularly when you are writing a novel of quest, pilgrimage, or search about a young man "on life's way," as Kierkegaard would say, to think of him going through the aesthetic stage, the ethical stage, and then the religious, although most of the novels are about the aesthetic stage.

**J.G.** Isn't there something to be said for living on the aesthetic stage, as Binx Bolling does initially?

**W.P.** Of course. Kierkegaard would certainly agree. His hero of the aesthetic was Mozart and his *Don Giovanni.* He loved Mozart more than any other composer. The aesthetic stage is the stage of the highest enjoyment—of artistic enjoyment. You don't have to leave it. Kierkegaard never said we exist in one stage altogether. All people are probably a combination of the three stages. The three generally overlap, though there are "pure" cases, mostly literary, like *Don Giovanni.*

**J.G.** When the English edition of *The Moviegoer* appeared in 1963, one Danish reviewer commented, "Binx Bolling seems to have given up his strange search, he has groped around until his thirtieth year, and perhaps that is just as well, for how much can Kierkegaard . . . and religion really help us?" [My translation]

**W.P.** The reviewer should have gotten the overt reference to Kierkegaard in the "Epilogue." Binx had gone through a stage, the aesthetic stage, he stopped going to movies, stopped playing those games about neighborhoods, movie houses, past experience, repetition, rotation. And he finally decided he wanted to do something, he takes Kate by the hand and he tells her it is all right for her to ride the streetcar alone. He takes responsibility. Binx's attitude to the stoic Aunt Emily is somewhat ambiguous. That's what I like about *The Second Coming;* it is not ambiguous. It is absolutely clear what Will Barrett is going to do.

**J.G.** Is Sutter Vaught in *The Last Gentleman* a stoic?

**W.P.** No, Sutter is desperate. He has exhausted the aesthetic sphere. I would go further than Kierkegaard; I would combine the aesthetic with the scientific. I think the two are parallel. I think Mozart and Einstein are on the same plane. They are both writing about how the world is. Music is cognitive and science is cognitive. And you have the observer writing about it, communicating with the fellow scientists and communicating with fellow music lovers. Sutter is in that tradition. He was a scientist, but he was also in despair. He understood the good news, the gospel; he knew exactly what was going on in that baptism when the priest baptized Jamie. But Sutter was an unbeliever, he didn't accept it. With him it was an either/or, either belief or unbelief, and he was an unbeliever. His sister Val was a believer. Sutter was in despair.

**J.G.** You seem to take issue with Kierkegaard on the function of knowledge in attaining faith.

**W.P.** Well, it is a classical dispute between Catholics and Protestants whether faith is a form of knowledge. I thought it was a very nice opposition to have Kierkegaard making a clear statement that faith *is not* a form of knowledge; it is a leap into the absurd. Thomas Aquinas saying in his classical thirteenth-century way that faith *is* a form of knowledge. It is different from scientific knowing, but it is a form of knowledge. I tend to agree with Aquinas there, even though I am more sympathetic with Kierkegaard. I am on his wavelength. I understand his phenomenology, his analysis of the existential predicament of modern man. Aquinas did not have that, but I think Aquinas was right about faith. It is not a leap into the absurd. It is an act of faith, which is a form of knowledge.

**J.G.** Kierkegaard might well ask, "What kind of knowledge?"

**W.P.** A knowledge that God exists and that man is created in His image.

**J.G.** But isn't that simply faith?

**W.P.** Well, I don't think so. In fact, the burden of my nonfiction is a demonstration that man is different from other creatures. That he has this extraordinary capacity to know things, a certain freedom, and he can find himself in a predicament. You can't explain these things by deterministic biology. Ordinary epistemology does not take account of news as a form of knowing. I addressed that in *Message in a Bottle.*

**J.G.** Does religion offer Will Barrett a solution to his existential problems at the ending of *The Last Gentleman?*

**W.P.** *The Last Gentleman* ends ambiguously, too. I had a priest tell me it was clear to him what happened at the end of *The Last Gentleman,* that when Will Barrett stops Sutter in the Edsel and goes off with him, he said, obviously what they both do is to go to Sutter's place and they both commit suicide.

What was intended was that: Will Barrett knew Sutter was onto something. Will Barrett has a good antenna, a good radar, and he knows when people know something or don't know something. Even at the end of *The Second Coming,* he knew this senile priest knew something he didn't know. He knew that Sutter knew what was going on, so he asks him. But Sutter is not going to tell him anything. He knows what it is Will wants from him and that if he told him something, he would accept it in a psychological mode.

It would be something like "How to Improve Your Life." So Sutter is not going to tell him anything. In other words, he is leaving it to him to live his own life. The implication was that Will Barrett was going to go back to the South, probably marry Kitty, and probably go into business with the Vaughts and their Confederate Chevrolet agency. That was the implication. But he didn't [see Percy's *The Second Coming*].

## II. Scandinavian Copy

**J.G.** At one point in *The Last Gentleman,* Sutter Vaught formulates man's choice as he sees it: "to live like a Swede. Or: to live as a Christian among Christians in Alabama? Or: to die like an honest man?"[1] Would you explain this passage to me?

**W.P.** I have forgotten I said that. If Sutter said that, he is rejecting both. When he says "Swede," he is talking about a purely materialistic society. When he is talking about Val, his sister, he is talking about an incarnate Christian society. She has this Christian community in South Alabama. And for Sutter "to live like a man" is simply to be oneself, to choose despair or whatever he chooses.

**J.G.** In your essay "The Man on the Train" you mention that the materialistic Swedes will not use the resort areas the Swedish government set aside for recreational purposes.

**W.P.** A Swede told me that his favorite place was up north. But to get away from the government reservations, to find a place which had not been set aside for recreation, he had to go to English villages. This again goes back to Kierkegaard; he was the first one to give it a name:

"a rotation." He says one becomes *Europa-Müde,* and if you live in Austria you'll go to the south of France. Or, if you live in Paris you'll go to the Munich area, and if you're German you'll go to the coast of Spain. And it is certainly true of this country, too. People are always looking. It is a favorite American pastime to go to Mexico to find an unspoiled village [see Percy's essay "The Loss of the Creature"].

**J.G.** One of your characters in *Love in the Ruins* seems to have made it into a career to bring others to his home base in Copenhagen.

**W.P.** If Art Immelmann was living in Denmark, he was an immigrant from Germany. For after all, the original Immelmann was a German World War I ace, and he invented the Immelmann turn. My father was a World War I flyer, and I remember him describing to me the Immelmann Roll. It was a combat tactic; he would loop and at the top of the loop do a barrel roll to escape. So I heard about him from my father, and Immelmann *was* a German ace. I don't know why I made him the Devil, but it seemed to be a good idea.

**J.G.** Art Immelmann promises Dr. Thomas More a job as a brain specialist at the University of Copenhagen.

**W.P.** [amused] I combined the best of both worlds:
German genius and Danish spirituality.

**J.G.** There isn't much Christianity in Scandinavian spirituality nowadays.

**W.P.** That is why the next saint must come from Sweden. You have to go all the way to the bottom to come back up. He is not going to come from Christian Carolina, I can promise you.

### III. Lancelot or Percival

**J.G.** Lancelot's plans for a new start with Anna in Virginia are by some Scandinavian critics seen as the preparation for a leap onto a religious stage.

**W.P.** It would be a sort of inverted religious stage, a caricature of the religious stage. After all, Lancelot was *not* in quest of the Holy Grail. He was in quest of the unholy grail. So, it was the religious stage turned inside out.

**J.G.** But at that time Lancelot had realized that there wasn't any holy or unholy grail.

**W.P.** True. But when he was headed for the Shenandoah Valley and Virginia to meet Anna, he was still planning what he called "a third revolution," a very violent, almost fascist revolution.

**J.G.** So Cleanth Brooks is right in lining up Lancelot with Adolf Hitler and Idi Amin?

**W.P.** If you subtract the Holocaust, the persecution of the Jews, he'd probably be more right than wrong. Lancelot liked to say the Nazis were stupid and that they could have accomplished the same thing without killing the Jews.

**J.G.** What about Lancelot's desire for a distinction between good and evil, his ability to act, and his readiness to accept a responsibility. Aren't these positive features?

**W.P.** Sure. He was in many ways like Aunt Emily in *The Moviegoer.* In one way he was worse, in another he was better. He was worse because he didn't have the ethical values of Aunt Emily; she would not have been in favor of killing the enemies of society. *He* would have. After all, he did kill three or four people when he blew up the plantation house. But in his own way he was "better" in the Kierkegaardian sense of being aware of a progression toward the religious sphere. He was "better" in realizing that the old methods of communication, the old cultural values, were dead, and there had to be a new world and a new life, some sort of rebirth. And he envisioned a rebirth and a new communication by tapping on the wall and through the wall, with Anna, the girl next door. And he saw the possibility of a new life with

Anna and the possibility of a third revolution, as he thought of it, in Virginia, which had its positive elements.

**J.G.** Would they, among others, be likely to get rid of the pornography and swinishness he had been fighting?

**W.P.** Yes, but also to get rid of Aunt Emily's values. To begin a completely new life, Aunt Emily would have gone back to the Greco-Roman Stoicism.

**J.G.** I had the impression that Lancelot's new life would be based on Aunt Emily's old values.

**W.P.** No! Lancelot was going to make it up from scratch and find his own way. He thought of *himself*. . . there is a scene where he sees a young man standing in one of the passes in the mountains of the Shenandoah Valley. I had several things in mind. One was a Confederate soldier: one of Stonewall Jackson's men crossing the Massanutten Mountain and about to defeat the Northern army. The other was Robert Jordan, the hero of Hemingway's *For Whom the Bell Tolls,* who is fighting in the Spanish Civil War. Remember the scene where he is lying with his gun waiting among the pine needles? And the third is a young Nazi storm trooper.—I spent a summer in Germany in 1934, and I lived with a family in Bonn. The father was a member of the S.A., *Schutz Abwehr,* and the son was a member of *Hitlerjugend.*

There was a tremendous excitement at the "rejuvenation" of Germany and the idea of new values in the Nietzschean sense: the death of God, the death of old values, and the creation of new values. I remember the young *Hitlerjugend* boy was very excited about the possibilities of the future. There was nothing about the Jews at the beginning. I had all this in mind when I thought of a young man standing in a pass of Massanutten Mountain, Virginia. Lancelot is a conscious combination of something quite positive and quite evil.

Maybe I was also thinking of Gabriel Marcel. He is French, a Jew, a Catholic convert who had the nerve to say: we tend to overlook something positive about the mass movements. It is easy to say how wrong they were. It is easy to overlook the positive things: the great sense of nerve and vitality. This was what I was very much aware of in Germany in 1934. It made it even more seductive; as in the movie *Cabaret,* when a young German stands up in a beer garden and sings.

**J.G.** I thought Lancelot Lamar was so deeply rooted in the values of the Old South that it would be impossible for him to escape his heritage and start from scratch.

**W.P.** That's true. What I was doing was to try to destroy the middle ground. I tried to see what would happen if he *lived up* to his tradition. And his tradition is similar to Aunt Emily's tradition. He was not a Christian; as a matter of fact I had less in mind Sir Lancelot than Ulysses. In the old Greco-Roman tradition, if you had been mortally offended, if suitors had moved into your house and had taken advantage of your wife, what you did was to go and kill them. So in my sneaky way—that's the only thing a novelist can do now is to be deceptive and sneaky—I try to raise questions which slip up on the reader. The question is:

why shouldn't Lancelot do this? Instead of dealing overtly with Christianity, I deal with the old Roman ethic:

what's wrong with him taking revenge in the way he did? Would Aunt Emily object to that? What he is doing is carrying Aunt Emily's ethic to its logical conclusion. If he has been cuckolded by somebody, a Hollywood producer, then what he does is *kill* him.

That's what Ulysses did, and we look on Ulysses as one of the great heroes of Western culture. Ulysses and Telemachus kill everybody! Lancelot only kills three people, I think, I've lost count, but Ulysses and Telemachus kill all the suitors. And we applaud Ulysses.

**J.G.** How does the murderer compare morally with his victims?

**W.P.** In the end, I regarded Lancelot as demented, as a man who has gone into the religious stage in a demented way. He has got hold of it in a sense, and he is a man of action. He is a man who believes in putting his beliefs into action. Do you remember he said at one point—I don't know whether I got this from Kierkegaard or Nietzsche—he said that: if one man comes along who believes something sufficiently, a man who is willing to act on his belief, then everybody will follow him. Because nobody else believes in anything, and nobody else knows what to do. What Lancelot did was partly admirable, partly crazy.—But the novel, like most of my novels, is also an attack on the twentieth century, on the whole culture. It is a rotten century, we are in terrible trouble.

**J.G.** Scandinavian critics tend to make Lancelot more of a true hero than you have intended.

**W.P.** But they leave out the other pole. The other pole is Percival. The critics are right in that the point of satire was to destroy mushy American liberalism. The mushy way of approving everything that is "life-enhancing," or "self-improving," or "cultivating your personality." To cut it down to an either/or—I'm always trying to cut it down to an either/or—it has either got to be one way or the other.

That is what Lancelot says to Percival: would you agree it has either got to be my way or your way—it is not going to be their way. That is the last question, and Percival says, "Yes." The reviewers are partly right, but they leave out Percival. Isn't that a sign of the times?

**J.G.** Is Percival the real hero of your *Lancelot?*

**W.P.** I was trying to do something there; I'm not sure it worked. It worked for some people. Percival, the priest, is never described. He was never in the story. Yet he was supposed to be present. He was listening—he was the one who is hearing all this. He only says about two words at the very end. It was my intention that his character should be known indirectly through what Lancelot said about him.

**J.G.** Virginia Woolf did something similar in *The Waves.* She also used the name Percival.

**W.P.** I didn't know that. When I first began to write that novel, I was going to write it about two men, as a third-person narrative. And the part about Percival did not work. So I wrote out Percival, and I wrote it as a dramatic monologue with Lancelot, which was the way it should be. But it confused a lot of people. They didn't realize whom Lancelot was addressing at the beginning—whether this person was real or not. A dramatic monologue apparently puts people off.

**J.G.** What is Percival's role at the ending? Is he a personification of the Church?

**W.P.** What does that mean? He went back to be an ordinary priest in a parish in Alabama.

**J.G.** Is that, as Lancelot said, copping out?

**W.P.** That is for you to decide. (Come to think of it, it is exactly what Kierkegaard wanted to do.) The issue is there. Percival agrees with Lancelot about the way the world is:

the world is a rotten place. They agree that there is a lot wrong with the world and that they ought to condemn what is rotten. But they do not agree what should be done about it. They have different ways. It is supposed to be a very conventional, classical statement of two different traditions. One is, well, Cleanth Brooks would call it gnostic, I hadn't thought of Gnosticism, but I was thinking of the good pagan–Greco-Roman–Nazi–and–so–forth tradition:

Aunt Emily on one side and orthodox Christianity on the other.

At the end of *Lancelot* I was trying to present two radical points of view; neither is accepted by most people—most Americans. One is:

Lancelot goes to Virginia for the third revolution, he rejects the world. The other is:

Percival goes to a parish in Alabama, and he hears the confessions of Buick dealers. They could not be more different, and yet they have something in common: they both know there is something radically wrong with the world.

## IV. Women and Insanity

**J.G.** Why is it that women reviewers are not satisfied with your women characters? Are there any "normal" women in your novels?

**W.P.** What about Allie in *The Second Coming?* She is crazy, but she is pretty normal. And what about Aunt Emily in *The Moviegoer?* She is not only normal but normative, as normative as Marcus Aurelius.

**J.G.** Why are the girls we like in your fiction mentally unstable?

**W.P.** Well, that goes back to a device I use consciously, namely to arrange the placement of the hero and the heroine so that it is always a question: who is crazy? Whether he is crazy and the rest of the world is sane or he is sane and the rest of the world crazy.

It is supposed to be a delicately balanced issue, so that many people can read it and say, "Well, I am also crazy." Allison is a crazy woman living in a sane world, or maybe she seems crazy because she is reacting sanely to an insane world. Someone like Allison, who is beginning a new life, starting afresh, and even creating a new language, maybe she is on the track to sanity. It is not difficult to make out a case that the world is mad.

**J.G.** Is it a trend in modern American fiction that the heroes are considered insane by society?

**W.P.** This is, of course, the thesis of R. D. Laing, the psychiatrist, that schizophrenics in their own way are sane. I think that most psychiatrists disagree, and they may be right in that Laing takes it to an extreme, but for literary purposes it is a convenient thesis. A schizophrenic may be on the track of sanity; he finds the world unbearable, and maybe the function of the novelist is to show that the world is, indeed, unbearable. And that there are certain strategies you have to take to live in it, and there are persons who are entitled to have a psychotic reaction. At any rate, it is a delicately balanced issue; the reader can read it either way.

**J.G.** The women in *The Last Gentleman* get a particularly harsh treatment.

**W.P.** Yes, and those in *The Moviegoer,* too. I don't know whether that is antifeminism on my part or the difficulty for a male novelist to create a woman. Good women writers have an easy time creating men. But, how many *women* did Hemingway create?

**J.G.** It seems they were all either whores or mother figures.

**W.P.** True, or, in my case, neurotic or psychotic. Maybe it is because men do not understand women. I didn't have any sisters, and maybe if I had sisters I'd do a better job. But to me "a normal" woman is an absolute mystery. I can only understand her if she is as neurotic as I am.

**J.G.** You did create some wonderful women for *Love in the Ruins.* They all seem, however, to be seen at a distance.

**W.P.** But the last one, Ellen Oglethorpe, she is drawn from my Georgia background. Part of my family comes from Georgia. My mother's family were Georgia Presbyterians. So I thought it would be nice to have a voluptuous Georgia Presbyterian girl. And she is not neurotic. She knows exactly what she wants. She may not be very deep; I wasn't too interested in her, I just wanted to have her there.—I plead ignorance, I don't know enough about women.

## V. Writer and Society

**J.G.** Do you think many readers cherish your novels for your satiric portrait of contemporary America?

**W.P.** Oh, sure.

**J.G.** In *The Second Coming* there are a love story *and* the continued satire of society. Do you fall between two stools?

**W.P.** It may be okay because that may be what saves me from being a very bad novelist. It would be a bad thing to write simply a novelistic explication of Kierkegaard, or Marcel, or whoever. But since I'm a Southerner and an American and since I get angry about a great many things that happen in this country—I am by nature a satirical novelist, and a humorist. I'm always pleased when people find the novels funny, because so many take them so seriously.

**J.G.** One of the features of your American society is that new Christian movements multiply. What do you think of them?

**W.P.** I have mixed feelings about them. I am a Catholic, and I have reborn Christians come and say to me, "Why don't you become a reborn Christian?" I would think that by definition a Christian is somebody who's reborn. So is it a question of being born a third time—or how many times?

**J.G.** What do you think of the support Ronald Reagan has received from these movements?

**W.P.** I think he is a little worried about it, a little uneasy about it. I think he is backing off from the embrace of Jerry Falwell. I think there are some good things in the new movements. They are reacting against some obviously evil forces in society: pornography in the movies, the decay of the American family. So I sympathize with their concern about that. But two things worry me about them: their wanting to get into politics, which goes against the grain, and the other is the commercialism of it.

There's a great deal of money involved: heavy media involvement with tremendous appeals for money. And it is not clear where the money goes or how sincere the ministers are. So I have mixed feelings about it.

**J.G.** The modern trends the new Christians seem to be fighting are the very same Lancelot rebelled against.

**W.P.** True—except Lancelot wouldn't have much use for Christians of any kind, at all. And, of course, Will Barrett in *The Second Coming* finds himself in the strange position of disagreeing with both nonbelievers and believers. He doesn't like either one. So he is looking for a *tertium quid.*

**J.G.** Does he find one?

**W.P.** Well, that's a good question. That's for me to ask you.

**J.G.** Will Barrett is also concerned that one place is much like any other place. Is the South much like any other place nowadays?

**W.P.** The South has a greater sense of place than other parts of the country, but the South is changing. The South is more like the rest of the country now. I regret it in some ways, not in other ways. I saw a map of what's happening to the demography of the country, and what's happening is that the population and the wealth are moving south. The Sunbelt is gaining, that's good in a sense, because there have been so many poor people, who have been in a wretched situation ever since the Civil War, so that is good. But it is a terrible price we have to pay. All you got to do is to drive through the suburbs of New Orleans and of Baton Rouge, and it looks like Los Angeles. There is a word for it; it is called "losangelization." The South is going through the process of losangelization. That's not good. The trick is, given the New South, which is not the South of Faulkner, not the South of Eudora, it is not the South of Flannery, but it *is* the South of Interstate 12 and Highway 190. It is the South of Los Angeles.

How to humanize that! How do you live with that? What I am trying to do is to figure out how a man can come to himself, living in a place like that. So at the end of *The Second Coming,* very deliberately, I've Allie and Will leave the greenhouse, go to a motel, the first coming together takes place in a Holiday Inn, which incidentally is a good Holiday Inn, I've been to one like that, where they have turnip greens, cornbread, and grits.—And from there . . . you know where he proposes to live with Allie, while they are going to build log cabins for old people. He proposes to move into a G.E. Gold Medallion home, a mass-produced home. And they could be happy there.

**J.G.** Are you writing any philosophical essays now?

**W.P.** That's what I am working on. I am working on a semiotic approach to consciousness. Consciousness itself, which American psychology, behaviorism, can't handle. It has no way of getting hold of it. So I am trying to get ahold of it by a science, and it is not going to be a conventional science of secondary causes.

**J.G.** Is the philosophy something you write to charge the batteries before returning to fiction? Or do you write fiction to relax between philosophical essays?

**W.P.** I don't know. When I finished this last novel, it was as if I had been a woman who had been pregnant four years. And, you know, women go into what you call a postpartum depression. I went into a terrible depression, and all I knew was that I would never write another novel again as long as I lived. What I can do is to write dry stuff like these semiotic essays

## NOTE

◆ ◆ ◆

1. *The Last Gentleman* (New York: Farrar, Straus and Giroux, 1966), p. 379.

# *Difficult Times*

## AN INTERVIEW WITH WALKER PERCY

◆ ◆ ◆ ◆ ◆ ◆

*January 29, 1985*

*The interview was conducted with Walker Percy in his home in Covington, Louisiana. Also present was Ann Ebrecht, a literary critic, who went to school with Percy's daughter.*

**Jan Nordby Gretlund** Why did you start your university education at Chapel Hill?

**Walker Percy** That was my uncle's [William Alexander Percy] idea. He chose Chapel Hill for me. He wanted me to attend a school of the solid Anglo-Saxon yeomanry, and his beloved Sewanee did not qualify, it seems. He also thought Chapel Hill was still small enough to have a relationship—as a school—with the community there. This was in the mid-1930s.

**J.G.** Why did you choose to study medicine?

**W.P.** Everybody in my family had been lawyers, it was a tradition in the family to be going into law. And I knew damn well I didn't want to do that. I had no use for it at all!

Traditionally, the only professions left were law, medicine, the military, and the priesthood. It was that way for a long time. I ruled out three immediately, so that left medicine. No, I guess it was more than that. I was interested in science, I was good in science in high school, and I liked biology and pre-med. I liked the science of medicine.

**J.G.** And there was no doubt in your mind that it was medicine you wanted to study?

**W.P.** No, there probably wasn't, because I immediately went into pre-med when I got to Chapel Hill. I already knew before I came. In a way it was a mistake—I say "in a way"—who knows?

In those days you took as many courses as you could in science, thinking that was going to help you when you went to medical school. So I took up a major in chemistry, a minor in physics, and I think I took maybe three courses in English. I took *one* English elective! I took freshman English, which everybody had to take, and one course in Shakespeare by a very good teacher at Chapel Hill named Taylor. That was all the English I had. I also took a minor in German.

**J.G.** Did you learn enough German to speak the language?

**W.P.** No, no, you didn't learn languages like that. You learned to conjugate and decline. I learned enough so that I could read German. I remember reading Thomas Mann's *Buddenbrooks.* And I remember taking a trip to Germany with my German professor after my freshman year, in 1934. We stayed with a family, at a friend of our German professor at Chapel Hill, they lived in Bonn. The father was in the S.A. and the son in the *Hitlerjugend.* That was in the early period of Nazism. What I was thinking of was the spirit of the *Hitlerjugend* at the time, which had not got into anti-Semitism and was full of brilliant German nationalism. We saw the good part of that; we didn't see the bad part of it.

**J.G.** In your novels we can read that our desperate trouble did not stop with the Nazis. A lot is still hopelessly wrong with the world. But you write and publish, which implies a hope that the world will be affected by your jeremiads.

**W.P.** After all, Jeremiah was not in despair, even though a jeremiad is supposed to be a desperate evocation of doom and gloom. But if he had been in despair, he would not have bothered. I mean, despair *is* a loss of hope, and he was saying all this in order to say, "Look, you have to turn to the Lord, to save yourselves from the mess you're in!" What else can you do?

**J.G.** Couldn't you voice your warnings in short stories, rather than in long novels?

**W.P.** Never, never. Never would it cross my mind to write a short story!

**J.G.** Wouldn't it be a challenge to write a good short story?

**W.P.** No, not at all. People don't read short stories. And you're too limited. It is like writing a sonnet, you have to figure out how everything works. In a novel you are free. I feel free in a novel, so I can follow where it goes.

**J.G.** With the possible exception of *The Second Coming,* your novels are pessimistic about our future.

**W.P.** I like to write about people who live in the shadow of catastrophe, people who are living in the eye of the hurricane. And when you think of it, when you take things seriously, if you are a writer and feel some obligation to write about the situation you are in, you can't help but compare your situation now with that before World War II and even right after. The world was a fairly safe place, even if the Germans had killed millions of people, even if the Russians had killed millions. It wasn't bad, things were going to look better. Surely this was the end of the last war of all. We didn't have the capacity to destroy ourselves.

Now the situation is so incredibly bad you can't even think about it! Nobody can think about it, which is an interesting situation to be in. It is the first time in the history of the world that we are actually sitting here with the power to destroy ourselves, with two fingers on the trigger, depending on whether some jerk in Moscow or Washington is going to do it. And nobody can think about it.

The mystery to me is that you are sitting over there in Europe acting cheerful [based on our correspondence, which began in February 1981]. You have the SS 20s trained right on you, and you got the American Pershings sitting in your back yard. And everything is great? But it may be the reason why people in Europe know how to appreciate life more than the people of South Dakota. The people of South Dakota are all depressed. They are not about to be killed by anybody.

**J.G.** Although it is a rejection, your 1956 essay on Southern Stoicism has a positive tone. Is Stoicism of any help to us in the present situation?

**W.P.** It *is* very positive. What I was trying to say was that Stoicism is the main Southern ethos, which is not ordinarily recognized in a certain class. According to Flannery O'Connor, it is Protestant Christianity which is the main spiritual source, fundamental Christianity, which mainly informs the South. She is right about that, about what *she* saw among the South Georgia people. But I was talking about the planter class, my uncle, his friends, and his ancestors, and the way they were brought up.

In the South before the Civil War, and even after it, there were little private academies all over, with professors of Greek. Everybody took Greek and Latin. And they called their cities Corinth, Ithaca, and Demopolis. All educated young Southern gentlemen knew their Cicero and their Horace, their Virgil, and their Seneca, as well as their Marcus Aurelius.

**J.G.** Were you saying in your essay that there is something wrong with the Southern tradition of Stoicism?

**W.P.** No, I was just trying to bring out the fact that everybody knows all about Fundamentalist Christianity informing the South and that people don't usually know how strong the Greco-Roman Stoic tradition was among the educated classes.

**J.G.** Why do you reject Southern Stoicism in your novels?

**W.P.** I don't! I don't!

**J.G.** "I don't. I don't! I don't hate it! I don't hate it!"

**W.P.** That was Quentin Compson. I didn't say that. No, it is altogether admirable, when I think of my two brothers, who are admirable fellows. They do great community work in the tradition of our uncle. How can I argue with that tradition?

Ann Ebrecht talked about the different cultural aspects of Catholicism, and I guess my main cultural character would be the idea of the good English Christian knight: Sir Thomas More, who is a righteous man, a good man, who will fight. He is a warrior. And the Knights of the Round Table, for example, Lancelot, I always liked him because he got into so much trouble. He was an adulterer, a violent man, and yet he was one of the two knights who saw the Holy Grail! I always thought that was a strange part of the legend.—I don't see Christianity and Stoicism as antithetical.

**J.G.** So you don't have to reject Stoicism to be a good Catholic?

**W.P.** No!

**J.G.** You said once in an interview that "the infinite mystery is also an infinite delight." How can a mystery be a delight?

**W.P.** I don't know what that means! What is "an infinite mystery"?

**J.G.** God, His ways, your faith!

**W.P.** So it bothers you that the solution to the search turns out to be a mystery?

**J.G.** Yes, it does.

**W.P.** All right. Faith consists of two or three mysteries: the Incarnation is a mystery, the Trinity is a mystery, and the real Presence in the Eucharist is a mystery. But that is the end of the search. That is the end of the quest, you don't go beyond that. Either you believe that or you don't.

**J.G.** Is the novel you are working on [*The Thanatos Syndrome*] an expression of your faith?

**W.P.** Yes. It is set a little further along than *Love in the Ruins.* I'm about halfway through. I'm having a tough time with it, but I've been working on it pretty well. It is not as optimistic as *The Second Coming.* I got a letter yesterday from a girl in Griffin, Georgia. She's a reporter on a local paper, twenty-three years old, she said she liked all of my novels, and she really wrote knowledgeably about the connection between Kierkegaard's philosophy and the actual situations in the novels. She understood it perfectly, but she could not understand *why* it was necessary that at the end of my novels a man had to fall in love and get married: boy meets girl, and sure enough boy falls in love and marries girl. She said, "Is that necessary? Do you have to get married?"

I hadn't thought about it, I guess they did mostly get married. It seems that the nearest approximation, humanly speaking, of happiness is human love. You would like for your characters to get out of the fix they are in and achieve some kind of happiness. The best way to do it, the easiest way to do it, is to fall in love. A man falls in love with a woman or vice versa. If both happen at the same time, that's pretty good. But Tom More is not doing well in his marriage right now. His wife is not very happy with him. They have fallen on difficult times.

# *Interview with Ron Rash*

WITH THOMAS BJERRE'S PARTICIPATION

◆◆◆◆◆◆

*Clemson, South Carolina, October 28, 2014*

Ron Rash. Courtesy of *Clemson World* magazine, Ashley Jones, university photographer

◆◆◆◆◆◆

*With some questions by Thomas Bjerre*

**Jan Nordby Gretlund** I would like to talk first about your novel *The Cove* [2012]. There are innumerable skills, it seems, that you had to have on a farm in the Carolina mountains at the beginning of the twentieth century. There were hard chores for everybody.—It seems to be important for you that we know what it was like to live on a small farm a hundred years ago, so your novel becomes a cultural history, as well.

**Ron Rash** It's a way to allow the reader entry into another way of life, almost a different world. I think part of what a writer can do is to help preserve a culture.

**J.G.** Some writers do, but hardly ever as detailed as you do.

**R.R.** I think such details make the story much more real. It allows the reader to go deeper into the characters' world. If you can get those details as right as possible, it keeps the reader in "the dream" of the novel. But what I also find interesting is that people read novels, which are "lies," in order to learn about real things.

**J.G.** I suppose we read to find out about real things in our lives *and* about our choices.

**R.R.** Oh yes, ultimately the work has to transcend the time and place to matter. If my work does not connect to readers outside my region, *their* experiences of being alive in the world, then I have failed.

**J.G.** You also take great care in getting the words and expressions right, for example the expression "lipping full." What is the origin of that expression?

**R.R.** "Lipping full" means so full that it comes to the lip of the bucket.

**J.G.** And the word "lief," which reminds me of Danish and German dialects?

**R.R.** Used in the expression "as lief," it means "rather," as in "I would as lief do something else." It was used by Shakespeare.—Many such words and expressions were still in use in the North Carolina hills, where I spent my summers at my grandmother's farmhouse, near Boone.—When I was older and in graduate school, reading Chaucer and Shakespeare, I saw words I had heard in Appalachian songs and speech. When the immigrants from the British Isles came here, they brought their ballads and vocabulary.

**J.G.** The traditional community in your novel *The Cove* does play traditional instruments such as the violin, called "the fiddle," the flute, and even the dulcimer, now known as an electrified instrument called a "cittern," in country music.

It struck me that another tradition you describe—the covering of the mirrors after a death in a country family—was also known among upper-class Charlestonians in the nineteenth century [see, among others, Pam Durban's novel *So Far Back* (2000)].

**R.R.** When I was growing up and when I was still young, there were still people in the Appalachians, and in other parts of the South, I'm sure, who were doing this. It was the belief that the ghost could come out through the mirror, yes that and stopping the clock, those kinds of things.—I grew up with a number of superstitions.

**J.G.** It is tempting to quote Flannery O'Connor's Hazel Motes: "As long as I'm doing it, it is still being done."

**R.R.** Right!

**J.G.** The farmers in your novel *The Cove* worry much about their reputation, the family's reputation. And they worry about their honor, the honor of Laurel and Hank, her brother. These preoccupations may be read as history through some romantic haze. The difficulty for the novelist is, perhaps, to also bring out the hardship and harsh reality of the early twentieth century in the Carolina mountains.

**R.R.** The one thing I *don't* want to do is to sentimentalize that era.—So I show how arduous building a well was. That's hard work.—Laurel works hard. Then you see those women in the dress shop who are condescending to her and how Laurel is targeted by the community's superstitions. But I hope the reader senses that I am also writing about the present.

Class consciousness is still with us today. In the United States we have wars started by the people with the power and wealth, but *they* never go, and their children do not go. It is the less privileged Americans who go to Iraq and Afghanistan. I think we should have kept the draft, because then we would have been much more cautious about what we were getting into.

**J.G.** Even though there is a town close by, everybody on the farm lives in isolation, and more so as they are living in the actual cove that the novel owes its title. The social classes can be divided by what radio station they listen to, from NPR to a country music station, and the few black people would listen to a third station. That is the setting. And your main characters are Laurel, who is unmarried and has a pink birthmark as an obvious facial feature, and a runaway German, who has little English. And out of these materials you create a most engaging love story. Well done!

If I had had to choose, I would probably have concentrated on the German flutist and how he is able to dodge all these people without letting on that he is "the enemy," a German!

**R.R.** He is a musician who comes into the "underworld" of the Cove, and even deeper into the underworld when he is digging for water. I use the Orpheus myth, but I wanted to alter the myth—the musician is finally ready to become a real artist, *because* he has now suffered. I would argue that very often, unlike Orpheus, the artist is the survivor. They survive the deep emotional wound, and the loss and pain are what allow them to become artists. In the original myth, Orpheus, before his loss of Eurydice, was able to move everybody and everything to tears, even inanimate objects.

**J.G.** I should have spotted your use of the Orpheus myth when Laurel's true nature is brought back by "a musical instrument," and by your art. You have people who play the flute and otherwise pretend to be mute and some people who speak up—and some who do both.

The time and the nationality are, of course, important, as the United States declared war on Germany in April 1917. But then all of a sudden, and in spite of all the German immigrants living in the United States, an extensive witch hunt for Germans—any Germans—was started. It was a hunting of Germans, even for those whose families had lived in the United States for generations. Who would have thought it possible?

**R.R.** In Schenectady, New York, pinochle was outlawed because it was associated with Germans. Drinking beer was viewed as unpatriotic in some places, and several people of German descent were lynched, even some who had been born in America. In the novel it is a tipoff that they are playing pinochle in the prison. In short, people were being victimized because of their origin and language.

**J.G.** So there is a direct connection between being victimized because of a birthmark like Laurel to being hunted as a German, like Walter in the novel.

**R.R.** And to jump into the future—that kind of phobia against certain groups is still with us. If, during the war with Iraq, you said, "I think entering Iraq was wrong," you could be accused of not being a patriot or even of being *a traitor.*

**J.G.** I think that your greatest achievement in *The Cove* is that you actually create a fascist—the kind of fascist that even the Europeans had not yet created—at the time of the novel. The creation of an American fascist in a small town in the South during World War I offers much insight into the human psyche. The novel deserves attention for its history, myth, poetry, drama, tragedy, and psychology.—The same could be said about your novel *Serena* [2008] with the history of the clear-cutting of the woods and the poetry.

**R.R.** I hoped readers sensed such things.

**J.G.** And *Serena* is a thriller, because the reader doesn't know what is going to happen.—I have not seen the movie yet—but it surprises me, based on the reviews, that Susanne Bier could not get more out of a novel that seems laid out in scenes like a play. The very first scene in the novel—when a young woman, her baby, and her angry father are at the station waiting for the train to arrive in order to confront the child's father, who is newly wed and arriving home to his estate with his bride—does seem to offer all the qualities of a dramatic opening. The same is true of the final scene where Serena, the evil woman, finally pays for her many crimes and her egotism. She is killed at her timber plantation in Brazil, and a guard identifies the killer in a photo of Serena's long-dead husband. The novel is a wonderful

Shakespearean tragedy. What more could Susanne Bier, or Hollywood, possibly want from the novelist?

**R.R.** I haven't seen the movie, but I've heard neither of those scenes is in it.

**J.G.** How can these scenes *not* be in there?

**R.R.** I don't know. I did not have any contact with the people involved, except for a few conversations with Christopher Kyle, the screenwriter, where he was asking some technical questions.

**J.G.** I read the screenplay, it is on the net. I have a copy in Odense, and it seems okay to me.

**R.R.** I had heard the screenplay was good.

**J.G.** The unfortunate thing was really that *The Hunger Games* had sequels. If there had been only the first film, that would have helped. Of course, somebody owns the actors, they are *investments.*

**R.R.** Yes, I suppose so.

**J.G.** Maybe the actors had not been in the game long enough to make demands.

**R.R.** It would be interesting to find out what really happened, because Bier is hinting in some interviews that there was a problem. But it does seem a shame that a powerful female director and a powerful female star could not depict a woman as strong as Serena. It makes me glad I am a novelist and have full control over what I create in its final form.

**J.G.** I hope that will be possible eventually, perhaps when they stop making *Hunger Games* movies.

**Thomas Bjerre** Many of your characters feel a deep attachment to the land, but some also feel entrapped by it, like Leonard Shuler in *The World Made Straight* [2006], who feels closed in. You use the phrase "landscape and destiny"; is there a tension between them?

**R.R.** It is something I sense among mountain people around the world. There are two responses to being in a mountain region, whether it is in Quebec or Switzerland or here. One is a sense of the mountains like a womb, protecting oneself from outside forces, so there's a feeling of safety in that. But there is also the feeling of being closed in—a sense of oppression and of being reminded daily of how small and insignificant your life is compared to the mountains that have been here for eons. I am fascinated with the psychology of someone who grows up in such places.

In a sense, the landscape is Laurel's destiny, to some degree it is for Leonard as well. The landscape has trapped Laurel in the Cove. There is a kind of inevitability, because the landscape has decided her destiny. In the novel the one way she can transcend that landscape and inevitable destiny is through a triumph of the imagination. Laurel creates the Vaterland in her imagination, the same idea Coleridge is getting at in "Kubla Khan."

In a very different way, Nick Carraway and Jay Gatsby in *The Great Gatsby* evoke the Midwestern landscape's expansiveness, the endless sense of the possible.

**J.G.** And Nick is a judgmental character as well, because what he finds in the East is corruption. So it becomes tempting to draw the rather naïve conclusion about the classic American novel: the closer you are to the land, the further you are from corruption.

**T.B.** In much of your fiction we meet characters who wish to escape our lies about family and society and expectations, often through education. But they are met with scorn and suspicion by their surroundings. Is this due to an anti-intellectual streak? Or is it due to the traditional gender notion:

real men don't read—they do physical labor?

**R.R.** In such a culture, men and women have defined roles. What very often happens with class, I am sure almost anywhere in the world, is that there is a sense that the moving out of one's class can be perceived as an act of betrayal. You are turning your back on your heritage. I have seen some of that in my own family. So there's always a tension between the need to escape and the need to stay.—I have a story, "Those Who Are Dead Are Only Now Forgiven," collected in *Nothing Gold Can Stay* [2013], where an ambitious young man wants to leave, but his girlfriend won't leave with him. In the last scene he decides he too will stay.

**J.G.** This reminds me of Percival Everett's *Assumption* [2011], a novel set among mountain meth people in the West.

**R.R.** I know the book you are talking about. Everett is an underrated writer in this country.

**J.G.** But Everett has removed himself from his origin in Columbia, South Carolina, to the West—and also somewhat from his racial history—trying to do other things in another place, which we just talked about. It has its price. But even in his western settings, it would be difficult to argue that he turns his back on his origin and background. But some readers may still feel betrayed.

**T.B.** As regards gender, to what extent do you see characters as guided or challenged by strict gender norms *today* (we already talked about it in the past). Are they still with us? Do you expect your wife to cook your dinner, or change the linen, or to do other domestic chores like that?

**R.R.** I think a lot of that is changing and has changed. My younger brother and I are English majors, but my sister is an engineer. She had times when she had to fight that condescending attitude toward her as woman. She could, she is as tall as I am, and she can be ferocious.

**J.G.** Are you going to—or maybe you already did—put your sister in some fiction?

**R.R.** She is as strong as Serena, but much nicer, thank goodness. Often Serena is connected to Lady Macbeth, but she is not like Lady Macbeth, who starts breaking down and feels remorse and, off stage, kills herself. Serena is stronger than that.

**J.G.** Have you ever met a woman like Serena?

**R.R.** Not yet, have *you*?

**J.G.** No, on the contrary.—Characters challenged or guided by strict gender norms are actually one of your *main* themes. Thomas Bjerre brings it up. When we talk about it, it is clear to me that we see society's expected gender norms mirrored again and again in your fiction and poetry.

**R.R.** I'm interested in *that* and how it is in different periods. Time is a kind of geography, because it takes you to radically different places, even within one's own country. What an artist wants is *conflict,* which is what makes novels and stories interesting. But to see these women, expected to react in a certain way, react against society is to me just a fascinating conflict to explore. Serena is the most obvious example of this.

**J.G.** Yes, I agree, but when we first see Serena, she has already graduated beyond anything society expected.

**R.R.** Yes, but we see Rachel going beyond what is expected of her by the local society, and we see her increasing strength. Laurel, of *The Cove,* is once again going against the dominating culture, for example by not betraying Walter, the German, as the local people would want her to do. She is obviously outside the established society; and so is Marcie when she protects her lover from Sheriff Beasley in the short story "Burning Bright," which became the title story of a collection in 2010.

**T.B.** Some of your short stories tackle subjects such as addiction and returning war veterans. But why is it that all your novels, except one, are set in the past? Is there a particular reason why you don't take on contemporary Appalachia in novel form?

**R.R.** Oh, *I think I do!* Contemporary issues are certainly raised. In *Serena,* there is the issue of environmental destruction, and this is happening right now in Appalachia with "mountaintop removal." Those are people within their own culture, and they are destroying their own world. But it is complex as they have families, and it is the best-paying job they can find in the region.—I would claim that every book I have written has been as much about the present as about the past. For example, *The Cove* is certainly about the xenophobia of the United States today.

**J.G.** Even if the issues are still with us, you *do* choose to set the novels in a particular past. Since Shakespeare we have known that some drama in the present is needed.

**R.R.** My new novel, *Above the Waterfall* [2015], is actually set in the present.

**T.B./J.G.** What do you consider the biggest challenges in your region today?

**R.R.** That is what I am going to be talking about in my new novel. Certainly, one of the challenges is environmental, and that has national implications, as well. What about our protected national forests—we have so many in western North Carolina—are they to be opened up for mining and fracking? Appalachia is now no longer able to insulate itself from the problems of the world. Those challenges are very much parts of the new novel.

# *Interviews with Dori Sanders*

◆◆◆◆◆◆

*York County, South Carolina, March 11, 1996; Aeroe Island, Denmark, August 23, 1997; Beaufort, South Carolina, January 29, 1999; Hilton Head, South Carolina, November 5, 2010*

Dori Sanders

◆◆◆◆◆◆

**Jan Nordby Gretlund** When we look at your two novels, it is obvious that *Clover* [1990] is the more popular. Is there a good reason for that?

**Dori Sanders** I think *Clover* became a harbinger of a trend yet to come. When it was published, it was described as "unique" and based on "an intriguing premise." And in a little way, it *was* a kind of first: a little black girl in the South tells the story of her life with a white woman, her stepmother. It was unusual then that the novel is narrated by a young girl. What makes it unique is that the novel is not laced with hate, and a lot of the bones that African Americans may feel pressed upon to pick are *not* picked. I am not an angry person, and for me to address anger, even in fiction, would not become genuinely real.

**J.G.** Why didn't *Her Own Place* [1993], your second novel, do as well as *Clover?*

**D.S.** I don't know why, I have yet to figure that out. It did *not* do as well. I think maybe it was because it was an old story told by an old woman. *Clover* was a *new* book, but there is not a new book in the Mae Lee Barnes story.

**J.G.** If we look at African American literature, how many old women like Mae Lee Barnes do we actually encounter?

**D.S.** *Not* very many! I sincerely believe that some of the critics found it difficult to understand that book!

**J.G.** Well, it is not a book for readers looking for *action.* I taught both novels, and *Clover* is easy to teach because things are going on, new things happen. But when we look at *Her Own Place* we are faced not only with a few interesting scenes but with *a whole life.*

**D.S.** Exactly!—It is slow. One critic wrote that the trouble with the novel is that Sanders leads us into an unbelievable group of women, who do nothing until forced to. It is a rule not to write the reviewers, but what I wanted to tell this one was: "I am so pleased that you saw a side of the South that truly does exist and that I was totally unaware of. I know that I wrongly depicted my Southern black women, because they don't sit on the front porch and shell peas and talk about what they are going to eat. Black Southern women are way ahead of that and have always been. For years, with the few hours they have, they have been busy challenging Einstein's theory of relativity. Thank you for setting me straight."

What do they do?

**J.G.** They work themselves to death.

**D.S.** It is true to life.

**J.G.** It brings out a Zora Neale Hurston reply and the idea of the woman as the mule of the world. And Angela Davis, Margaret Walker, and Alice Walker would agree.—Do these writers mean anything to *you* now?

**D.S.** They truly do!—I have read them. It is just that you have to realize, when you think about it, that every Southern life, even if you are a *Negro,* does not necessarily follow all that happens. Many African Americans wrote of the hardship of lives spent as sharecroppers under the harsh hand of a terrible white owner. But in my case, I am here, and now as a woman, sixty-some-odd years of age, that's me. . . .

**J.G.** Sixty-one!—Weren't you born June 8, 1934?

**D.S.** Yes—sure, they [that is, this interviewer, in the *South Carolina Encyclopedia*] got it wrong! When somebody ever puts your age in your favor and you are a woman from South Carolina, you make no correction.—But if they *add* one month to your age, you start screaming and braying like a white-mouthed mule: "You got my age wrong!" But if you make a mistake the other way, especially if you make a wonderfully *good* decision, we start to mull and we say nothing, because you have given us much joy!

**J.G.** You should not be worrying, you look about forty-eight. So, start mulling.

**D.S.** Well, all right.—Remember, going back in time, that my daddy bought the first eighty-one acres of farmland around 1915–16. So I go back to a time when my stories are *certified* stories—I know because I lived with my grandfather at an early age. He was a man who had very little memory, because he had been so harshly treated as a little slave boy carrying water.

**J.G.** When we talked about this in Conway, I got the impression that in your work in progress your grandfather plays an important part.

**D.S.** Yes, but *not* on that side, though. The story I am writing now is of my paternal grandmother. She was a wonderful mixture, which I think is true of every race on the face of the earth, because Hitler was unable to fulfill his lurid and wretched dream. That mixture is there, and I have a Native American heritage from my paternal grandmother. But of what tribe is not clearly definable.—I strongly suspect a tribe, but since my work in progress might veer from that tribe, it is better for me to leave it unknown.

◆ ◆ ◆

**J.G.** In *Her Own Place* a certain hammock is brought to our attention at least eight times, sprinkled throughout the novel, and that's often enough to become a symbol.

**D.S.** It *is* symbolic, and characteristic of a sense of a certain place. The hammock in our front yard seemed to me, growing up, to offer a sense of comfort and belonging.—Not that I could get in and out of it without getting myself bundled up, entangled, and "all tore up." I *never* mastered the art of entering or leaving a hammock.—My father doubtlessly knotted the mesh and made our hammock, because he made every piece of furniture we had, chairs, desks, and lawn furniture.—I couldn't envision my home without our hammock.

**J.G.** You strongly associate your home place with your father. What are the differences between the fictional character Gaten Hill in *Clover* and your own father?

**D.S.** There are differences only in time, only through the time span. My daddy had that little weird sense of humor that Gaten has in the novel. I would be standing in the kudzu vine and he would come up to me and say, "I'm looking for my little girl, have you seen her?" And I would say, "It is me!" Then he showed that sense of play and began to describe me in great detail as I actually was, and I cried, "That's me, I am that little girl!"

He was a man with five boys and five girls, and each of us a strong presence in his life. He was so real to each of us and was *there* for every one of us. But now beyond that, there was the peach growing and the feel that he didn't let you go too far off on a tangent:

"You saw a bear in the woods? Are you sure it was a bear?" Or "A rabbit was in the field, it was *that* long!" And my father would say, "Are you sure it was *that* long? Now let's not get carried away." In the novel Clover would say, "I'm trying to wash the cancer off my body." And Gaten would say, "Now Clover let's not get carried away!" There are obvious parallels.

But my father could not have met a white woman, as in the plot of *Clover,* because I grew up in a totally segregated society. Integration did not even begin to usher itself into our school system, or into our area, until very late in the 1960s. It gets to our neck of the woods and to all the community schools in the early 1970s.—And my father was not killed in a traffic accident, and obviously my mother didn't die in childbirth. They both died in old age.—But a sense of *professionalism* applies to my father's image.

**J.G.** Your father was an elementary school principal here in York County, wasn't he?

**D.S.** He left the teaching profession in 1912 to re-enter a community college to study algebra and Latin. He said later that it was the only worthwhile job he had ever had, because he so yearned for higher learning.

I think my father would have been proud of me, and I think he would have understood *why* I didn't yearn for learning. It was because he exposed me to it every day of my life. And once a child is exposed to such a studious pattern of reading, you sort of tire of it, at least I did. But it serves as a basis for my writing. We had wonderful books.

**J.G.** When I read *Clover* and Kaye Gibbons' *Ellen Foster* [1987], I get the sense that we are in a period of female Huckleberry Finns.

**D.S.** I have, of course, read Mark Twain, absolutely. My problem with *Ellen Foster* is that I have yet to read it. It is just that early on, when *Ellen Foster* and *Clover* were both published by Algonquin Books, I shared readings with Kaye. So I felt in my head that I knew everything that book contained, but I really didn't. I only know it from the portions I heard Kaye read.

I used Clover as my young narrator in order to illustrate the real life of the children of my area. What did they really have to say and think about? I shaped Clover from a little boy that lived on the farm. He would mostly come with his shoelaces untied, and I would shout, "You'd better tie them shoelaces or you're gonna fall and break your neck!"—his nickname was "Smudge"—and he would shout back, "Oh, it's a style!" It was fashionable not to tie the laces, craziest thing I've heard in my life.

Smudge would sometimes ride his bike up to the peach shed and brag about this new friend he had. He bragged about this friend every day. I believe he called him "Jake," and he was the most important boy in the world! I got so tired of hearing about this boy, but, yes, I formed a mental image of Jake, a little boy larger than my friend Smudge, and I had an image of a boy with a crazy hairdo. Then one day, after three weeks in the month of July of hearing about this boy, Smudge finally brought him by. Guess what Jake looked like:

a little blue-eyed, freckle-faced boy with red hair. Smudge had never ever mentioned that Jake was white and stammered! My mental image had been of a boy much like Smudge, but race didn't matter to the boys. And I tried to shape Clover to fit in with the age group where they look at people for who they are and what they can do for you.

**J.G.** In your Clover there is still a lot of the Huckleberry who has to see the ugly world of the grown-ups, much too early.

**D.S.** Of course, Clover is much like little Huck. I have also come to that conclusion, but I wasn't consciously trying to shape Clover that way.

**J.G.** Some of the criticism of *Clover* was that you were too positive, too optimistic! Some people called your novel a fairy tale too removed from reality. You answered the criticism by saying these were the experiences of your life and the way you had seen it.—If we talk of the future, do you think that optimism about biracial harmony is reasonable?

**D.S.** I am pleased that some find the novel optimistic. As I said, it is not an angry book. Some people feel that it is sugarcoated.

**J.G.** African American critics?

**D.S.** Some of them whites! But some of these people fail to see the cutting edges in *Clover*, and they do not get the other side of the criticism.—In short, they do not read my mail! I have boxes of mail from across the country saying that I have not been fair, in many ways, to the white race.—Somebody wrote that maybe if the characters cared as much for people as they do for animals, they would be better off.—So, do you see how hard it is?

**J.G.** It is the aim of all good fiction to create a debate and to call attention to some very real problems. And the reactions to *Clover* prove that your fiction does exactly that!—To what extent is *Clover* a truly African American novel?

**D.S.** To the extent that when Sara Kate comes to the Hill house, everyone in the family gathered around when she rode up, except Gideon who kept eating his slice of watermelon and spitting out the seeds.

**J.G.** You describe the "strange, uneasy feeling" that fills the house and "settles upon them." This reads as symbolism of the two races in the same house.

**D.S.** Definitely!

**J.G.** When I interviewed Reverend Martin King Sr. in the Ebenezer Baptist Church, he said that the only great problems facing successful integration are the psychological barriers between the races, and "you can lead a mule to water, but you can't make it drink!" Clover and Sara Kate are "Two people in a house. Together, yet apart." Are Clover and Sara Kate actually overcoming the psychological barriers?

**D.S.** I would say that in this case, it would be true, especially for Clover. And, remember we do not get into Sara Kate's head. All I did was to get Clover to say what *she* thinks Sara Kate is thinking.—Clover is aware that if she stands up for Sara Kate, which she does, the family will let her know about family loyalty *to them.* This is mainly voiced by Aunt Everleen. So Clover has to live a double life, depending on who is present.

**J.G.** If we look at the jealousy between Aunt Everleen and Sara Kate, the trouble is not necessarily a *racial* issue.

**D.S.** No!—They are two women fighting for territorial rights. And also there is the well-known accusation "I do all of this, and you do nothing!"

**J.G.** The dispute is perhaps even more about who will bring up Clover, which does imply white versus black values, even if they do try to unite their efforts.

**D.S.** Exactly! The two women do bond in their efforts to bring up Clover, and for that they have to create a racial harmony in the family.

**J.G.** Sara Kate knows her CPR when Uncle Jim Ed, a big black man, needs it; nobody else knows what to do. She saves him by giving him mouth-to-mouth resuscitation. It is implied that the interracial taboos may only be ignored in a life-or-death situation.

When the whole black community are together welcoming Sara Kate and studying her, they are disappointed that she is *not* a "poor-white-trash" woman, as most of them had expected. Many are jealous. The novel is *also* about class.

**D.S.** Exactly! Everleen thought at first that Sara Kate would be a stringy-haired girl from the mills. They were hoping she would be "poor white trash"; then they would have had something to pick.—But Clover is no Pollyanna, she knows what is happening, and Jim Ed has to correct the women: "the white woman is not coming from where you thought she was."

**J.G.** We have now established that the novel is not only about *race* but also about *gender* and *class.*

**D.S.** The black community had already picked the piano teacher to be Gaten Hill's wife, and they would not have accepted anybody else—even if she had been a black woman.

**J.G.** I noticed that the main character's full name is Clover Lee Hill, and the "Lee" part reminds me that this is very much a Southern book. Did you call her "Lee" to bring in Southern history?

**D.S.** Yes.—Clover is not really a name for a girl, although it is an endearing name, as you know, it is a town. But once you have a little girl named Clover, you got to make it real and to solidify, so I had to bring in the "Lee."—In *Her Own Place* the main character, Mae Lee Barnes, also has "Lee" as a part of her name.

**J.G.** My thinking on *Her Own Place,* and the reason why it did not take off as wildfire, is that to a certain extent it doesn't read as fiction but more like biography.

**D.S.** Yes, it does, and there is a lot of biography there. I didn't spice it up too much—or fictionalize that story. To tell you the truth, the book is an autobiographical sketch of *every woman* in my town.

**J.G.** You emphasize the words "every woman," and in today's literary climate *Her Own Place* is, of course, instantly categorized as "women's literature," because here you are entering sister-bonding territory.

**D.S.** The point of departure for that is World War II, as that was the time when women in my world were able to find the little trace toward independence that would serve them for the rest of their lives. Because for the first time they were able to get off the farm and find jobs! Just north of here is where the old munitions plant stood. It was just called the "war plant."

Last summer [1995] the last remaining portions of that plant, which I never had a chance to revisit, was torn down. On a hot summer's day, a man who worked for a television station up here loaded his car with every relic and remembrance he could find, in front of the bulldozers, and brought them to me. They are housed in a little hut soon to be a museum of that period.

**J.G.** You talk like you worked in that plant yourself. Did you?

**D.S.** It is kind of hard to say. . . .

**J.G.** So we are back to the enigma of your age. Well, if you had worked in a munitions plant in 1945, the last year of World War II, you would, according to your official age, have been eleven years old!

**D.S.** Let me tell you, I am now the same height as I was then. I was the tallest kid on the block. A lot of us went to work there, even though we were not quite old enough. All you had to do was to be tricky and change your age. Nobody in our community had any birth certificate. The plant was out in the middle of nowhere.—And I worked too hard!

**J.G.** How much did they pay you?

**D.S.** Very, very little, but more than we had ever earned; sometimes they would let you work around the clock, seven days a week.

**J.G.** Were you an all-black women crew?

**D.S.** No, there were white and black women. It was just that the whites got the best jobs. Of course, most of them worked in the office or in the cataloguing department, where they decided what was to be shipped where.—We did hard work such as torching and painting the shells, but we were trained to do it.

There was one thing that was very sophisticated about the whole operation—the jobs were rotated. They did not want you to get too good at any one particular skill or to know too much about what was going on. So they had the rotation of jobs. Maybe if you knew too much about it. . . .

**J.G.** You would make yourself a shell!

**D.S.** You got it! [laughing]

**J.G.** When was this job over?

**D.S.** As soon as the war was over.

**J.G.** Do you still have friends from that time, who worked with you?

**D.S.** Yes, I still have some friends from that time.

**J.G.** What was the plant called?

**D.S.** To begin with it was the "the war plant" or "munitions plant," and then it became the "shellplant" and finally just "the plant."

**J.G.** There is an emphasis also in *Her Own Place* on hard work and on race, gender, and class, as in *Clover.* In your fiction men are repeatedly saying, "A woman should not work that hard," but they work the women hard anyway.

**D.S.** And if you think that's bad.—If a woman is struggling on her own land, trying to make a living from farm land that belongs to her *and* she has proved to be good in the kitchen, some well-heeled white woman would want to lure the black woman off her land and into her kitchen. She would just be putting you down:

"You shouldn't be out *there,* it is much nicer and cooler in my nice kitchen."

Most women work in their kitchens. All the young women in my family grew up working on my father's farm. He said, "Children, this is *your land,* this is something that will be forever."

**J.G.** Gaten Hill is a positive male figure in *Clover,* although dead in most of the novel. In *Her Own Place* all the men, save maybe the white landowner, are unreliable or at least fickle, you can't depend on them, they disappear. Sociology shows that many black families are without grown-up males. Is or was this true also in the country?

**D.S.** Oh, absolutely! I felt pressed upon to write about that particular aspect of the African American male in *Her Own Place.* But if I looked to my father and my brothers, the only images I could have portrayed would have been positive. But then I realized that not every man in the community was like my daddy and not every young man like my brothers. So I figured in *Her Own Place* I had better become realistic. One of the things that happened, when the war was over, was the return of young men. And they said the war had changed them. They found that there no longer was a place for them. *They* were changed, but what they did not realize was that *so were the women* they returned to! The women had now experienced bringing home checks with their own names on them.

**J.G.** *Her Own Place,* like Ralph Ellison's *Invisible Man,* reads like a history of a period: the coming of electricity, women in industry, civil rights, integration, black people returning from the North, et cetera.

**D.S.** I was doing a life of Mae Lee Barnes, and you can't put aside change if you do a life. And I try to put it all into the novel.—My editors and a several critics feel that *Her Own Place* is by far the superior work.

**J.G.** I think it is, in terms of rendering the black American experience. But I don't read fiction to be educated in history. I like fiction, and the history and the sociology belong in there, but I want to know Mae Lee Barnes not as an abstraction of history but as a fully rounded human being, and I do. But in *Clover* I get *to know* several people.

**D.S.** Aha, aha!

**J.G.** It is a strong community you write about, everybody helps bringing in the crops. And everybody knows everything about everybody.

**D.S.** That is absolutely true. When you live in a community, you know everything about everybody. You also know everything about every white person, because—who is in the kitchen?

**J.G.** Your father takes up a lot of space in your mind, but your brother Orestes is even more present in your life, it seems. You often mention him.

**D.S.** The reason is that we were the only ones stupid enough to till the farm. Everybody else was smart enough to leave. Out of ten children it was Orestes and Dori who kept the farm going.—Right now we are having some wood cut and every day I remind Orestes about that, because he has to do a lot of bushwhacking.

**J.G.** But he is not a young man.

**D.S.** Orestes is in his eighties.

**J.G.** And you are the youngest?

**D.S.** No, my sister is no. 10.

**J.G.** If a crop failed, you once told me, Orestes would say to you, "We need us another book." I feel we need us another book, too! You told me that the third novel will be about a little boy who got a cracked skull from the overseer's whip. And the plan was to include some real trouble, when a white man jumped the line and wanted his cotton ginned first. I think I saw traces of that in your little brown book essay called "Promise Land:

A Farmer Remembers" from 2004. Are you still planning a new novel?

**D.S.** I am thinking about reworking that manuscript.

# *Interviews with Eudora Welty*

◆ ◆ ◆ ◆ ◆ ◆

*1119 Pinehurst Street, Jackson, Mississippi, February 9 and June 8, 1978*

Eudora Welty

◆ ◆ ◆ ◆ ◆ ◆

**Jan Nordby Gretlund** In an essay on Jane Austen, in 1969, you wrote that "the interesting situations of life can, and notably do, take place at home." Was your childhood home full of "interesting situations"?

**Eudora Welty** No, not especially. My family wasn't the *usual* kind in the South, because both my parents came from away. So there were no blood-kin aunts, uncles, grandparents, and so on. Different ones came from time to time, but in those days people couldn't lightly travel from Ohio and West

Virginia to visit. So it was mostly our immediate family circle. Of course there were things going on. I had two younger brothers. But in the homes of my friends, who grew up with large families around them, that's where I got that insight—and when I went to my parents' homes, especially my mother's in West Virginia, where she had five brothers. But in the Jane Austen essay, I was writing a generalization of something I believe; I wasn't drawing it out of my own life in particular.

J.G. It is obvious from your fiction that you take great pleasure in oral narratives. Was there a tradition of storytelling in your family?

E.W. Yes, on my mother's side they were big storytellers. When her brothers came here to visit, they would renew the stories of their youth, funny things that happened in West Virginia out in the country. They grew up on a farm. Every name they mentioned would bring out gales of laughter and reminiscences and there would be songs: "Remember how we used to sing?" So they would all sing it.

J.G. In *Delta Wedding,* Laura says that Uncle George "evidently felt that old stories, family stories, Mississippi stories, were the same as very holy or very passionate, if stories could be those things." Can they?

E.W. To some people. Oh yes, sure—Laura is trying to comprehend that sort of thing. Family stories are where you get your first notions of profound feelings, mysterious feelings that you might not understand till you grow into them. But you know they exist and that they have power.

J.G. Some of Laurel McKelva's memories center on the library of her childhood home. Were the classics mentioned in *The Optimist's Daughter,* that is, Tennyson, Dickens, and Gibbon, in your parents' library?

E.W. Yes, they were. Besides Mark Twain, Henry James, and Ring Lardner—he is a classic to me. My parents always had books, for which I am deeply grateful. I grew up in a family of readers. No book was prohibited to me. As far as Dickens goes, he meant a great deal to my mother. She had been given a set of Dickens as a little girl, as reward for having her hair cut. She had chosen that over a pair of golden earrings to pierce her ears, in those days much favored by little girls, especially in Virginia and West Virginia. Her father was a very poor country lawyer with a large family, but he ordered the books from Baltimore, and they came up the river packed in a barrel. She adored those books, so that later when she was married she brought them to Jackson. When our house caught on fire, she went back into the burning house, although she was on crutches at the time, and began throwing that set of Dickens out the window to save it.

J.G. You have said recently that parts of *The Optimist's Daughter* are "literal memory." To what extent are the West Virginia scenes your literal memory?

**E.W.** The physical memory of how it looked—the shoals, the mountain—and how it sounded—the memory of the entire setting.

**J.G.** You have mentioned that *The Optimist's Daughter* meant more to you personally than *Losing Battles.*

**E.W.** Yes, because of the strictly personal memories: the way my uncles looked coming home at night through the far-off fields, just white shirts showing down the mountain, and the sound of the horses. All the physical sensations were memories of about age 3, when you really have very sharp sensory perceptions. I still recall this, and I just put it all in there.

**J.G.** You have often pointed out that you never write about people you know, about real people. And you take great pains to stress that Morgana and its inhabitants are fictitious. Miss Katherine Anne Porter, for one, has not accepted your disclaimer in *The Golden Apples.* Below it, in her copy of the book, Miss Porter wrote:

"All right honey, we *shorely* believes you!"

**E.W.** Well, this is the first time I heard about *that!* Of course, any character you write has bits and pieces of somebody, but they are really conceptions of the imagination, which are invented to carry out what I want to do in the story.

Of course, I endow them with things I have observed, dreamed, or understood, but no one represents a real person. I could not do it; it would defeat me in my fiction. I'm sure Katherine Anne was not being literal in the way you imagine. "Morgana" is a made-up name in the tradition of Delta names.

I don't know if the Delta looks like itself any more. It was settled rather late, not early like Natchez and so on. People dug out the logs from the abysmal swamps, the kind Faulkner wrote about hunting in. That's the way the whole Delta looked like up around Coahoma County. And when these people hacked it out and made places, they named them usually after themselves or someone near, or they made a place name out of a family name.—I just noticed this, no one told me.—After Mr. Benton the town would be named "Bentonia." A lot of them were women's names, "Flora" and all sorts of things. I made it Morgana because of the Morgans that were there, although I made it Morgana first and *then* got the Morgans to name it from. I also like having the idea of *fata morgana,* to show that they were living absorbed in illusions. It all went of a piece like that.

**J.G.** If your fiction is not autobiographical, will you accept it if we call it very personal?

**E.W.** Oh yes, it is very personal; they aren't the same thing at all.

**J.G.** Do you feel that a critic has any right to be interested in your personal life?

**E.W.** It all depends on for what purpose. If it is about my work and bears on my work—but not just an idle question. It always reaches the point where people begin to ask you out of curiosity. That gets me edgy. Elizabeth Bowen used to say that every time she gave a public lecture, when they asked questions after, it always reached a point where someone in the audience said, "Do you write better when you're in love?"—And that was the point when she said, "Thank you very much!" and left the platform.

**J.G.** Obviously, Jackson, Mississippi, is a place that has meant a great deal to you. Is that what is implied by the famous statement, supposedly first made to Miss Porter and later quoted by Flannery O'Connor, that you are usually "locally underfoot" in Jackson?

**E.W.** That's just an expression—it means I am always moving around here. "Underfoot" just means present. It is a localism, and it carries some tinge of being in the way.

**J.G.** I admire your house here in Jackson and also the southern houses in your fiction. Do buildings such as the Shellmound Mansion, the MacLain House, the Renfro Farmhouse, and the McKelva House have a special meaning for you?

**E.W.** They have a value in the work of fiction because they convey, I hope, the kind of person, the kind of background, the kind of economic background, to which they belong. It is just as evocative to a knowing reader as saying, "They never went to school," "They make so-and-so much a year," or "They are poor whites," or "They are ambitious people on the make." You can't make a mistake in something like that and write well. I think it is important not strictly that you see the house in your mind's eye but rather that you know these facts.

**J.G.** Mr. Walker Percy has written that "town and writer sustain each other in secret ways." Jackson, Mississippi, has obviously sustained you all your life, but is it necessarily "in secret ways"?

**E.W.** No! Unless he means "the ways are not very easy to communicate" and they probably have no bearing on what the writing is. The relationship exists, but it should be of no interest to the reader of a piece. I certainly agree that the ways are many and profound.

**J.G.** Do you feel that the essential part of what you say about fellow Mississippians could have been said with equal validity about anybody else?

**E.W.** Think of it like this: what I was trying to say about Mississippi was like being drawn to a magnet of that one place—well, there is another magnet in the next place! I think the same kind of relationship exists, but the things related would not be the same things. Mississippi and Alabama and maybe parts of Georgia would be sort of alike. Tennessee is very different. Louisiana is totally different. Virginia is different. They all have their own truths. I think the same relationship would exist, but the same bindings would not be there. Of course, this country, as you can see everywhere, is changing. Places are not as different as they were when I began writing.

**J.G.** Is it still possible here in Jackson to send your taproots down far enough to give you a sense of origin?

**E.W.** I don't know about the ones coming along now. But everybody I grew up with has that same feeling of roots. Children growing up now have lived in five or six houses by the time they are ten years old.

**J.G.** Does that make the children rootless and restless?

**E.W.** I suppose, and every place is getting to be somewhat alike. In the future, it is not going to be the same. But I think there will still be a deep sense of family to people who have grown up with that. I can't help but think that.

**J.G.** Judge McKelva is buried with a view to the new interstate highway under plastic poinsettias by Fay, his second wife. Is the portrait of Fay, "the little shallow vulgarian," a portrait of the future?

**E.W.** God, I hope not! But I did mean to suggest that she might have that element in her.

**J.G.** Fay does not seem to have a past.

**E.W.** And she doesn't miss it! She doesn't know what it is. I don't know if you happened to see the French reviews of *The Optimist's Daughter* when it came out in France? I am not a very good reader in French, but I did get the point—which was that the only sympathetic character in the book was Fay!

**J.G.** Are you fascinated by the Stovalls, Peacocks, Chisoms, Sistrunks, Reids, et cetera?

**E.W.** Oh yes, I love them all!

**J.G.** Are you a little bit horrified also? It has been suggested that you are "looking down your nose" at these people.

**E.W.** Suggested by whom? That's absurd! I understand them very well indeed. I love them. I know just what's going on in their minds. I don't look down my nose at anyone among my characters. I wouldn't invent somebody in order to look down my nose at them. No, I see the absurd qualities in everybody, and it doesn't matter who they are. I saw the absurd qualities in Judge McKelva, who was of a different order, and in Edna Earle, who is sympathetically telling the story about all the people she herself looks down on.

**J.G.** Is Judge McKelva a "Compson"?

**E.W.** Yes.

**J.G.** Are the Stovalls just "Snopeses" who are taking over in the South?

**E.W.** Let us not be literal about things. People won't stand for being divided up like that. In the red clay hills, farther to the north and east of Yoknapatawpha, there is quite a different social structure. There is nobody else except what you would call poor whites. Yoknapatawpha has an entire gamut running from Compson down to Snopes, with many in between. So there is the friction of Snopeses trying to take other people's places. Nothing like that goes on in the red clay hills because nobody has anything. The only reason that the Stovalls are different from the others is just that they are *meaner.* None of them has a dime.

**J.G.** You have said that in the early '60s there wasn't much difference between Compsons and Snopeses.

**E.W.** It was not I but a friend who made the remark. That was when I was talking about my character in my story "Where Is the Voice Coming From?" when someone told me that I had made my murderer a Snopes and he was a Compson. The remark meant that some of the people who are born so to speak in the Compson neighborhood or family had just as rotten ideas about race at that time as the Snopeses. People who could be racist could be in any part of society. It was meant only in that respect and only at that time, I think.

**J.G.** When you left Jackson to study and work in the North, did you ever feel like your character Laurel McKelva? Did you feel you were also running off leaving somebody that needed you, just to call yourself an artist and to make a lot of money?

**E.W.** I always felt guilty when I left home. I never did want to make the money part. I never had that sort of dream, because I knew it was impossible from the start. The kind of thing I wanted to do was only to. . . . But I always had such a family feeling. I was always conscious of my family here, and I knew they'd miss me. I had an awful guilt feeling all my life about going away. Whenever I was on the Pullman leaving town, we would ride, as the train pulled out of the station, past that sign up there:

"Where will you spend eternity?" I used to think, "Oh God! That's reproaching me." I don't mean I really took it literally and seriously, but it was just my last view of Jackson.

My family was always willing and anxious for me to go away and be things. They never opposed it. They paid for me to go. And there was no reason for it, except I just felt I ought to be back here. That was early on. After I grew up a little, I saw that they could quite well do without me and I without them, periods of the time.

**J.G.** Laurel overcomes her existential crisis and seems to liberate herself from Mount Salus. Doesn't she lose something valuable when she leaves Mississippi?

E.W. Yes. I did not mean that she shook off everything there and went forth a free soul. She was enormously enriched by all she had gone through, and it was her understanding she had gotten. She did not abandon anything. She took it with her, but in a form of accepting it and understanding it for what it was.

J.G. In her story "An Exile in the East," Flannery O'Connor called New York "no kind of place." You have called it a "no man's land," and you have said you can't write stories which take place in New York. Would it ruin your sense of place if you were to use a Northern setting?

E.W. All I meant was that you could not confine anything that you said if you wrote about New York. I love New York; that's why I wouldn't call it "a no man's land" except in the depiction of a character in a story. It was not out of my lack of affection. But as far as using it as material, I find even a town like Jackson too big for me to manage. I have to have a small enough stage, a small enough arena, to confine it and to be able to manipulate what I am doing.

J.G. You were in New York at the beginning of the '30s. It seems to have been a good time to be there.

E.W. It was indeed. It was a good time for me. It was my chance, the first I had ever had, to go to the theater, to the museums, to concerts, and I made use of every moment, let me tell you. I was taking a business course, which meant I didn't have to study at all, so I went to the theater. In those days there were many theaters running, the way they are in London now. And you could go on the night you decided to go. Furthermore, you could get a ticket at $1.10 for the cheapest seat, at the cut-rate drugstore in Times Square. You could buy tickets for a show and rush straight over and see it. Also I didn't mind standing up for anything.

Everybody that was wonderful was then at their peak. People like Noel Coward, all the wonderful music hall stars—Beatrice Lillie, Bert Lahr, Fred Allen, both the Astaires, Jack Benny, Joe Cook, and Ed Wynn. Wonderful dramatic stars, even Nazimova! Katherine Cornell, the Lunts—if I sat down to it, I could make a list of everybody on God's earth that was playing. Martha Graham was dancing solo in a little cubbyhole somewhere. I would go and watch her dance. And Shan—Kar! Everybody was there. For somebody who had never, in a sustained manner, been to the theater or to the Metropolitan Museum, where I now went every Sunday, it was just a cornucopia. We had a good group of people from Jackson there at Columbia to start with, so we had company for everything we wanted to do. We could set forth anywhere. We could go dancing in Harlem to Cab Calloway. We went a lot to Small's Paradise, a nightclub in Harlem where all the great bands were playing then; whites were welcome as anybody else.

I was there at the opening of Mercury Theater, during the WPA days. I remember seeing the opening of the black *Macbeth,* which was put on in Harlem, directed by Orson Welles. The play's location was changed from Scotland to Jamaica. The witches were voodoo priestesses. The queen wore crinolines, the banquet was outdoors under swinging paper lanterns, and the witches were playing the voodoo drums. Hecate was played by a black man dancing on a drum without any clothes on. After the opening night I believe he was made to wear something.

◆◆◆

**J.G.** In a *Paris Review* interview [1972], you said that you do not think of yourself as writing out of any special tradition. Do you acknowledge a kinship with other Southern writers?

**E.W.** Oh yes, I feel that we are all like bathers in the same sea. We all understand and know what we are partaking of. But I think we are each going about it in our own way. So far as I know, we haven't had any definite effect on each other's work. There could be many unconscious effects; I read all the time, I love to read, and I live in books a lot. But as far as the art of writing goes, I have never felt the touch of any other imagination on mine as I write. I think that must be true of all of us. I can't imagine, for instance, three more different writers than Katherine Anne Porter, Flannery O'Connor, and myself.

**J.G.** Do you still keep up with Miss Porter?

**E.W.** Yes. She is a dear friend. She is a great lady, whose work I admire from the bottom of my heart. She came here to give a lecture at a college in March 1952. I drove her down to the Gulf Coast. We looked up Elizabeth Spencer—she lived down there—and we all had a good time together. We drove round the Coast, then pretty unspoiled; it bears no resemblance to what is there today after Hurricane Camille. Katherine Anne loves that part of the world, we were getting near—you know she is from Texas near Louisiana—so driving into southwest Mississippi and Louisiana, we were nearing her bailiwick, and I think she felt that. And she lived in Baton Rouge a long time, where I first met her. All of that country meant something to her, which Jackson didn't.

I saw her a couple of years ago in Maryland after she had been ill. She had moved to the apartment out near Silver Spring where she lives now. She had had cataract operations and a broken hip but had most courageously and indomitably recovered from these. She couldn't see very well yet, but she was getting used to her cataract glasses. She had a secretary to help with her work; she was keeping up with everything. I was in New York and asked if I could stop by and see her. "Darling, do you like catfish?" she said. At that time I had never eaten a catfish in my life. I don't know why. I lived in catfish country where you could get all you could eat for a dollar eighty. But she said she was going to cook some. She is a wonderful cook. So when I came down from New York, Katherine Anne had been cooking all morning. She had cooked these dainty little catfish fingerlings, I guess you call them, little tiny things which you dip in something. She had fresh asparagus. It was early spring, and we had champagne and strawberries. We celebrated. We sat and talked, ate, and drank champagne all afternoon. It was an affecting, really an indelible visit, and we laughed so much all the way through. It was a wonderful reunion.

I haven't seen her since she had her strokes. But I have talked to her on the telephone. Yes, I keep up with her.

**J.G.** From an unpublished Flannery O'Connor letter, it appears that you were on a program with her in November 1962.

**E.W.** That's right. That was in South Carolina. That's how I met her. I admired her work a lot. She "hated me," she told me, because I was supposed to have gone to the University of Chicago once and had illness at home and couldn't leave at the last minute. Flannery went in my place, and she said, "It was the most awful blizzard I landed in and I got pneumonia." She had an awful time, and she said, "I ought to hate you, really."

But we turned out to like each other. We got to talk, but I *never* did get to talk to her just by herself; it was always in a crowd or a group. We wrote now and then. I always had it in my mind that we were going to get to talk again. I felt I knew her well and loved her work. I always regret that I didn't have that next meeting.

**J.G.** During a press conference at Oxford, Mississippi, in 1977, you were asked if you had been influenced by William Faulkner. You answered briefly, "Not any!" Is it as simple as that?

**E.W.** Of course not!

**J.G.** Are you simply fed up with the question?

**E.W.** I was sort of fed up with the question, and at a press conference how could I go into that? I think the answer is *no.* The answer is no, because I think what was meant by the question was whether or not he had helped me in specific and personal ways. It was a sort of arithmetical question. Just his existence and his works mean a great deal to me. Certainly they influenced me; they meant so much to me. He also in very specific ways taught me so much; how he had done things just dawned on me. I was telling you a while ago about houses. He showed me above all in his work how in Yoknapatawpha every single segment of society is represented by place and house and so on. He knew so *much* about all that. He wrote about a much vaster world than anything I ever contemplated for my own work, and he made all of that so visible and exactly right. Every speech that comes out of a character's mouth *would* be made by a person in that situation, in that kind of family, at that time. He can't go wrong. He showed me the marvelous usage of dialogue and, well, of everything.

**J.G.** Have you consciously tried to avoid rewriting Faulkner?

**E.W.** No, I think that was what I was answering, too, when I said, "Not any!" It is not so self-conscious a process as that when you write. I think, in the act of writing, "How am I going to handle something" and not "How would so-and-so have done it" or "I mustn't fall into this pitfall here." It is just trial and error on my own.

**J.G.** Two of your stories particularly remind readers of William Faulkner's work.

**E.W.** What are they?

**J.G.** "The Burning" and "Clytie."

**E.W.** As for "The Burning," I think that is a bad story. I don't know why I tried to write anything historical. It is almost the only time I ever tried to write something which is not in our time and place. But I certainly never consciously thought. . . . Heavens! I would hate to be assigned "try to write something influenced by Faulkner." My pen would drop from my hand.

**J.G.** In retrospect, can you see why some critics would be tempted to see the Faulkner influence in those stories?

**E.W.** I think that my faults in "The Burning" were the kind of things they blamed Faulkner with. I think the story is too involved and curlicued around with things. I haven't gone back to read that story, but recently Shelby Foote, who is getting together an anthology of Civil War stories, wrote and said he wants to use "The Burning." I wrote back, "I hate for you to use it; I think it is the worst story I ever wrote." He said, "I think it is a good story, and I'm a Civil War expert; you're not." I still didn't go back and read it, but I thanked him and told him to go ahead.

As far as "Clytie" goes, I am sure the answer is that there is "not any" Faulkner influence. I have seen here and there a family going to seed right in the public eye. These things exist in life; of course, Faulkner saw the same kind of thing in Oxford.

**J.G.** It has been taken as proof of the value you place on the concept of the family band that Robbie (Reid) Fairchild returns to the family in *Delta Wedding*. Is this justified?

**E.W.** Is proof needed? Without realizing it, I seem to have repeated a pattern like that in many stories. It is partly because for my point of view in that novel, I have to have an observer come in. In *Delta Wedding* it was the child; Robbie was another outsider. I think the Fairchilds would have accepted her as much as they could accept anyone. The same way that Gloria in *Losing Battles* and Fay in *The Optimist's Daughter* are different types of interlopers with different results.

**J.G.** Is it the purpose of the watermelon fight in *Losing Battles* to point out the negative side of a close family life?

**E.W.** I wanted to show that the relationships run the whole gamut of love and oppression. Just like any human relationship has the possibilities of so many gradations of affection, feeling, passion, resistance, and hatred. But "negative" is not the word I would use.

**J.G.** The families of *Delta Wedding* and *Losing Battles* are united. But in middle-class Morgana this is not so.

**E.W.** *Delta Wedding* was very middle class. It was just a different kind of family from those in *The Golden Apples.* All those in Morgana seem to have been smaller families, and they were not isolated on a plantation; they were living in a town. The Fairchilds had a sort of family kingdom in the Delta. And the people in *Losing Battles* had a sort of kingdom in the poor red clay hills, but they were isolated from community life. The family is what they had nothing else but. And Morgana was a whole town, and everybody was sort of like a family itself.

**J.G.** Is it fair to say that it is the community that makes Virgie "a little tart" and drives Miss Eckhart to madness?

**E.W.** I suppose in a superficial way it is. A community that tightly knit can be very exacting of penalties and especially for someone who does not belong. And both Virgie and Miss Eckhart qualify. They had more power of feeling than the other people did, and they were pecked down.

**J.G.** You once said about a plot: "There has to be a story to bear it." *Did* you worry about the plot when you wrote *Losing Battles?*

**E.W.** Yes, I did, because, *owing* to circumstances, I wrote it over a long period of time, so things had time to worry me during the intervals when I was not working. I had so much more than I needed, I could have said things in a hundred different ways. So the plot worried me in that respect, how best to show it.

**J.G.** I know you cut *Losing Battles* substantially. Did you cut it enough?

**E.W.** I think so. But I haven't read it again; I don't like to read my work over. I think there were complaints that it was too long. I am sure that disturbed some people. To me everything in there had its place, or I would have cut it. I can be very ruthless in cutting. I don't put in things because my loving hand wrote it. I felt they were there for a reason.

**J.G.** You have said that you feel more comfortable with the long short story. And you indicated that this is because you feel that less is resolved, more suggested, in a short story.

**E.W.** That's true, and yet in the short story you don't have the demands of a novel, where everything has to be accounted for. The short story can be suggestive for its own sake. You don't have to develop what you don't need, whereas in the novel you have to carry everything through. Short-story writing is a freer, more imaginative way to work. Yet it is even tighter knit than a novel because it has to keep its sustained quality. You can't let it down in the middle; it has to be just right.

**J.G.** Is it true that you had written half the stories of *The Golden Apples* before you realized that you were writing about the same people?

**E.W.** Yes! That was so exciting. Until I was in the middle of the story "Music from Spain," I thought that was a separate thing from the rest of the stories. And so in a way I always felt guilty that I dragged that in, but I think it dragged in all right.

**J.G.** I accept that you do not want to call *The Golden Apples* "a novel."

**E.W.** Good! Thank you. Because so many people say, "I don't accept that you don't call this a novel, so therefore, since it is a novel, will you answer these questions about why don't you do so and so?"

**J.G.** Why is *The Golden Apples* not a novel?

**E.W.** Well, for the reason, I guess, that they were conceived as stories. Also, I didn't want the responsibilities of trying to connect them, as they would have to be in a novel—because it would mean tearing down all I had. What I wanted to do with those characters is what I did, and that means stories. I thought also that it gave me a freedom to show these different things about Morgana in a way that seems more life-like—things being developed along straws of the story. Sorry it sounds vague; I never have tried to express this that I know of.

**J.G.** Some critics feel that the meaning of the individual stories cannot be fully understood until the ending of the collection.

**E.W.** Well, that's good. I am glad for it to be like that. Let them make their own work for what they are.

**J.G.** One of the differences between a short story and a novel is supposed to be that the characters in a short story are born "fully grown." Yet the characters in *Losing Battles* seem fully grown from the very beginning.

**E.W.** Some are and some aren't. You know the E. M. Forster classification:

some are round and same are flat. The flat ones never change, and there are plenty of flat ones that don't ever change in *Losing Battles.* But all the main characters have many possibilities. There is a character like

Aunt Beck, who is always gentle yet puts her foot in her mouth when she says things. The very time she wants to be most tender, she says something that can really hurt, without knowing that she does it. There is Miss Lexie, who started out as a flat character, but all kinds of complications come in when we know about her life in nursing Miss Julia. All the torments she went through—I considered that *that* happens to her. I think Miss Julia is the factor that shows the depth of the others, the ones that were touched by her. And Judge Moody, who might have started as a flat character, is far from it. Everything is aroused in him by what happens. And Jack, who is not by any means just a straight hero type, has deep feelings. He is deeper than Gloria, who claims to be the sensitive one. He feels where she can't. If she hadn't had that shallow streak, she would have done better by Miss Julia.—Yes, I feel that *Losing Battles* did give me room to develop the characters.

J.G. Do you still feel that "character is a more awe-inspiring fish" than situation in a short story?

E.W. A novel can do so many more things and develop so many more things than a short story. Its situation and scope, all of that is a different kind of thing, so that you might have more important things you can develop in a novel than you could in a short story. But character is a more profound subject than situation in either short story or novel.

J.G. In 1951 you said that "in a story, character and place have almost equal, or even interchangeable, contributions to make." Do you still feel that this is true?

E.W. Now I wouldn't say "interchangeable," but I think that place can be almost a character in a story. Place can have really important and even dramatic significance.

J.G. To what extent do you make conscious use of Greek and Roman mythology in your writing?

E.W. It is conscious, clearly. I have lived with mythology all my life. It is just as close to me as the landscape. It *naturally* occurs to me when I am writing fiction. It is not a far-out, reached-for something. I feel no sense of strain when I use mythology. Maybe I use too much of it; I don't know. I have grown up with legends and fairy tales, and I have always loved them. I still like to read folktales from all kinds of other lands.

J.G. Critics have been quick to refer to Frazer's *Golden Bough* and Bullfinch's *The Age of Fable* [1855] for aspects of your fiction. Are the critics overdoing it?

E.W. I have read the one-volume edition of *The Golden Bough,* but I didn't read that till I was out of college. But myths themselves I've read all my life.

Many of my childhood books were of Greek and Roman myths, also Norse and Irish. The whole Andrew Lang series of fairy tales and fables and *Aesop's Fables* were in my house.

**J.G.** Did you read Thomas Bullfinch's *Age of Fable?*

**E.W.** Never have read that one. I am interested in fables as *told.* I truly haven't read enough of the critics to make a sweeping statement. But I think that anyone who attributes my stories to myths very specifically and thoroughly is overshooting it. I would rather suggest things.

**J.G.** The ending of *The Golden Apples* is a case in point. When Virgie is sitting alone on the courthouse steps, she is joined by a black woman. One critic has seen the black woman as Minerva, the stealing servant, *and* Minerva, the goddess of wisdom.

**E.W.** Oh, that really drives me crazy. It makes me sort of frantic. The end of my book was the most natural thing in the world. It was a drawing together of two people without a roof: the old black woman, who has nothing, and Virgie, who is bereft at that moment.

Yet they both have—something; one of them has got a chicken, and the other has got all these things in her mind. No! When I hear something like that, it drives me to the other extreme of saying something literal, like what I just said.

**J.G.** In your children's book *The Shoe Bird,* Arturo cannot recognize the phrase "shoes are for the birds," which he invented, when it comes back to him.—Is there a parallel here to Hans Christian Andersen's story "It Is Perfectly True!"?

**E.W.** I can't remember that story, if I ever read it. I am not sure I have—although I have read Hans Christian Andersen. I think that in a way I prefer the folktale, as collected by the Brothers Grimm, to tales invented by one person. But I loved the Andersen tales. They always were so sad to me when I was a girl. He always upset me, when I was little. His tales worried me so much, and they affected me as if they were not fairy tales but real—real stories where you really felt for the people as people, which they were. The pity may hurt his stories—it is a comedown to be asked to cry.

**J.G.** Is this also true of fiction in general?

**E.W.** I just finished reading all of Chekhov again that I could. I mean all the stories. And you don't cry in those, although you could, because it is so encompassing—at the same time they are not sentimental. Although I haven't read him recently, I think maybe Andersen was sentimental in a way, wasn't he? I liked "The Little Match Girl," when I cried. I cried in "The Snow Queen," I was really frightened. It was so terrible with that ice in her heart.

**J.G.** Can we expect more shoe bird stories from you?

**E.W.** I think that was not well thought of. It was the only thing I ever did with someone else asking me if I would write something. I was asked by my publisher if I would write a children's book. I don't think it has been in print for ages. I don't think anybody thought much of it, including me. I did the best I could on it, and it was when I couldn't work. My mother was ill here, and I wrote in the dining room, where I could be close by. I thought it would be so easy to write it, because I had children in the family then that were the right age. I wanted to write for them. Somehow it was very strained. I know its mistakes. I still enjoyed it, though.

**J.G.** In an introduction to an interview with you, Ms. Alice Walker has maintained that "the past will always separate" the races. Do you believe this to be true?

**E.W.** I don't think so. I have black friends who agree with me that it isn't so. Recently I was at Yale with some humanities scholars, answering questions. The woman sitting next to me was black, and they were all talking about the problems of the '60s. Several of the scholars were from foreign countries, asking questions about the situation here, how strained the situation was. And the black woman said to me, "You know, during it all, when it was just at its worst back in the '60s, and I was a schoolteacher, my mother said to me, "Why aren't you all upset about this?" and I was laughing. I said, "I guess it is because I am a Southerner." Which I really loved. I, too, always knew we would understand each other; we always have in the past.

**J.G.** Your 1942 essay, "Ida M'Toy," is one of your great portraits of black women, but where is the genuine black and white friendship in your fiction?

**E.W.** I see it in a good many places. I meant to convey that Missouri, in *The Optimist's Daughter,* is a true friend of Laurel's. Missouri is her maid in the household, but they were also big friends, and both of them knew it.

**J.G.** Does Missouri help Laurel much?

**E.W.** I think she does. When Judge McKelva's body is being carried out, it is Missouri that stands with Laurel and helps her. She helps her with the bird, too, doesn't she? I mean, in these really wrenching experiences that Laurel is going through by herself, Missouri's instincts are perfect. She is always sensitive to what is going on. In *The Ponder Heart,* too, Narciss is the mainstay of the family.

**J.G.** In one of your manuscripts for *The Ponder Heart,* you wrote, "I think they only asked [Miss Teacake] because she was somebody white. The rest of their testimony was black as midnight."—Was this deleted for artistic or for political reasons?

E.W. It isn't good writing. Nothing political had anything to do with it. I am sure the reason I took that out was that it was out of character for Edna Earle to say that.

J.G. In the early '50s you showed great political interest in the career of Adlai Stevenson. Has there been anything in politics to be enthusiastic about since then?

E.W. Neither before nor since. He just really touched my mind and heart. I was so enchanted to have a person like that wanting to be in public life. I happened to be in New York at the time he was running so that I got to hear him in person. I think a lot of people in this country felt the same way I did, wanting so much to help Stevenson be elected. If Stevenson had been elected, we don't know about the forking of the paths. I mean there would have been other paths to fork from. All kinds of things could have happened. When he didn't win, I lost interest again.

J.G. It has been claimed that you are indifferent to the larger social and political problems of your region. Is it true that you overlook the regional problems?

E.W. Whoever has claimed this, it isn't accurate at all. What is true is that I don't think of myself as a writer of fiction who seeks to make it a platform for my opinions. I am a very interested citizen and try to keep informed on everything and to vote. But I don't think fiction is the place to air those principles, except for the moral principles of right and wrong and these I try to let characters show for themselves. I tried to put all this in a piece I wrote for the *Atlantic* [October 1965] called "Must the Novelist Crusade?"

J.G. It is clear that the object of your fiction can't be social criticism, but can the novelist *avoid* crusading?

E.W. You can't avoid dealing with moral matters, because that's what life is about. But I think it is wrong when somebody like Steinbeck crusades in his fiction. That's why Steinbeck bores me so. The real crusader doesn't need to crusade; he writes about human beings in the sense Chekhov did. He tries to see a human being whole with all his wrongheadedness and all his rightheadedness. To blind yourself to one thing for the sake of your prejudice is limiting. I think it is a mistake. There's so much room in the world for crusading, but it is for the editorial writer, the speechmaker, the politician, and the man in public life to do, not for the writer of fiction.

J.G. How can you claim that fiction is "stone deaf to argument" and then go on to write "The Demonstrators"?

E.W. I think that was right and true, because I was letting all that speak for itself. "The Demonstrators" is written right out of that kind of situation, in the thick of it.

**J.G.** And the issues are implicit?

**E.W.** Yes, and the fact of the great complexity of it, how inexpressible some things are. And how so many of the people who would feel the most are powerless and so many of the wrongheaded people have all the power. To me it was consistent to write "The Demonstrators" and say what I did.

**J.G.** Yet readers of your well-known fiction find many topical elements. In *Losing Battles,* for instance, you deal with electioneering, depletion of woods, bad teachers' training, and a poverty-stricken orphanage, just to mention some of the potentially political issues.

**E.W.** These things are there. And there are people there who are living with all these handicaps and things that should be righted. *Losing Battles* was written about the '30s, when nobody had anything with which to do it. Injustice was staring everybody in the face—and they were living in spite of it, and through it, and with it. I am not saying that is a good way to be; I am saying it is a terrible way to be.

**J.G** You do not seem to be interested in the concept of "sin" or in the idea of "evil." This is so uncommon in an American writer that perhaps it deserves a comment.

**E.W.** I am, though. Not in "sin"—not from a Roman Catholic point of view like Flannery O'Connor, because I am ignorant of that religion. But I do believe that there is "evil." I believe in the existence of "evil," or else your reaching for "good" could not mean anything. I do feel there is "evil" in the world and in people, very really and truly. I recognize its power and value. I do! I thought there was "evil" in Fay in *The Optimist's Daughter.* And there is "evil" in a society which does wrong things.

**J.G.** It seems that you think very little of organized religion.

**E.W.** I don't know where you got this opinion. I am not a frequent churchgoer, but I am a reverent person.

**J.G.** In your fiction you have always treated the prejudice between denominations with scornful humor.

**E.W.** Or amusement, I'd say. Up in the East, when Carter was running for president, everybody said, "How could a Baptist ever be president!" In the South, that is the structure of the society of a small town. It is in a churchy society that most Southerners are brought up, and it is what they mention in every other word in their conversation.

In a small town like Banner, if the Baptists couldn't be against the Methodists, they'd have nothing to talk about. My amusement has nothing to do with reverence or with God, it is *society,* and I am writing about it in that aspect.

**J.G.** It is obvious that you don't like it when critics use novels as "fishponds" for their criticism. Isn't it surprising then that you yourself have written so much criticism?

**E.W.** Not especially, because I do think I write out of a fellow feeling for fiction writers. I'm really trying to get at what I think they were trying to do. I am not trying to take something there and put it here; I am trying to understand what *they* did. I like it when someone writes that way about me, which many critics do. On the whole I feel that I really do approach other fiction writers with the feeling of a fiction writer, instead of the feeling of a critic. I like to write about the process of writing that I have discovered through my work and what I think I have learned reading others.

**J.G.** In *The Eye of the Story,* your new book of nonfiction, you chose not to include pieces like "The Abode of Summer" and your essay on the nature of the fairy tale. Why did you leave them out?

**E.W.** Only because I thought they repeated material already in the collection. I took out the one on fairy tales because I had a piece called "Fairy Tale of the Natchez Trace." I cut a great number of things because I wanted to make a sort of balanced selection. I liked "The Abode of Summer," too, but I thought I had enough on Mississippi, such as "Notes on River Country," a more considered and longer piece. I chose among things of a kindred type and tried to take the one that I thought well developed.

**J.G.** You have included most of your purely critical essays in the collection, such as "Place in Fiction," "Words into Fiction," and "The Short Story."

**E.W.** Yes, just about all of those, because they were considered essays on my part. I really worked on those—they were my long-time thoughts about fiction—whereas a review is something done with a deadline. You do the best you can, but it is not something you've worked over for months.

**J.G.** There isn't anything by "Michael Ravenna," your World War II pseudonym, in your book of nonfiction.

**E.W.** No. I didn't save any of those reviews because they weren't worth saving. I don't even know what they were.

**J.G.** For how long did you write under a pseudonym?

**E.W.** This is to exaggerate my signing another name to an occasional book review. I didn't work at the *New York Times* very long, just through a summer [1944]. And I was writing reviews under my own name at the same time, holding down a full-time job. So I didn't have too much time to be "Michael Ravenna."

**J.G.** Has your book reviewing stolen time from the fiction you wanted to write?

**E.W.** I like reviewing books. I take my pick. I couldn't write about a book I really don't like, you know. It is a source of pleasure to write about books I do like, and I do that and other things to earn a little money on the side. That includes going around lecturing. I have had a year of that, which is unusual. I like it, but it takes a great amount of time and even more energy.

**J.G.** Are you working on any fiction at present?

**E.W.** That's what I'm waiting to do. I have just now finished writing a piece for Mr. Bruccoli. This was an "Afterword" on a novel called *The Great Big Doorstep* by E. P. O'Donnell from 1941. This is in the Lost American Fiction Series. I was asked if I had a nomination for such a series, and I nominated this book. I was thrilled when I was asked to write the "Afterword." That's all. That is the last assignment that I promised. I can get back to my fiction—after this interview!

# *Seeing Real Things*

AN INTERVIEW WITH EUDORA WELTY

◆◆◆◆◆◆

*1119 Pinehurst Street, Jackson, Mississippi, May 20, 1993*

**Jan Nordby Gretlund** On the basis of your early story "Acrobats in a Park" I assume that you have read the poetry of Rainer Maria Rilke.

**Eudora Welty** Of course, I have, but I do not remember when or where.

**J.G.** There was a translation in 1939 by J. B. Leishman and Stephen Spender of the *Duino Elegies.* . . .

**E.W.** Yes, I love those. I remember reading those long ago.

**J.G.** And in that edition there is a print of Picasso's painting "Les Saltimbanques," and one of the elegies is on that painting.

**E.W.** It could be that I saw it—not with the poem, but I saw the Picasso. I saw his paintings pretty early. I have always been fascinated by painting, and especially by that school. I used to see most things in Chicago at the Art Institute, which is a marvelous museum, and they were the earliest people I saw.—When I went to the University of Wisconsin in Madison, I had no idea what I saw, but I used to go down to Chicago to see the Impressionists, whenever I could. I went frequently.

**J.G.** I know that you are a painter yourself.

**E.W.** You couldn't take anything I did in painting seriously. I loved it, and I studied it, but I had no serious ambition about it. I wouldn't dream that I had any ability for that, I just loved painting. I studied art when I was growing up here. There was a good painter named Mary Hull who gave lessons to young people right here in Jackson. I knew a number of Jackson painters. There was quite a number as I was growing up. And when I got to the University of Wisconsin, [and when] I was a junior, they had a wonderful art history course, and I minored in that. I majored in English and minored in art, because they had such marvelous professors and marvelous chances to see the real thing. I could go into Chicago and see the real things—that was just wonderful.

It's very different from studying writing because that was something you had to do almost in solitude. You can go to many good classes in literature, which I did, but the act of writing I didn't think I could learn that way. Any practice in it is of course valuable, that's the way you learn.—I had some marvelous professors in English literature, which meant everything, I would have chosen them any day over a professor in writing. The one I liked and got most from was at Wisconsin, his name was Ricardo Quintana. He was a Swift and Donne man.

**J.G.** Did you read Swift and Donne?

**E.W.** I did read Swift and Donne, but I read everything contemporary, too. I just read whatever came to hand, I just read all the time. I was coming along when you could read Proust and Thomas Mann, all those people were publishing. And Chekhov—I sort of dictated my own, what I would read, by my own taste. It wasn't that I spurned anything else, but it was just that I was so eager to read them. By Thomas Mann I read *The Magic Mountain,* of course. My mother was reading *Joseph and His Brothers,* but I never did read that, although I meant to. I read *Buddenbrooks,* and later probably in the early '40s or maybe late '30s I read some of the tragic shorter things that he wrote. I don't think they were translated in the early 1930s, or maybe they were and I didn't know it.

What happened in those days was that the Modern Library was invented, and Proust and Mann began to appear in print. I think Proust was one of the first things that came out, and *Swann's Way* was the first. I remember going down to Macy's, I was in New York, and there used to be fights in the aisle over getting hold of them, everybody was so eager. And Macy's and Gimbel's, the store across the street, had price wars on who was going to make it cheaper. There was a day you could get it for seven cents! That's when I was going to Columbia, 1930–31, I think. Although it could have been other times I was in New York, because I went every time I could. Anyway, that was a marvelous gift to everybody, to start the Modern Library.

**J.G.** I see you as more of an Agrarian than most people do.

**E.W.** I just don't know about it. I didn't write with a philosophical basis to what I was doing. I had no philosophy I was pursuing, and no aesthetics, I'm just writing as a tale-teller. But they were very good to me at the *Southern Review;* they were just like godparents to me. They accepted my work and printed it. It was a godsend. But there was no philosophical or any other theoretical connection.

**J.G.** But wasn't there a spiritual kinship? After all, my count shows that you were the darling of the *Southern Review,* as you had more stories published in the first series than anybody else.

**E.W.** Really! I didn't know that. It was just that Peter Taylor was a little younger than me, or he would have been ahead of me.

**J.G.** Did you ever read *I'll Take My Stand?*

**E.W.** Eventually I did. I think I must have just read it out of curiosity, probably because it was written by these people whose other work I liked and who had been good to me, but I didn't read much like that. I was a big fiction reader. I didn't take any part or even much interest in the Agrarian pursuits. I didn't know enough to begin with. I didn't have a good background. And I had no philosophical convictions that I would apply to writing. I remember when I met Robert Penn Warren, much, much later, I didn't meet people in those days, and Jackson is quite a distance from Baton Rouge, but I went to Baton Rouge one time to drive a friend, the journalist Herschel Brickell, down there. And we met Katherine Anne Porter. She had invited me to come and see her, and she was then married to Albert Erskine, and we all three went to lunch at their house.

It was a good while before I ever met Cleanth [Brooks] and Red [Robert Penn Warren]. But when we all did meet, they were so likable and wonderful and so good to me that I didn't feel out of place.—I was pretty shy about the whole thing. I felt that I would never be of interest to them, because they had such a philosophical investment in all this, and I didn't have *any.*—This was in the late 1930s. Katherine Anne wasn't married to Albert for very long. The whole thing was a big mistake. He died recently. When I moved from Harcourt, Brace, my agent Diarmuid Russell wanted me to go to an editor I liked, and he had asked different people that might be interested. One was Albert Erskine. He had then gone on to be president of Random House. I hadn't seen him since these days at Baton Rouge, when he was a bridegroom really, and he was so good to me. He published *Losing Battles.*

**J.G.** In *Losing Battles* you have two academics, Julia Mortimer and Judge Moody, with names that seem to mock them. And there is a critical debate about the novel opposing the values of academics and farmers. Do you blame the farmers for their willful ignorance, or do you mock the academics and praise the family?

**E.W.** Yes. The family above all, and also the love of the tale, the talking. The way you keep the family going is through the stories. I'm glad that you felt that.—The names are good old Mississippi names, I wasn't trying to be cute or anything. I always liked the name Moody. Don't you like that?—I laid it in the part of Mississippi that is the most rural and uninvaded. I chose a place on purpose that had not been infiltrated by anything else. Far from being the Old South, and all that stuff, these people—all they had was each other. And there are so many people in Mississippi like that.

**J.G.** And the setting is definitely Mississippi? A few critics have argued that the novel is really West Virginia transplanted.

E.W. My mother is from West Virginia, you know. It is the same strain of people, but those people did not come here from West Virginia. The heat, the drought, and the dust is Mississippi; it's not West Virginia. But there is a simplicity and a directness and a relish of tales and things like that, which they have in common.

J.G. Isn't it surprising for the author of "Place in Fiction" to hear the argument "Welty wrote about the northeastern corner of Mississippi, but it is really West Virginia!"

E.W. That's absurd! I tried to get a part of Mississippi where they had nothing, Tishomingo County, because I wanted to show what they did have was each other, and the family tales, and the family solidarity. That's all they had. And I thought that was a good basis for a novel.

J.G. Baton Rouge is not a presence in your fiction, but New Orleans certainly always was, from "The Purple Hat" to *The Optimist's Daughter.* Mississippians seem always to have been fascinated by New Orleans. It appears that it was only rivaled by Memphis.

E.W. That was literally true, I think, when I was brought up. People had one city or the other to which they went,—to go to when they had to consult specialists of any kind or to make an important purchase, such as a bridal gown, or something like that. And also it was a place of pleasure, where you went for your flings. Of course, in North Mississippi, Memphis is the only place. And here in Jackson people were divided between Memphis and New Orleans. Always it was just one or the other. You didn't go to both!

New Orleans is such a wonderful stage, a wonderful theater, for anything to be acted out. It is native to it, to be like that. It is much more of a change from ordinary life than Memphis is. Memphis could be almost like Jackson, but New Orleans is like a French place. It still is. It is very deep. I mean it is layers of life, and not easy to know. It is mysterious, a good city. When I wrote "The Purple Hat," I was trying to show off having been to a gambling hall. We used to go down there on dates, to meet with friends. In those days we would go and dance to wonderful jazz music that we'd just walk in to, right off Royal Street. It was very easy to go down there and get into this completely different world. I didn't know Memphis very well, but it was, I think, much more countrified; New Orleans was an old, old city, and fascinating. It cost very little to go there, but you had to have enough money to afford what was little, which not many of us did.

But I remember being able to catch the streamliner train that began to come out of Jackson, Tennessee, to New Orleans, it would go through Jackson [Mississippi] at some time between five and six in the morning and arrived at New Orleans about 10 o'clock or 10:30. You could get off the train and walk around all day—you couldn't afford a hotel, you had nowhere to sit down. We had no money, but we were young and did not need a place to sit down. You could walk all through the Quarter and eat one good meal there, at Galatoire's or something, and have one drink in Pat O'Brian's Courtyard, and then walk back to the train at six o'clock in the evening, get on, and ride home. You could do the whole thing for about ten or fifteen dollars! It was the only way we could have done it during the Depression. We always went from the station to the French Quarter and just stayed there and went up and down. If we had enough money, you could go into the Hotel Monteleone, which is on Royal Street, and if we ever spent the night, it would be there, because you'd just walk out into the French Quarter in the morning. All those little streets down there, you had certain places you went to, to revisit.

I never did go for shopping. I didn't care about going to the shops. But I went to get to hear the wonderful jazz by the old people in the Preservation Hall, since it started. I remember Sweet Emma played the piano. She would come in wearing a housedress and her hat, and she'd put her purse and a bag of groceries to take home afterwards on top of the piano, an old upright, and sit down and start in. I have some of her records. She was just like a good housewife coming to give it a good cleaning down where she played.

**J.G.** But most of the traveling performers you saw right here in Jackson.

**E.W.** Yes. They really were nationally known, and the only reason we ever got them here was that they had to lay over one night between Memphis and New Orleans. This was when I was nine or ten years old.

**J.G.** When did you hear Fats Waller play in Jackson?

**E.W.** That came a good deal later. I didn't go to hear Fats until . . . he didn't come here until in the '20s. I had all his records already, he didn't burst upon my horizon, he had already done that. I never would have set out to do "Powerhouse," because I wouldn't have thought I could. I was just so keyed up that I just did it. I did have the good sense to know that I had no basis to rewrite anything, I just didn't know anything except what I wrote down.

**J.G.** Sometimes fiction becomes fact. Your Mike Fink story in *The Robber Bridegroom,* in which he rides into an alligator, is now registered as an official Mike Fink story in Blair and Meine's *Half Horse Half Alligator.*

**E.W.** Oh, I just made that up. But it is in the spirit. I mean, the whole thing was in the spirit of that extravagant time. I tried to make it like a tall story. Mark Twain, you know, referred to all those things, too, when he wrote *Life on the Mississippi,* and when he wrote *Huckleberry Finn.*

**J.G.** But you add an element of sadness. Your Mike Fink is a depressed mail rider of modern times. It is sad to see him in his reduced state.

**E.W.** I know it. It's like in the fairy tale tradition. Well, those were people who frequented the Trace, really. Mail riders had to go there. I had to have somebody like that for another character. I read a lot of histories of the time. . . .

**J.G.** *The Devil's Backbone,* perhaps?

**E.W.** I have read that one, and another one by Jonathan Daniels, but there are plenty of histories of the time, which you can read. It was really true, really a fact that. . . . Did you read a story I wrote called "A Still Moment"? The three men that meet there on the Natchez Trace,—that could have been physically possible, because the three people were around there at the same time. I just imagined what it would have been like, but it would have been possible. I read a lot of things that made me write it, like the letters of Lorenzo Dow, the mad, they say he was mad, evangelist. He made dates a year ahead that he would be back at this clearing in the wilderness, and he would be there. He and his wife exchanged letters while he had this life. I read those letters, they are just wonderful. It was a time of extravagance and romantic ideas. It was the times that made me write those stories.

**J.G.** Did you know that "A Still Moment" is probably the story by you most often referred to and commented on?

**E.W.** Really? It is just as well. I don't know what to say. That really is strange! I'm very proud of the fact that Robert Penn Warren told me he liked that story the best. That part about Audubon, I guess, is based on the truth.—Not Audubon in my story.—He was all down in there, painted his way down. I've seen some of his paintings in old houses down there. And in his diaries he would write about his horror as he walked the streets of New Orleans and saw great tables in the market of slaughtered songbirds for sale, just to eat! It's fascinating to read. It is the only time I ever wrote out of things I've read instead of out of living. Those were such romantic "facts."

**J.G.** Your fascination with the early history of the Natchez Trace is expressed with much humor. And the humor has stayed with you right up to *The Optimist's Daughter,* in which it comes out as satire on the social classes, especially in Fay's mourning scene.

**E.W.** I got one review in French that said the only person worth saving in that book was Fay and that all these other people were trash!

**J.G.** And that is not exactly what you had in mind?

**E.W.** Not exactly.

**J.G.** Was the French critic right in so far as your criticism was leveled at all social groups in Mount Salus?

**E.W.** It is against the humans. What it is against are the people who do not know the meaning of their own experiences, as I came out and baldly said about Fay: people who don't know the meaning of what's happened to them. They are not sensitive to what's going on around them. They don't see. And it has nothing to do with the classes or anything like that. It is just the human ability to know what your own experience means. Some people never learn what happens to them.

J.G. Do the Fairchilds of *Delta Wedding* ever realize their shortcomings? They don't always treat their black laborers as human beings.

E.W. Which was probably exactly what was going on at the time. They didn't even realize what they were doing.

J.G. I have the impression that Troy Flavin, the overseer, is having a relationship with one of the black girls on the plantation, that is, with Pinchy.

E.W. I get more letters about Pinchy. "What does it mean," they say, "Pinchy is coming through." Well, I should have explained that. It is just a term that meant that you would get religion. She was going through that, which I had heard from time to time. But a lot of things I didn't have the wits to realize would need to be explained, I just took it for granted that everybody would know what that was.

J.G. Wasn't it unusual for Ellen Fairchild, the plantation mistress, to go down and witness the "coming through"?

E.W. Not if she liked Pinchy. I guess it was a family feeling toward the people she was looking after. No, I think that would be taken for granted. You'd help them whatever they were going through. It was what they would call maternal. I'm sure it wouldn't be accepted now. I mean, it would be very strange now, I guess. I know whenever it was cold weather here, we used to take blankets and go over to where our maid lived and take her more covers. One was called Arlene. They relied on us; when a sudden freeze came down, they wouldn't be prepared. Jackson was smaller then. All of us were closer together than now. Our maids lived on the other side of Greenwood Cemetery.—Of course, that's terribly looked down on. You're not supposed to be paternal, or that kind of thing, but that was the need of the moment:

they were cold. Nobody would do that now, for everybody's sake. They would think we were looking down on them. "You should have paid them more to begin with," you know.

◆ ◆ ◆

J.G. Talking of racial relations in Mississippi, what do you think of the efforts to bring Byron De La Beckwith to trial again?

E.W. He is a monster! Of course, he should have been convicted in the first place. He is a horror! I don't know what is up right now. You know my story "Where Is the Voice Coming from?" is about him, the one I wrote the night it happened. The reason I wrote the story is that I thought, "I should know exactly the kind of person this is." And I did know, except as somebody told me, "You thought it was a Snopes, and it was a Compson." But I wouldn't exactly agree, I don't think De La Beckwith is a Compson.

**J.G.** What do you think of black–white relations in Jackson today? Are there any?

**E.W.** Well, I may not have an ear close enough to it,—so far as I can tell, at least it seems to me to be open always. You can always talk. And there are a good many black leaders who are prominent now, and people in office. I mean it is doing all right, it is slow, too slow, too late, but . . . not too late, it can't be too late.

**J.G.** Is there any part of Jackson where it is too dangerous for white people to go?

**E.W.** I wouldn't know it, if there was. And it might be just as dangerous for bad white people being there as for any black people. Things seem to be awfully slow. When I fractured my back and went to the hospital, the fracture mended, and I did exercises and came home. They sent me with this nurse, Daryl Howard, and said, "Keep her!" And that's what I've done. I can't really afford to, but I do. I really am fortunate. Daryl comes at seven o'clock in the morning, brings me some coffee in bed, and then she stays through breakfast and lunch, half a day every day, just to get me going, and she tells me most of what I know about the black situation. She's black and she's highly intelligent, you know, well-educated children and so on.

The other night her daughter, who has a night job, was standing outside the place where she works, just one of these all-night places, a decent place, but the hour was bad, and a man drove by where she was standing at the curb and said, "Throw your purse in the car or I'm blowing your brains out!" They mean it, too, when they say that. She was really terrified, and who wouldn't be? She did what he said, she threw her purse into the car. And she was terribly upset, of course.

**J.G.** Was it a white man driving the car?

**E.W.** I don't know. I don't even know if she knew. It could be either.

I mean, it happens with either. Anyway, the poor girl was hysterical after it happened, as she well would be. She's married, but her mother went over and spent the rest of the night with her. It was such a terrible thing. She went down to look at a lineup to see if the man was the one, but she didn't find him. But that kind of thing goes on, too much—and among decent, educated, self-sufficient, self-respecting people that are going about their business. And this kind of thing happens, and it is just entirely too much, and I don't know what's being done about that. It's gotten more rampant, and more taken for granted, I believe, than it ever was before.

◆ ◆ ◆

**J.G.** The identification with your place that you just demonstrated is characteristic of your fictional characters. But, it has been argued that the male MacLains in *The Golden Apples* are not really of their town, because mostly they are not in Morgana.

**E.W.** That's their part of being of Morgana. They are of it; that's why it matters. That's just a fact. I can remember things like that happening here. It just enters into the legend of a town:

"Remember about Mr. So-and-so, he left his hat on the banks of the Mississippi River and disappeared."

**J.G.** Are the male MacLains essential for an attempt to define the identity of Morgana? And is this why Randall MacLain is elected mayor?

**E.W.** I think so. And also, their stories never die. Everybody's crazy about them, and for the reason that's the way they act. They are just so . . . romantic figures. I can remember some in my childhood.

**J.G.** There is another critical idea that I would like to hear your reaction to. Its origin is the scene in *Losing Battles* where Granny Vaughn, after the celebration of her ninetieth birthday, invites Vaughn, the youngest boy, to come to her in bed. It has been argued that this scene shows the dark side of humanity in your work. I disagree.—I believe the old woman sees the outline of Grandpa Vaughn's hat on the boy and in her exhaustion believes she is addressing her late husband.

**E.W.** You are probably right. It was just natural for her to say that. You know she was the mother of them all and would just welcome them. . . . I am sure that was it: she was thinking of Grandpa, or. . . . She was able to take care of anybody's problem, no matter what.

**J.G.** If readers are looking for the dark side of life in the novel, they could take a look at Miss Lexie's nursing of Julia Mortimer. Why does she starve her patient?

**E.W.** Yes, that's a horror. There are people like that, and there are some nurses like that—I don't know. There's some kind of cruelty in some forms of nursing. I don't mind saying this, we had a whole lot of nurses in our family. I had to have a whole lot of them for my mother, and I had that same thing, called "good country ladies with no home ties." They would advertise:

"Settled white Christian lady with no home ties will come and stay with you and help you nurse your. . . ." And that's just what she needed, but it depended on the person. There were some that were just horrors, but some of them were just as kind as could be. They were old ladies without anything to do, and they would say, "I am glad to get this job because it's getting to be cold weather," you know, time to come in, just country people that were alone.

I had to get somebody to help. Just the need to be two people to lift mother. She was very particular about who she had. She fired one nurse because . . . well, I had her read to her, because I was busy somewhere else. This nurse mispronounced "gesture"—as in "he made a gesture"—and my mother said, "You're fired!" She was hard to please. You would be too, if you loved to read and couldn't. We read all day long to her. I read, and we had recordings for the blind. I read whatever she liked to hear. She liked the Bible. She liked the Book of Esther, she loved the King James version of the Bible. She loved the sound and loved the poetry of it. She was an intelligent person. And she relished the sound of it. She wasn't too crazy about the recordings I got her. She liked *me* to read.

◆ ◆ ◆

**J.G.** I read your fiction as a contribution to the tradition of realism, specifically to a Chekhovian brand of realism. What is the relation between "a sense of place," with its emotional connotations, and your idea of realism?

**E.W.** The physical surrounding has to be exact and has to be right. That's how you make it right: use place to identify . . . an emotional content. I'm just thinking of it also as a tactic in the writing of fiction that you can use place "to place" things, in the verb, and it identifies. Well, it is like that long piece I wrote on place.

**J.G.** It is the emotive content of your aesthetics of place that makes it impossible for critics to distill it into a few words. How can you hope to define the principles of something which is based on emotions?

**E.W.** I don't know. I wouldn't be able to.—And is it really necessary?

**J.G.** I believe that the best way to study the Weltian concept of "a sense of place" is to read your fiction, book by book.

**E.W.** Yes, that's where it exists!

**J.G.** I like your phrase from "Some Notes on River Country" where you wrote, "A place that was ever lived in is like a fire that never goes out."

**E.W.** It's very poetic, I'm afraid, but I believe it, though.

**J.G.** What was the origin of your famous essay on "Place in Fiction"?

**E.W.** We were to give a series of lectures at Cambridge University, and this was the opening one. And I was panic stricken to think I would be addressing Cambridge students. Also more than that, they were from all over England and taught American subjects at English schools. I was trying to think of something, I had tried to think of something that I could legitimately bring up. I'm not a scholar or anything like that, that is why I thought that place in fiction was the bridge.

I was sitting there panic stricken before I read my first speech, and one of the teachers that came in, while I was sitting there, just seemed in passing me to get a telegraphic message from me, probably because he was a Scot. Anyway he stopped and said to me, "You will do grand!"—which was so kind of him. I was petrified.

**J.G.** Who invited you to Cambridge?

**E.W.** It was something they have every year, English teachers of American subjects in sixth-form schools and colleges and universities, the teachers of all these come to sometimes Oxford, sometimes Cambridge. And it was funded by two groups. I think Britain paid for the passage over on a boat, and the United States paid for your maintenance. We had to go on an American boat one way and an English the other. It was a terrible American ship, the *America* or something. The English ship was a Cunard, but not one of the big boats. It was fine. In fact I loved and enjoyed it both ways.

They want some on all subjects, I mean not just English. There was another on English literature, I can't remember his name now. He's from Cornell. This was a perfectly nice man, but we weren't especially congenial.

The ones I liked were the English teachers of American subjects, and we had a long enough time to become really acquainted. It was a wonderful experience. John Hope Franklin was there, and many other good people. So it was like a faculty, just like in a college. It lasted six weeks. It was three lectures to do twice. The sixth-form teachers had a second assembly, and we also had to address them.

**J.G.** Did you simply repeat "Place in Fiction"?

**E.W.** No, it was in three parts. It was longer than what I used for printing. I had quite a lot of examples which I thought they needed and which I wouldn't have left in, especially in America. I worked on it, months and months I think, trying to get something. They were going to invite one writer. The others were all teachers. I was invited as the only practitioner.

So I wrote a paper as a practitioner about using place. I tried to get something that would join us together for my speech. I was so scared. I had never made a speech anywhere before, and I just started out at Cambridge University! I could not turn it down, it was such a chance to go over there. We stayed at Peterhouse, and I made lots of friends that I kept for years, in fact some until they died.

◆ ◆ ◆

**J.G.** It must make you sad that many of your friends are now dead.

**E.W.** It's just terrible. It is. I feel terrible about it.—I'm very glad to still be alive, and I really don't think about old age too much. The only thing, the worst thing about it, is that on account of arthritis I'm not very well able to travel. So all the things that I love to do . . . for instance, I wasn't able to go to the funeral of my editor Albert Erskine. The funeral was in Connecticut, his home. I had planned to go, but the doctor told me not to try it. I felt so bad about it, he'd been so good to me.

I haven't been to New York now for several years. Some of the people I always went to see are still there. I always stay at the Algonquin, still do.—It's just that I don't want to be on anybody's hands. What I would do would be to get a car and a driver that could be mine while I was there. I tried with taxis, which was very hard; getting into the taxi and getting out is hard for me. But if you get a car and a driver, I still do that, I have them meet me at the airport and be waiting for me when I get off the plane, and they take me straight to the hotel. And that's very helpful. You can do things to make it easy for yourself.

**J.G.** Do you have manuscripts that you are still working on?

**E.W.** No, I just wish that I could get some things written that I want to write. It is just too physical, writing.

**J.G.** Couldn't you dictate, maybe to a tape recorder?

**E.W.** No, I can't do that. I can't dictate or any other thing. I need to do it myself. I just don't think in the terms of sound, the page is where I work.

**J.G.** And yet some of your stories are at their best when you read them aloud.

**E.W.** Well, that's good. I mean, I make some of my living doing that. I'm glad I got some that fill that bill. I'm often asked to read "Why I Live at the P.O."—It has to be short, and that means it has to be early. I got more long-winded as time went on. I really enjoy reading. It is the only thing I will do. I don't lecture.

**J.G.** Is the last piece you have written for *The Norton Book of Friendship?*

**E.W.** Yes. Of course, that wasn't writing but editing, except for the introduction. I'm not sorry I did that. We [Ronald Sharp] had a good time doing it.

**J.G.** It gave you a chance to pick some of your favorite people and place them in an anthology.

**E.W.** Right!

## INDEX OF AUTHORS AND WORKS

◆ ◆ ◆

www.ingramcontent.com/pod-product-compliance
Lightning Source LLC
LaVergne TN
LVHW010353080826
844660LV00004B/262

* 9 7 8 1 6 1 1 1 7 8 7 6 0 *